D0933711

Pilgrimage
and Healing

Pilgrimage and Healing

Jill Dubisch and Michael Winkelman, Editors

The University of Arizona Press
Tucson

The University of Arizona Press

© 2005 Arizona Board of Regents

All rights reserved

♾ This book is printed on acid-free, archival-quality paper.

Manufactured in the United States of America

10   09   08   07   06   05   6   5   4   3   2   1

Library of Congress Cataloging-in-Publication Data

Pilgrimage and healing / Jill Dubisch and Michael Winkelman,
    editors.— 1st ed.
        p. cm.
    Includes bibliographical references and index.
    ISBN-13: 978-0-8165-2475-4 (hardcover : alk. paper)
    ISBN-10: 0-8165-2475-0 (hardcover : alk. paper)
        1. Pilgrims and pilgrimages. 2. Spiritual healing. I. Dubisch,
    Jill, 1943– II. Winkelman, Michael.
    BL619.P5P519 2005
    203'.51—dc22
                            2005011397

Contents

Preface

*P*ilgrimage may evoke the idea of an antiquated religious ritual, but this perennial feature of religious devotion has remained a vibrant and dynamic activity in the modern world. While some may marvel at the near fanatical devotion of millions of pilgrims who make the arduous trek to Mecca, we Americans now throng to our own pilgrimage sites at the World Trade Center in New York City and the Federal Trade Building in Oklahoma City. The perennial attraction of a special sacred site that meets our personal, social, and spiritual needs has something of an anomalous status in the modern world. Why do these sites found in the religious traditions around the world still hold such powerful appeal?

This volume brings together anthropological and interdisciplinary perspectives to understand these persistent forms of popular religious participation. The contributors help expand our understanding of such traditions in light of an increasingly secular trend in pilgrimage activities, exemplified in the Burning Man Festival now held annually in the desert of Nevada. These new developments in pilgrimages are not, however, a fundamental change in the motivations and purposes of pilgrimages, or in their relationships to institutional structures. While often found within the broader domains of major religious traditions, pilgrimages have also been in opposition to dominant hierarchical structures and their efforts to control religious activities.

The contributors to this volume were invited to address a specific focus on the healing dimensions of pilgrimage. Their success allows this volume to make a contribution to medical anthropology and its efforts to understand the myriad of therapeutic resources utilized by populations around the world. The grounding of these chapters in specific cultures and pilgrimage traditions has also permitted them to make contributions to the concerns of other disciplines as well. These include not only religious studies and social movements, but also women's studies and contemporary spirituality.

As our world increasingly adopts a secular and atheistic perspective in many domains of experience, these studies remind us that the spiritual quest remains a potent force for all—pre-moderns, moderns, and post-moderns alike. As we reinvent our spiritual traditions, the pilgrimage sites of old become pilgrimage sites of new traditions that often eclectically borrow from the past in creating new sources of spiritual engagement. Because of the power of place, tradition, imposing architecture, and natural structures, these ancient pilgrimage traditions are often at the focus of both traditional and New Age religious responses (e.g., see www.sacredsites.com).

The reasons for the persistence of pilgrimage as a significant source of personal engagement with spirituality are examined by the contributors. The power of pilgrimage lies not only in its ancient functions as a healing journey, but perhaps more so in its broad transformative powers. The chapters here illustrate how pilgrimage exerts its influences at personal, interpersonal, social, class, political, and nationalistic levels, as well as provides symbols and processes for linking people together across these and other dimensions of difference.

As humanity experiences an increasing splintering of intimate social groups and anomie, pilgrimage may come to be a central feature of those reinvented traditions that help us reconnect with others and community. The contributors to this volume are to be thanked for sharing their understandings of how these ancient spiritual traditions still offer important resources for humanity.

Michael Winkelman
Tempe, Arizona

———⑥

Introduction

The Anthropology of Pilgrimage

Michael Winkelman and Jill Dubisch

*A*lmost three decades ago, Victor Turner, commenting on the lack of anthropological studies of pilgrimage, made the following observation: "[pilgrimage] was a great popular process, demographically comparable to labor migration, involving millions of people the world over in many days and even months of traveling, rich in symbolism and undoubtedly complex in organization, and yet very often ignored by the competing orthodoxies of social science and religion" (Turner 1974: 187).

Since Turner wrote these words, the anthropological literature on pilgrimage has burgeoned, due in no small part to the work of Turner himself, and of his wife Edith Turner. As anthropological perspectives on pilgrimage have developed, the Turners' analysis of pilgrimage as a rite of passage has inspired both emulation and criticism. And pilgrimage itself, far from dying out in a "postmodern" world, has continued to flourish, and has even experienced a renaissance, at both well-established and newer sites. This growth in both popular and anthropological interest in pilgrimage has similar roots. Pilgrimage is a highly flexible ritual that can be adapted to a range of needs and spiritual beliefs, thus drawing a wide spectrum of participants. This flexibility both reflects contemporary trends in spirituality and accords with anthropology's current emphasis on the dynamic and creative dimensions of ritual practice (e.g., Grimes 2000). Thus pilgrimage is at the same time a traditional practice within established religions and a ritual that can be melded with the eclectic activities and orientations of new contemporary forms of spirituality.

Anthropologists have examined pilgrimage through a variety of lenses, focusing on the ritual structure of the journey (Turner 1974; Turner and Turner 1978), pilgrimage's relationship to issues of local and national politics and identity (e.g., Crain 1992; Dubisch 1995), day by day accounts of the journey (Frey 1998), the sites at which pilgrims converge (Dubisch 1995), the religious context of pilgrimage (Gold 1988), and accounts by pilgrims themselves. Pilgrimage has political implications derived from individual and collective movement into a relationship with the sacred. Pilgrimage may reflect localized concerns and be associated with new or resurgent forms of nationalism or religious identity. Pilgrimage may even have shamanistic elements, altering consciousness and bringing one into contact with the spirit world to achieve healing. And as anthropologists seek ways to understand transnational forms of culture and community, the global nature of pilgrimage also has attracted anthropological attention (e.g., Coleman and Eade 2004). If rituals are, in Rosaldo's terms, "busy intersections," that is, places "where a number of distinct social processes intersect," (Rosaldo 1989: 17), then pilgrimage, a ritual in which the intersection is both literal and metaphorical, is one of the busiest intersections in the ritual world.

Although pilgrimage is motivated by a variety of needs and desires, and lends itself to a wide range of individual and communal motives, a powerful common theme that emerges from both historical and contemporary pilgrimage accounts is the search for healing.

The healing effects of pilgrimages can be termed "biopsychosociospiritual," encompassing physical, psychological, social, and spiritual dimensions and engaging the personal, social and political bodies (Scheper-Hughes and Lock 1987). For the pilgrim facing serious personal health problems, the approach to the "sacred other" provides a context for reconciliation and creation of a peace with one's circumstances, and even with impending death (see Justice 1997). Healing dynamics embodied in pilgrimages include 1) a physical journey with social, symbolic and physical effects; 2) an act of personal empowerment; 3) an assertion of the individual's identity in relationship to sacred "others" that integrates self within collective models; 4) the particularizing of individual suffering within broader frameworks that provide meaning; 5) a sense of social solidarity from an active connection with a community of fellow pilgrims; and 6) alteration of consciousness, eliciting psychophysiological dynamics conducive to supporting a range of bodily healing responses. The ritual journey, the power adhering to specific sacred or spiritual places, and the connection of pilgrimage sites with important cultural myths combine to provide a particularly compelling and potent context for healing of both physical and emotional ailments.

This role of pilgrimage as a source of healing has provided the impetus and focus for this volume. While recognizing the increasingly sophisticated anthropological analyses of pilgrimage in recent years, we also seek to retain a certain "grounding" of this anthropological subject matter by not losing sight of the fact that, for many who undertake such ritual journeys, pilgrimage is about everyday concerns and about the expression, and the search for resolution, of the human experience of suffering.

Thus the material offered here examines the healing effects of pilgrimage in a variety of cultural forms, from Nepalese shamanism to Catholic shrines to gatherings in the Nevada desert. These diverse cases also suggest a range of meanings embodied in the concept of "healing" itself, from healing of specific physical ailments, to redressing social suffering, to healing the wounds of the past, to creating a better world. Collectively and individually the chapters raise important questions about the nature of ritual generally, and healing in pilgrimage in particular, and about why so many participants find pilgrimage a compelling and effective means of addressing the problem of suffering.

Although the authors in this volume have engaged in the participant observation that is the hallmark of a specifically anthropological approach to the subject of pilgrimage, they reflect a variety of relationships to the phenomenon they are studying. Some are more observers; others are "observing participants." In some cases, as in Peter's Nepalese pilgrimage, the anthropologist undertakes the journey as a fully involved pilgrim himself, a "participating observer." These roles may shift across time, illustrated in Jill Dubisch's case, where at first she was simply going for a long motorcycle ride, and only later became both a pilgrim and a scholarly observer.

Because of this often intimate relationship with the subject matter, most of the authors seek to give a "feel" for pilgrimage in their chapters, describing their own experiences of a site or a typical pilgrimage journey. While such descriptions in part reflect recent trends in experimental writing and reflexivity in anthropology, they may also reflect the power that pilgrimage rituals have even for those who are not believers in the traditions that shape the pilgrimages. Many of us who have studied pilgrimage have experienced its totalizing nature, an experience that cannot be adequately represented in detached, academic prose alone. Pilgrimage is, after all, a highly physical and sensory experience that needs to be rendered in as much of its color and complexity as possible if we are to understand the nature and appeal of pilgrimage itself and to apprehend its healing power.[1]

Anthropological Approaches to Pilgrimage

In initiating the systematic anthropological study of pilgrimage, Victor and Edith Turner (Turner 1974, Turner and Turner 1978) drew upon Victor Turner's earlier work on ritual developed from van Gennep's (1960) concept of rites of passage. Van Gennep proposed a universal structure for rituals that move participants from one social status or stage of life to another. In such rituals, individuals or groups are symbolically (and often physically) separated from their former state or position, go through a period of ritual transition, and then are reincorporated into society in their new status. Turner focused his analysis on the transition stage, a liminal period of important ritual transformations characterized by *communitas*, a sense of commonality among participants. These key concepts of liminality[2] and communitas played an important role in the Turners' approach and their subsequent anthropological analysis of pilgrimage.

The Turners compared liminality in tribal ritual with similar phenomena in societies dominated by historical religions. In *Image and Pilgrimage in Christian Culture*, they contrast pilgrimage as a religious activity with monasticism and mysticism. "While monastic contemplatives and mystics could daily make interior salvific journeys, those in the world had to exteriorize theirs in the infrequent adventure of pilgrimage. For the majority, pilgrimage was the great liminal experience of the religious life. If mysticism is an interior pilgrimage, pilgrimage is exteriorized mysticism" (Turner and Turner 1978: 6–7).

Pilgrimage, the Turners argued, allowed its participants to leave behind the conflicts, difficulties, guilt, and "occasions of sin" of everyday life. The pilgrim finds freedom from the mundane in the course of the journey, becoming "increasingly circumscribed by symbolic structures: religious buildings, pictorial images, statuary, and sacralized features of the topography" (Turner and Turner 1978: 10). They noted that the generally optional and voluntary nature of pilgrimage contrasts with the obligatory rituals of tribal society, but that pilgrimage shares common elements in "rituals of affliction" undertaken in such societies to propitiate or exorcize forces that cause illness or misfortune. Rituals of affliction, however, have "a systemic and quasi-pragmatic character" in that the action of the ritual is normally expected to produce the desired result. Pilgrimage, on the other hand, the Turners suggest, is not expected to produce such an automatic result but rather depends upon the intervention of a holy figure who produces, at his or her will, a miracle. (Although they do acknowledge that pilgrimage often contains its magical elements as well.) Therefore, "the curative, charismatic aspect of pilgrimage is not thought of as an end in itself. In the paradigmatic Christian pilgrimage, the initiatory quality of the process is given priority, though it is an initiation to, not through, a threshold. Initiation is conceived of as leading...to a deeper level of religious participation" (14–15).

As anthropological studies of pilgrimage have expanded, the Turners' model has been criticized on several grounds, from its concepts of liminality and communitas, to its focus on the ritual structure of pilgrimage, to the model's neglect of pilgrimage's wider contexts and its deterministic approach in linking a highly variable phenomenon to specific social processes. As Michael Sallnow put it in an early collection of such criticism, "The study of pilgrimage, by the very nature of the phenomenon, demands that *a priori* assumptions concerning the relationship between religion and society be abandoned.... The link between ritual and secular processes should be regarded as analytically determinable in each case, rather than simply assumed" (1981: 179).

Many critiques emphasize that the Turners' general assumptions about the meaning of pilgrimage may be counterproductive, constraining analysis to a predetermined analytic structure that obscures or distorts the pilgrimage's critical features. Such generalized analytic structures may fail to account for key elements of pilgrimage that occur outside the ritual structure of the pilgrimage journey. For example, pilgrimages made in fulfillment of vows may be said to begin when the vow is made, rather than when the physical journey itself is undertaken (see Greenfield and Cavalcante, this volume). Moreover, at any one pilgrimage site, pilgrims come for a wide range of purposes, and find highly variable, and even conflicting, meanings of the site and pilgrimage (see Bowman 1991; Crain 1992; Murphy 1993). The Turners' model also overlooks the range of individual motivations that inspire pilgrims to undertake the journey (see Morinis 1984). Making contact with the sacred, fulfilling a vow, seeking healing for physical or spiritual ailments, marking a life passage, doing penance, affirming cultural identity, and simple curiosity are among the diverse motivations for undertaking pilgrimage.

Another criticism of the Turners' model is its focus on the ritual and experiential dimensions of pilgrimage, to the neglect of social and political dimensions. Pilgrimages are often associated with important national and historic events that produce powerful meanings and provide the focus and timing of major ritual events at these sites. An emphasis on the internal dynamics of the pilgrimage ritual, and on the pilgrims themselves, also may obscure the important roles played by communities and individuals who host the pilgrims along the way (see Dubisch, this volume; Michalowski and Dubisch 2001).

In some cases pilgrimage may not even be the original motivation for an individual's journey. Sometimes it is only after the journey is underway, or after the events connected with it have been experienced, that an individual comes to see the journey as pilgrimage and becomes transformed into a pilgrim. Some of those attending the Burning Man festival described in this volume by Gilmore, for example, only saw their participation as a pilgrimage after the event. Coleman's chapter suggests that perhaps it was through the actions performed by the friends he accompanied to Walsingham that they were transformed into pilgrims in the process of their visit. And the veterans on the Run for the Wall, the motorcycle pilgrimage to the Vietnam Veterans' Memorial described by Dubisch, often begin their trip thinking they are "just going for a ride." It is only when they find themselves caught up in the rituals and emotions along the way that they realize that they are on a ritual journey and acknowledge their need for healing of the wounds of war.

These criticisms of the Turners' schema raise a wider issue: given such variability, can we even fruitfully speak of "pilgrimage" as a unitary cross-cultural phenomenon? While Catholic pilgrimage traditions have widespread similarities from historical connections, other cultural traditions with ritual journeys may have no single word corresponding to the English term (see Dubisch 1995: 45–47). In Islam, for example, there is a distinction between the Hajj, the pilgrimage to Mecca, which is obligatory for all Muslims and timed to the lunar calendar, and the *ziyara*, a journey to a religious shrine such as a saint's tomb (Eickelman 1976: 173). In Israel, the term *aliya*, which refers to a pilgrimage to a shrine, also means a Jew's return from the Diaspora to live in the homeland, the passage to heaven of a saint, or a man's being called to bless the Torah in the synagogue (Sered 1992: 19–20). In Greek, the word *proskinima* refers to a ritual journey to a shrine, as well as the devotional acts performed upon entering any Orthodox church (Dubisch 1995). And as

Gemzöe points out in this volume, the Portuguese term *romaria* is applied both to a pilgrimage and to the traditional feast associated with saints' days.

Although these cases raise important caveats for cross-cultural application of the term *pilgrimage*, we feel our use of the term here is justified and is both analytically and ethnographically fruitful. Despite the differences in semantic range of culturally specific terms, the idea of a special or sacred journey seems worth distinguishing from other, more mundane forms of travel, whether we are analyzing pilgrimage from the point of view of the participants themselves or within a broader theoretical and comparative framework. A visit to a medical doctor, no matter how far one has to travel, differs from a visit to a saint's healing shrine, even if both have the goal of seeking a cure. Differences lie not only in the ritual nature of the journey, but also, as the chapters in this volume illustrate, in the *totality* of the event. Indeed such totality may be one of the keys to pilgrimage's efficacy as a healing journey.

Recent anthropological work on pilgrimage has moved away from criticism of the Turners' model and toward the examination of pilgrimage in wider theoretical and/or geographical contexts, including the relationship of pilgrimage to tourism (e.g., Jackowski and Smith 1992), transnational connections (e.g., Eickelman and Piscatori 1990), and the symbolic dimension of the pilgrimage destinations (e.g., Preston 1992). Some studies also focus on the ways that contemporary pilgrimage differs from pilgrimage of the past. Post, Pieper, and van Uden (1998), for example, suggest the "modern" pilgrim, while still motivated by the concerns that have stimulated pilgrimage in the past (resolution of personal and family problems, enhancing spirituality, traveling to places of particular spiritual importance), is also motivated by curiosity and the desire for relaxation and sociability. Certainly many pilgrimages have their touristic or recreational side, however serious the pilgrim's principal motivation for the journey (see the chapters by Greenfield and Cavalcante, Gemzöe, this volume). However, we should keep in mind that such motivations were not entirely lacking in "traditional" pilgrimage.

Nonreligious pilgrimage also is increasingly the object of anthropological study (e.g., Reader and Walter 1993). Such "secular pilgrimages" nonetheless exhibit characteristics associated with more traditional forms. These include the ritual nature of the journey, the power of the special site, the connection of the journey to powerful cultural myths, the social and spiritual connections established on the journey, and the transformative nature of the undertaking, including the transformation from illness to health.

The objects of such nontraditional pilgrimage may vary greatly, as do the pilgrims' motives for undertaking such journeys. Graceland, Elvis Presley's home and now a museum and shrine, gives Presley fans inspiration and comfort in the closeness it brings to "the King" (C. King 1993). Death and tragedy may also create secular pilgrimage sites, such as the home of the Liverpool soccer club where many came to mourn the ninety-four soccer fans crushed to death in a soccer game at the Hillsborough stadium (Davie 1993). The site of the bombing of the federal building in Oklahoma City, and more recently, the World Trade Center in New York City, have also become destinations of pilgrims, many of whom seek healing or "closure" for the grief and loss such tragedies have caused. And the Run for the Wall, the motorcycle pilgrimage to the Vietnam Veterans Memorial, is a secular pilgrimage whose aims include both collective political activism and personal healing (Dubisch this volume; Michalowski and Dubisch 2001). Labeling such pilgrimages as "secular," however, should not obscure the fact that they may have important spiritual meaning for the participants. As Gilmore's description of the Burning Man festival shows, the line between secular and religious may be difficult to draw, as ritual itself is a creative process, and one that both reflects and constitutes new spiritual meanings and experiences.

Victor Turner (1974) referred to pilgrimage as an "anti-modern" ritual, based as it is on faith and the belief in miraculous powers. The belief in the healing powers of pilgrimage and shrines contrasts with science, rationality, and the modern "disenchanted" world. At the same time, pilgrimage can also be seen as a ritual form particularly suited to the postmodern era. As institutionalized forms of spirituality have waned, pilgrimage accommodates itself to individual spiritual searches and individual needs (see Weibel, this volume). The following statement by Post, Pieper, and van Uden clearly applies to much of contemporary pilgrimage: "Unexpectedly and often outside the sphere of the organized church...there is an enormous interest in rituals and symbols.... In many places there is a flowering of rituals, public and private, which also...includes rituals from popular religious culture" (1998: 1).

Even when contemporary pilgrimage takes place within institutionalized contexts (as in Catholic pilgrimage), it is nonetheless at least partially structured by individual pilgrims and their needs. In some cases it is even conducted in defiance of authorities who may refuse to grant official status to a pilgrimage site or who seek to discourage certain types of activities. Green-field and Cavalcante point out that many of the sites that are the object of veneration in Brazil are not officially sanctioned by the Catholic Church, and Gemzöe offers a vivid description of a church official's failed attempt to lead the crowd of pilgrims in a hymn during a religious festival at the Por-tuguese shrine of Fátima. In many situations, even visits to officially estab-lished sites involve an unmediated interaction between the pilgrim and the holy figure to whom a shrine is dedicated. In Dubisch's work at a Greek Orthodox shrine, she noted that most pilgrims never encountered a priest, but appealed directly to the Panayia (Virgin Mary) for a miracle (Dubisch 1995). Moreover, pilgrimage's ritual form is readily adapted to new, emerging and self-creative manifestations of spirituality and to personal needs and beliefs, as is seen in Weibel's discussion of "religious creatives." These individuals seek spiritual experiences at the shrines of various religions but assign their own meaning to these shrines and the experiences.

It is clear that any single label—whether "traditional," "modern," or "post-modern"—distorts or obscures pilgrimage's complexity and flexibility. The multiple possibilities, the flexibility of pilgrimage ritual, and the powerful effect of both the journey and the arrival at a special place give pilgrimage wide appeal in the contemporary world. Increasing affluence, greater ease of transportation, and various media (including the internet; e.g., sacredsites .com) that make pilgrimage sites more widely known within both local and global contexts also contribute to this popularity. An additional attraction, especially in the West, may be the fit that pilgrimage enjoys with the desire for more participatory, somatic forms of religious practice, and pilgrimage's role in contemporary searches for identity, from the local, to the national, to the global. Thus the Wixárika described by Schaefer affirm their identity through pilgrimage to the land of their ancestors, while Vietnam veterans con-nect with important American symbols on their cross-country pilgrimage to the Vietnam Veterans Memorial, and the "Religious Creatives" described by Weibel assert a spiritual identity that draws eclectically on ancient and con-temporary traditions. The relative elasticity of meaning of pilgrimage and the ways in which pilgrimage accords with contemporary spiritual search also make it an attractive ritual experience. Indeed, almost any journey may be termed a "pilgrimage" these days, its meaning defined by inner feelings and motivation rather than by external institutionalized forms.

Pilgrimage Sites:
Places of Power, the Power of Place

Although the notion of purely spiritual pilgrimage has played an important role in some religious traditions (especially Protestantism), pilgrimage commonly involves an actual journey to a physical place. Pilgrimage sites themselves shape the pilgrimage, and the particular nature and history of the site shapes its power, including its power to heal. While many kinds of places can become the object of pilgrimage, such sites, whether sacred or secular, tend to have in common what Preston has termed "spiritual magnetism" (Preston 1992). Such "magnetism" may be rooted in a site's association with major mythological or historical events within a specific religious tradition, as in the case of Mecca or Jerusalem, or in the association of a site with a particular person (e.g., saints' tombs; see Sered, this volume; Mernissi 1977). The association need not even be religious, as pilgrimages to Graceland and to the site of rock star Jim Morrison's grave in Paris demonstrate. In some cases, such as the Irish holy wells, the reasons for the power of the site are lost in antiquity and only the belief in their power remains. Miraculous occurrences, and especially apparitions of holy figures, may establish new pilgrimage sites, or enhance the reputations of existing ones. Miracles of healing following such apparitions confirm the power of the site and lay the groundwork for pilgrimage.[3] In other cases, the physical features of the sites themselves draw pilgrims. In China, for example, mountains are believed to have spiritual power and are often the destination of pilgrims (Naquin and Yu 1992). Astronomical, geomagnetic, and other properties may also give sites their power, leading thousands to flock annually to such places as the red rock "vortexes" of Sedona, Arizona, to experience their spiritual and healing forces.

Pilgrimage exemplifies the belief in the power of place, the inherent healing energies of specific locations. Pilgrimage's movement into sacred space involves engagement with special energies and powers, often embedded in the landscape and architecture. These physical notions of sacred space are especially emphasized in New Age or "Religious Creatives" pilgrimages (see Weibel's chapter) in which we find the creative adoption of Christian sacred places, based not upon Christian theology, but upon notions of inherent energies of place. The burgeoning literature on the positive health effects of magnetic force, radiation, electromagnetic energies, weather phenomena, and geological processes also provides a rationale for the pilgrimages of many New

Age enthusiasts (Devereux 1990; King 1992; Cowan and Silk 1999; Merz 1985; Pettis 1999). Such phenomena may be seen as explaining the power of specific sites and their ability to heal.

Records of healing often accumulate at particular pilgrimage sites, providing dramatic evidence of a shrine's healing powers and adding to a site's spiritual power. The crutches left at Chimayo, New Mexico, for example, testify to the shrine's ability to restore the ability to walk to its petitioners. Ex-votos of various types offer another common display of a site's miraculous powers. These range from the Greek *tamata*, small metal plaques that depict the nature of the healing performed or requested at a shrine (Dubisch 1995), to the original "home-made" ex-votos of Brazilian pilgrims described in the chapters by King and by Greenfield and Cavalcante. Tales of healing often circulate at a shrine, and beyond, adding to the site's reputation and attracting even more pilgrims.

Some pilgrimage sites are established spontaneously because of miraculous occurrences at the site, or because of felt emotional or spiritual need (as at the site of tragedy). In some cases, a pilgrimage site was not intended or foreseen, for example, the Vietnam Veterans Memorial in Washington, D.C., which since its inauguration has become an important pilgrimage destination for veterans and nonveterans alike (see Berdahl 1994). Other sites are promoted by both religious and secular authorities, prompted in part by pilgrimage's important economic and political effects, which include pilgrimage's contribution to local economies (Greenfield and Cavalcante, this volume) and the opportunity it offers for the expression of nationalism or regionalism, as well as for the strengthening of religious faith (see, Crain 1992).

The Purposes of Pilgrimage: Pilgrimage as Transformational Quest

Despite the various critiques of the Turners' work and the multiple directions of recent anthropological studies of pilgrimage, many authors in this volume find the Turners' emphasis on pilgrimage as a rite of passage, and on separation and leaving "ordinary life" behind, a fruitful starting point for analysis. This is in part a consequence of our focus here, which is the passage from illness to health, whether the passage involves the healing of self, family, or community, or even the search to heal society as a whole (e.g., Gilmore, this volume). This transformational approach highlights the ritual power of pil-grimage, a power that links the diverse forms of pilgrimage and illustrates its dynamic and creative nature. This section addresses the personal transforma-tion of pilgrimage and its empowerment, while the subsequent section addresses pilgrimage's healing power; however, the two functions or effects cannot be clearly separated.

Self-Transformation

Turner and Turner's (1978) view of pilgrimage as engaging in separation is manifested in the transformation of daily life patterns. Pilgrimage produces a movement into a sacred space that has both temporal and spatial dimen-sions. The movement of pilgrimage out of ordinary physical and personal space provides a social marker readily noted by others, and a sacralizing of the pilgrim's status as a special marker of faith and devotion. Pilgrimage typi-cally implies a temporal reorientation involving a multiplicity of relationships to the past, a form of reference to historical, prehistorical, and imagined tra-ditions of the sacred. As many of the chapters here illustrate, these relation-ships to the past often express an adherence to tradition, as well as entail a resistance to current hierarchy, orthodoxy, and power. Pilgrimage involves a movement into sacred space, symbolically, socially, and physically. In this respect, pilgrimage can restore one's relationships with aspects of the sacred, illustrating how pilgrimage is an inherently healing (whole-ing) process.

A central aspect of pilgrimage is the effort to connect with something beyond self, an encounter with the divine "other," which is the most preva-lent of spontaneous religious experiences (Stark 1997). This primordial effort to establish a relationship with a "sacred other" is a healing process, a dynamic of self-other relations that has developmental and healing implications (Winkelman 2000). These processes combine personal identity within sym-bolic and historically situated social reference systems that contribute to a ref-ormation and assertion of the sacred self (see Pandian 1991; Csordas 1994). The participation in ritual can provide a sacred aura to the pilgrim, a special social role that is recognized and rewarded. Pilgrimage exists outside of, and in some respects in opposition to, the ordinary demands and requirements of life and society and the pilgrim's normal roles and status.[4] These roles and requirements are often suspended for the duration of the ritual journey, a journey in which not only is everyday life left behind, but also in which the only status that counts (ideally at least) is one's status as a pilgrim. This social recognition provides validation that reinforces completion of a new identity that incorporates a sense of sanctity, or at least a new sense of "wholeness." Pilgrimage can place one in the context of traditions that provide a historical and sacred context for identity and transformation, balancing the relationship of self to society and cosmos, and consequently, integrating self into community.

The accounts offered here attest to this transformational process of pilgrimage in which the self is altered and affirmed in relationship to others, both social and sacred. These transformations of identity occur at many levels, and with reference to several "others." Pilgrimage commonly offers a reference to the sacred past where models of the self are expressed in deeply embedded cultural traditions. The incorporation of sacred identities can be part of this process, as manifested in the Wixárika pilgrimage (Schaefer, this volume), where reenactment of creation myths enables pilgrims to assume the persona of deities. The bonding with others that occurs in pilgrimage provides mechanisms for transformation of identity, a result of experiencing one's individual identity in relationship to others.

Life-transforming experiences are at the core of both "traditional" and more contemporary forms of pilgrimage. As Gilmore illustrates with the Burning Man festival, the remote destination requires a reorientation in time and space that permits a release of aspects of the self. This is both a letting go of "baggage"—the things no longer desired—as well as a form of radical self-expression, that is, a manifestation of core aspects of the inner self not supported by ordinary social contexts. Participants build an entire, temporary city in the middle of the Nevada desert, a city in which all are equal and in which many of the ordinary rules and practices of society (such as buying and selling of goods) are suspended or even forbidden. These forms of psychological release are healing, a release of those tensions created in ordinary life by the lack of a supportive and accepting community for self. The opportunity to engage in a process of self-reflexivity, combined with a connection with kindred spirits, promotes the assertion of true identity, enabling an integration of self in the processes of connection and renewal. The rituals of the "burning man" provide a symbolic release and purification. One can leave the old self and its constraints and be reborn with a new socially accepted identity.

The curative aspects of self-transformation are explicit in Peters's characterizations of Nepalese pilgrimage. These practices provide the context for an initiation process and embodiment of spirits that fulfills the quest for personal empowerment. The reacquisition of self is exemplified in the soul retrieval processes, reestablishing control over vital aspects of self through overcoming evil spirits that have compromised personal integrity. Schaefer reveals these self-transformation processes in the Wixárika pilgrimage as well, in which the transformational journey brings a sense of vitality in connectedness with family and community, reinforcing cultural pride. The pilgrims go "to find our life," engaging in a life-renewing process that provides contexts for resolution of personal problems.

Pilgrimage may itself be viewed as part of the dynamics of self-development, and hence as both model and metaphor. For the Christian, pilgrimage emphasizes a model of life, enduring trials and tribulations to arrive at a sacred destination. (And conversely, life itself may be viewed as a pilgrimage, especially in the Protestant tradition.) The Christian pilgrim acquires a sacred role, engaging in pious acts that demonstrate faith and provide a public recognition of the person's state of sanctification.

Pilgrimage as Popular Empowerment

Pilgrimage attracts some individuals more than others. While certain pilgrimages, such as the Hajj to Mecca, may be enjoined on all devout members of a faith, in most cases pilgrimage is voluntary. This voluntary character and the sense of empowerment and of personal connection with spiritual power that pilgrimage can provide make it an appealing ritual for the socially disadvantaged and marginal. Pilgrimage can also provide a means of protest against that marginalized condition, a protest that may itself become part of healing. King shows that the "spiritual contract" entered into by the individual Brazilian pilgrim with a saint bypasses any intercession by religious authorities. This "silent rebellion" against the religious hierarchy gives the impoverished inhabitants of the backlands of Northeast Brazil a sense of empowerment and a creative role in their own healing, as well as expressing resistance to rigidly defined social roles and expectations.

As King's study illustrates, pilgrimage is often carried out in a context in which the pilgrims are engaged in a popular and individual act that is in tension or even outright conflict with established hierarchies of the church or of society. This is because of the direct contact it affords with the divine, a contact unmediated by church powers and representatives. In addition, pilgrimages have often exemplified the struggle between local traditions and church hierarchy, a struggle in which local autonomy is asserted. As Sered shows, the marginalization from the culture of the Jewish religious hierarchy experienced by the poor and powerless can be redressed by engagement by Jewish pilgrims in activities that bring one into direct contact with the sacred.

Such local empowerment is also exemplified in contemporary pilgrimages, as Gilmore illustrates in the Burning Man festival. The rejection of consumer lifestyles, commodification, and vending are salient statements against dominant value orientations. A counter-materialist ethos is emphasized in the festival's gift economy, a sharing that creates binding ties in a new community of identity. An antihierarchical stance is exemplified in the lack of an official way to engage in ritual, which is dictated by the individual, not by theology. These individual approaches provide meaning and personal empowerment, a self-integration of body, mind, and spirit within a new system of evaluation. Pilgrimage serves as an act of empowerment, an active engagement in the creative aspects of self-expression that provides healing.

Gender is also an important element of pilgrimage related to issues of empowerment. There are several reasons why women predominate in pilgrimage in certain religious traditions or historical periods, or at certain sites. Pilgrimage can provide a legitimate excursion for women whose lives are otherwise restricted (see Gemzöe, this volume; Dubisch 1995; Hirschon 1983; Mernissi 1977). Women's responsibility for the health of their families and the special concerns of women (such as fertility, child-bearing, and the health of children) often lead them to engage in pilgrimage. In both Catholic and Orthodox Christian traditions the identification of women with the Virgin Mary is an important element in the popularity of Marian pilgrimage (see Gemzöe, this volume) and women often seek her aid for issues related to birth. And Sered's analysis shows that Israeli Jewish women's pilgrimages to the tombs of the "three Rachels" provide understanding of the particular social suffering they experience.

Women's particular responsibilities for the care of children and families and their health, and the need for spiritual assistance and assurance in meeting these role expectations, produce a female dimension to pilgrimage. Gemzöe emphasizes the ways in which the pilgrim's focus upon intimate, emotional and personal relationships to Mary as a mother figure enables her to perceive Mary as a source of solutions to her problems. Sered's assessment of the role of the "Rachels" in Jewish pilgrimage shows how these mythological models provide many symbolic referents for self—the woman as symbol of vulnerability, the dynamics of exile, and renouncement of personal needs in service to others. The lives of the Rachels provide models for the Jewish woman, exemplifying and reinforcing patience, endurance of suffering, and acceptance of loss.

There is also an intimate relationship of women's bodies and pilgrimage. In Brazil, women may offer part of their bodies at the shrine of St. Francis, cutting off their long hair and leaving it with the other *milagres* (Greenfield and Cavalcante, this volume). Greek women's extreme performance of pilgrimage vows, such as ascending to the church on their knees or walking barefoot, has been described by Dubisch as a kind of "poetics of suffering," a dramatic and visceral demonstration of their devotion to their roles as mothers and caretakers of their families (Dubisch 1995). In her discussion of women pilgrims in late medieval England, Morrison suggests that

> Many women traveled for the sake of the family, which was often centred on the woman's body.... But if this body could not function properly—if it were sterile, if the child it carried miscarried, if the child it carried died or was sickly...if the body could not produce milk to feed the child—then the body, a metonymy for a healthy, functioning family, needed to be cured. The woman's body, then, stands for the family. If the woman's body is healed, so is the family.... It symbolizes the state of her family's health. (Morrison 2000: 3)

Sered notes that Israeli Jewish women suffer from more physical and psychological ailments, and are seen as weaker in body, than their male counterparts. She suggests that this in part stems from women's continuing sense of "exile" and alienation. Pilgrimage to the tomb of Jewish female saints helps to ameliorate their sense of disconnection. In northeastern Brazil (King, this volume) women's somatization of their doubly subordinate status within the oppressed and patriarchal culture of the poor leads to a host of physical symptoms for which they seek relief at the shrine of St. Francis of the Wounds.

The body and bodily images play an important role in pilgrimage in a broader sense as well. Not only do pilgrims bring their bodies to the pilgrimage site, but pilgrimage also is a highly physical experience, one that often involves hardship or suffering as well as incorporating the sights, sounds, and other sensual experiences that accompany the pilgrim's travel. And as Gemzöe points out, in the Portuguese community, a healthy body is a gift of God and a healed body a sign of God's divine intervention. Body parts and whole bodies are modeled, molded, and depicted to leave as offerings at shrines. And individuals may crawl on their knees, walk barefoot or for long distances, or perform other physically difficult and even painful feats as part of their supplication or fulfillment of vows at a pilgrimage shrine. Such acts may even be liberating, bringing the pilgrim to a profound altered state of consciousness. Peters recounts how, when he inadvertently left his shoes behind before embarking on his shamanistic pilgrimage in Nepal, not only did he not feel any of the hazards littering the roadway, he felt himself dance more freely than he ever had before. And as Dubisch argues, for the Vietnam veterans making the pilgrimage to the Wall, riding their motorcycles provides both an escape from the psychological and emotional problems that haunt them and an absorbing visceral experience that is part of what gives the Run for the Wall its healing power (Dubisch, this volume; Michalowski and Dubisch 2001).

Men may also seek healing for problems specific to their gender. As Gemzöe points out, men's vows in the Portuguese community where she worked tend to be related to their own safety within the particular hazardous conditions they might face, such as being fishermen or serving in the military. The primary participants in the Run for the Wall are male Vietnam veterans who did not feel they received a "welcome home" when they returned from the war, but rather were shunned, their experiences ignored, and their status as veterans perceived as a stigmatized one. The Run for the Wall allows them to reclaim a sense of identity or pride as veterans and to be honored as warriors by offering them a context for acceptance, which is a part of this pilgrimage's healing mission (Michalowski and Dubisch 2001).

Pilgrimage is often undertaken on behalf of others, not just for oneself or one's family. In the Brazilian pilgrimage described by King, pilgrims carry milagres (ex-votos) for those back home who cannot make the journey, and bring home religious souvenirs or holy water from St. Francis' shrine (see also Greenfield and Cavalcante, this volume). On the Run for the Wall, one of the slogans is "We ride for those who can't," exemplifying the pilgrims' belief that their political and spiritual agendas link them to other veterans, both the living and the dead (Dubisch, this volume; Michalowski and Dubisch 2001). In his account of Nepalese pilgrimage, Peters speaks of "bringing healing back to the community"; thus the shaman's journey benefits those at home, not only those who go on pilgrimage. And many of those who attend the Burning Man festival described by Gilmore see themselves as taking some of the "culturally transformative" power of the event home with them. In these ways, the healing power of pilgrimage reaches beyond those individuals who physically participate in the pilgrimage itself.

While pilgrimage is often undertaken at the initiative of the pilgrim, some religious traditions emphasize pilgrimage more than others. (For example, pilgrimage is a less common ritual activity in Protestantism than in Catholicism.) And pilgrimage for the purposes of healing is also more emphasized in some traditions. It is in part for these reasons that the material collected in this volume tends to focus on Catholic pilgrimage in a variety of settings. At the same time, the absence of other religious traditions, and particularly of Islam, from our collection should not be taken to mean that healing pilgrimage is completely absent in those traditions (see, Betteridge 1992; Mernissi 1997).

But what, exactly, do we mean by "healing" in this context? Does pilgrimage in fact bring about healing, and if so, in what ways can we understand this to occur?

Healing Processes in Pilgrimages

The use of the term *healing* in the chapters here encompasses a broad range of meanings. Using Kleinman's distinction between "curing" as the elimination of a disease as defined by the biomedical system and "healing" as the broader restoring to wholeness (whether or not a "cure" is effected as well; Kleinman 1988: 3–6), we note that many pilgrims are seeking a cure for very specific physical ailments. Some of these ailments are addressed by the biomedical system, but others are deemed incurable within that system. Pilgrims also search for healing in a communal or global sense (as with the pilgrims to the Burning Man festival described by Gilmore) or in a spiritual or psychological sense (as with the Vietnam veterans who seek healing for the emotional and psychic wounds that are the long-term consequences of their war experiences). This healing reflects meaning-making processes derived from relations established between the individual sufferer and broader patterns of cultural representation, particularly those embodied in mythological and spiritual systems and in the symbolic, social, and physical properties of places.

While the desire to heal physical ailments may be a less common (though by no means absent) reason for undertaking pilgrimage in countries with advanced biomedical systems, such a desire continues to be important where there is a lack of biomedical resources.[5] Individuals may ask God, a saint, or other spiritual figure for healing of a physical problem, vowing to visit a specific shrine if their prayers are answered (as discussed here in the Greenfield and Cavalcante and Gemzöe chapters). Sufferers may request help for chronic conditions that biomedicine does not effectively address or even recognize, such as demonic possession (Dubisch 1995), Post Traumatic Stress Disorder and somatization (see the chapters by Dubisch, King, and Sered in this volume).

In the contemporary United States and in parts of Europe, the search for psychic healing, cultural healing, self-fulfillment, and spiritual identity (rather than the healing of specific physical ailments) has increasingly become the focus of "modern" pilgrimage. For example, Presley fans who make the pilgrimage to Graceland do not seek physical healing but instead are drawn by the desire for a spiritual experience associated with closeness to the shrine of "the King." "His fan clubs act as a communion of saints and believers, while pilgrimage at his grave is part of the shared experience of being a Presley fan. . . . Pilgrims to Graceland attest to how Elvis makes them feel; how he 'lifts their spirits' and makes them young and whole" (C. King 1993: 98).

Similarly, the Vietnam veterans described by Dubisch are not seeking a cure for specific physical problems when they participate in the Run for the Wall, but are looking for psychological and emotional healing from the long-term wounds of war, and for ways to express and heal the grief and guilt they still feel for the loss of comrades who died in combat. Their healing is also social, an acceptance of warriors who decades before returned to a society in which they were viewed not as heroes, but as villains.

Social Healing

One form of the healing that takes place in pilgrimage is the "healing" of social status. Such healing may be viewed in the context of social suffering. Social, economic, and political forces can lead to both the physical ailments of poverty or war and the emotional and spiritual illnesses that accompany them, whether or not such social suffering is acknowledged by the pilgrims themselves (see Kleinman, Das, and Lock 1997). Thus the Brazilian pilgrims described by King not only suffer from a variety of physical ailments readily categorized by conventional medicine, they are also victims in a larger sense of the political and economic conditions that have condemned them to a life of catastrophic poverty. The collective movement of pilgrimage provides contact with broader social others, with a wider community of reference. These relationships have many healing dimensions, embodied in the effects upon self and other, particularly through emotions and community bonding (see below).

The power of a pilgrimage site for social healing may be tied to larger political and historical events. The Church of the Madonna of the Annunciation on the Greek island of Tinos, for example, is associated historically and mythically with the very beginnings of the modern Greek state and, more contemporarily, with important Greek patriotic holidays such as Greek Independence Day (March 25). Thus, major religious events celebrated at the church are patriotic celebrations as well, tying together religion, nationalism, and the desires and motivations of pilgrims who have undertaken pilgrimage for entirely personal reasons (Dubisch 1995).

Similarly, Coleman shows that while pilgrims to Walsingham may come for the healing of physical ailments, they are also provided a place and occasion for "history to come alive." This allows Catholics to assert their legitimacy within English Christianity and to heal "the destructive mistakes of the past." Sered's contribution shows ways in which Israeli Jewish women find healing through the "understanding" of three major female saints who are intimately tied to Jewish mythology, ritual, and history, as well as being associated with matters of particular importance to women (fertility, romantic love, marital harmony). In these ways, individual suffering and illness are placed within meaningful narratives, rather than being seen as solely personal. Such narratives may derive from cultural myths, as in the shrine of the three Rachels described by Sered, or may reenact the mythic past, as in the case of the Wixárika and Nepalese pilgrimages described by Schaefer and Peters.

Healing thus emerges in the realignment of self with broader cultural patterns, defining self and other. Divine contact can provide the basis of a sacred narrative relationship, bringing the pilgrim's identity into relationship with the models exemplified in the divine other. These models and metaphors from the spiritual realm enable personal problems to be placed in broader social and cosmological contexts, thus providing healing in the sense of "wholing." As Schaefer points out, among the Wixárika healing involves finding a wholeness of self, a theme echoed in other pilgrimages as well. "Healing," then, encompasses not just physical ailments but also life problems, spiritual loss, social alienation, and the fragmentation of self.

Symbolic Healing and Metaphoric Processes

Symbolic processes are central to the healing dynamics of pilgrimage. Dow's (1986) model of symbolic healing is explicitly invoked as an explanatory framework by Sered in her explanation of the healing power of the pilgrimage

for Jewish woman. Kirmayer's (1993) model of symbolic healing emphasizes the healing power of metaphor as a system for linking the levels of the
body through the conceptual processes of metaphor. The mechanisms of symbolic healing involve meaning, an active relationship of self to a message that
is expressed in thought, feelings, and imagination, as well as social interactions.
Kirmayer argues that the healing efficacy of the ritual derives from metaphorical processes that produce psychophysiological effects. These effects are
derived from expectations found in the larger social context. Metaphor transforms the person by juxtaposing sensory, affective, and cognitive concepts and
reshaping experience through this combined information. Metaphor has
effects by providing meanings that link the mythic level of narratives, the
archetypal level of the body, and the level of the personal situation. Myth,
metaphor, and archetype, respectively represent social, psychological, and
bodily contributions to meaning. Meanings shared among bodily, psychological, and social processes provide mechanisms of symbolic healing. Metaphors
are derived from our experience of embodiment, including social relationships,
which are also embodied forces that we feel. Myth organizes the structures of
thought and behavior and has the power to evoke and reorder life experiences.

Kirmayer's model emphasizes three mechanisms of healing: 1) through
structuring conceptual domains, 2) by evoking strong sensory/affective associations, and 3) by bridging the archetypal and mythic levels of experience
that are natural categories that conflate the biological and experiential meanings of body and society (Kirmayer 1993: 176). Metaphor heals by integrating
the conceptual levels into the felt meanings within sensory and emotional
processes and physiological levels. The healing efficacy of myths derives from
their ability to unite within a narrative the disparate aspects of human experience, especially deep contradictions. Archaic myths associated with pilgrimage still work today because they tap into the pilgrim's archetypal
structures, uniting the abstract and concrete thoughts in bodily feelings. The
sensory and affective foundations of metaphor are integrated in verbal expressions, synesthetic and sensorimotor experience, and social life. For metaphor
theory, meaning is not simply mental representation. The meaning of
metaphors is presented through and to the representational systems of the
lower levels of sensory affective processing and bodily experiences. The mechanisms of symbolic healing derive from a kind of truth or knowledge, in turn
derived from the immediacy of bodily felt experiences that are grounded in
archetypal patterns shaped by cultural and social factors.

Meanings, Emotions, and Stress-Reduction

The power of pilgrimage to heal includes effects derived from emotions and meaningfulness. Pilgrimage's social and symbolic processes have direct effects upon physiological processes, particularly those related to anxiety and stress. Ritual healing can modify emotional distress through the provision of explanations and mechanisms for obtaining relief through social and symbolic processes. Ritual has effects on basic responses of the autonomic nervous system (ANS) through associated cultural symbols and social processes, as well as through direct physiological manipulations that produce relaxation in the ANS (Winkelman 2000). Ritual can alleviate high levels of pituitary/adrenal activity of the resistance stage of the stress reaction through changing interpretations, and consequently emotional responses. The physiological processes of stress can be elicited by social situations and symbolic meanings, which leave the body activated and mobilized. This contributes to the development of many conditions—ulcers, hypertension, cardiovascular problems, migraine headaches, and the like. The stress—psychological and physiological—results from the self's inability to manage social, psychological, and emotional aspects of life, particularly those related to fear and threats to self. Stress responses that evolved to deal with threats to physical survival are also elicited by interpersonal interactions and the broader macrosocial context—economic, political, and symbolic processes that affect the individual's well-being. The human organism faces these emotional threats with the same physical defense systems used to deal with enemies (the flight or fight syndrome). But symbolic threats generally don't allow for a physical struggle, so chemicals generated by symbolic occurrences arouse the body but are not used. Symbolic management of these emotional effects is central to the healing of pilgrimages, providing a sense of assurance of well-being that can directly stimulate the limbic brain, reducing fear, anxiety, and the physiological dynamics of stress.

Pilgrimages use both symbols that alleviate emotional trauma and social support and activities that provide healing processes that transform attachments and emotions. Dubisch's description of Vietnam veterans' Run for the Wall, for example, illustrates the contemporary role of pilgrimage in addressing the psychosocial wounds of trauma and of abandonment and neglect by society. The collective support provides a context for grieving, addressing guilt, and reconnecting with dead comrades. The social dynamics of this pilgrimage address emotional trauma by constructing a coherent sense of self, removing the negative stigma associated with the past, and creating a sense of pride and self-respect. This healing process transforms personal consciousness, as well as public and social consciousness regarding veterans, providing social support and bonds of brotherhood that empower self-transformation.

Faith and the Power of Belief

Central to the healing processes of pilgrimage are the effects of belief and faith. Vivid testimonies to extraordinary miraculous cures and a vicarious sharing in that healing experience are central to pilgrimage. The special destinations of pilgrimage often have a rich history of curing, a history that elicits positive expectation and hope. These positive expectations provided by history, the story telling of fellow pilgrims, and the "miraculous" cures on site mobilize the pilgrim's positive expectations.

Pilgrimage may also be carried out as a form of request for divine response, an offering made for future benefits. This illustrates the central emotional dynamics of addressing fears and instilling hope and expectations, key elements of the healing process. The belief in the power of faith for healing extends beyond the act of pilgrimage. A repeated theme (e.g., Gemzöe, Greenfield and Cavalcante) is that the pilgrimage is an act carried out in fulfillment of a promise made, contingent upon a divine response to a situation of acute danger to self or family members. This enactment of pilgrimage in fulfillment of a previous contract for healing, including the healing of others, raises some questions. Does the vow, one's faith, or the conditional offer of pilgrimage in exchange for healing have effects upon others?

The pilgrim engaging in arduous activities also provides a social statement of faith, countering the doubts of self and others' about the pilgrim's possession of the faith necessary to receive healing. The pilgrim may then be able to deflect blame of insufficient faith, attributing lingering illness to God's will or plan. A significant feature of pilgrimage is the surrender to higher powers, whether it is the power of tradition, personal guidance from the spirit world, or the power of liturgy or God. This acceptance of the effects of spiritual influences upon one's life exemplifies the qualities of spontaneous spiritual experiences, the sense of presence of a spiritual other who has a purpose for humans (Stark 1997). This relationship with the holy provides healing, exemplified in the common Indo-European linguistic roots of *holy, whole,* and *heal.*

Community Dynamics and Opioid Elicitation

Whether pilgrims travel in groups of known acquaintances or with strangers, the sense of community with fellow humans on a common mission is central to the healing power of pilgrimage. Gilmore's assessment of the Burning Man festival illustrates this effort at forging a sense of community in which there is trust of fellow humans. The sense of connection, release, and renewal provides for a redefinition of self in relation to others at multiple levels—symbolic, social, personal, and physical. The contact with others can lead to the creation of a sense of relationship to others that is both personal and physical, and the elimination (at least to some extent) of social distinctions.[6] The physical contact of pilgrims—cramped in buses, pressed together in masses—engages the body at levels that are inherently therapeutic. A sense of connection with others, a community that enables expression and validation of identity, provides tangible benefits through reinforcing a sense of self-worth (see e.g., Post, Pieper, and van Uden 1998). While the vacation-like festive and social atmosphere of at least some of pilgrimages might be discounted as an unintended side-effect of the pilgrimage,[7] these social relations might be central healing mechanisms. The social and recreational dimensions of pilgrimage may play a role in distracting attention from serious physical ailments, or they may provide the social relations necessary for affirming sense of self and self-worth. The social contact among pilgrims can be one of community and bonding, providing multiple mechanisms for healing.

Social and ritual practices that enhance social cohesion have the potential to elicit psychophysiological mechanisms that release endogenous opiates (Frecska and Kulcsar 1989; Winkelman 1997, 2000) and elicit psychobiologically mediated attachment responses that are based in the body's natural opioid mechanisms. A normal part of the human condition is the release of opioids as part of the mediation of human bonding and attachment. The emotionally charged cultural symbols that have been associated with physiological systems during attachment socialization provide a basis for linking mythological and somatic spheres and elicitation of the opioid system. Some pilgrimages also engage the penitent in strenuous physical activities that can elicit the response of the endogenous opioids, including extensive dancing and other exhaustive physical activities (e.g., clapping, walking), temperature extremes (e.g., sweat lodges), stressful procedures (e.g., fasting), painful stimuli (e.g., flagellation, crawling on one's knees, self-inflicted wounds), and long-distance motorcycle riding (Dubisch; see also Prince 1982; Winkelman 1997).

This opioid release may stimulate healing responses through the elicitation of emotions and physiological processes, including endocrine and immunological systems (Frecska and Kulcsar 1989), enhancing psychoneuroimmunological responses. The opioid release also produces a sense of euphoria, as well as feelings of certainty and belongingness that address the psychophysiological dynamics of stress and anxiety. These ritual processes for opioid elicitation reflect dynamic functions of the psyche that provide coping skills and mechanisms for maintenance of bodily homeostasis (Jilek 1989), as well as facilitating environmental adaptation, enhancing the biological synchronization among members of a group, and providing mechanisms for the reduction of pain and enhanced tolerance of stress. This opioid elicitation also produces experiences that strengthen social relationships. This sense of identity with group members and community identity can facilitate the dissolution of self-boundaries, enhancing identification with others and their needs.

Altered States of Consciousness

The physical movement required by pilgrimage often involves a form of suffering, either through the inconvenience of travel, entering harsh environments, or enduring rigorous austerities (e.g., walking or even crawling for hundreds of miles). Pilgrimage may also entail arduous activities, deprivations, troublesome engagements and tribulations, serving to impress upon the pilgrim the value of the pilgrimage and the importance of its messages. These sufferings may provide exculpation for misdeeds and a release of the psychodynamics of guilt. These painful activities, especially when combined with fasting and sleep deprivation, praying, chanting and singing, are also potent mechanisms for inducing altered states of consciousness (ASC) and their healing potential (Winkelman 1997, 2000). Thus the pilgrimage journey is a physical, psychological and social alteration of consciousness that provides many mechanisms for self-transformation.

The induction of ASC as part of the healing dynamics of pilgrimages is explicitly addressed in the chapters by Peters, Schaefer, and Greenfield and Cavalcante. The latter develop models of healing based upon the psychophysiological dynamics of hypnosis and its ability to reduce stress, pain, and psychosomatic illness and to reinforce immune system dynamics. They emphasize the effects of beliefs and cultural expectations upon physiological processes. Some of the pilgrimages reported here engage in the deliberate induction of ASC (e.g., Peters on the Nepalese shaman-pilgrimages, Schaefer on the Wixárika use of psychoactive plants). Pilgrimages may also induce ASC through less explicit procedures, including praying, chanting and singing, food and water restrictions, fasting, prolonged sleeplessness, and the rigorous austerities often undertaken during the ritual journey (e.g., walking or crawling for hundreds of miles, extended periods of riding a motorcycle). These and other ASC induction procedures that evoke basic neurological responses with recuperative properties have common overall physiological effects upon brain processes and functions (Mandell 1980; Winkelman 1992, 1996, 1997, 2000). The overall physiological dynamics involve an activation of the autonomic nervous system to produce a parasympathetic dominant phase. This may be produced by stimulation of the sympathetic system until exhaustion leads to collapse into a parasympathetic dominant state, which may also be entered directly through withdrawal, relaxation, and internal focus of attention. This activation of the parasympathetic system induces the body's relaxation response, part of the cycles of homeostatic balance in the nervous system providing natural recuperation and healing.

There are a wide variety of ASC within what Winkelman (2000) refers to as the integrative mode of consciousness. This is a natural function of the brain, attested to by the presence in all cultures of procedures for producing ASC. The overall effect of the integrative mode of consciousness is to integrate information from the whole organism, particularly stimulating emotions and memory into the frontal cortex. This integrates nonverbal information from the emotional and behavioral brain structures into the personal and cultural systems mediated by language and the frontal cortex.

ASCs have therapeutic effects: reduction in stress, anxiety, and psychosomatic reactions; regulation of psychophysiological processes underlying emotions, social attachments, and bonding; providing access to subconscious and unconscious information; and integration of behavioral, emotional, and cognitive processes (Winkelman 1992, 1996, 1997, 2000). Rapid induction of the parasympathetic dominance causes erasure of conditioned responses and increases suggestibility and placebo effects. Activation of preconscious brain processes facilitates their integration into consciousness and the resolution of repressed conflicts that affect emotions and physiological responses. Stimulation of limbic system functions and associated affective, self, and social identity processes contributes to healing through producing an integration of emotional information into consciousness, an enhanced integration of cognitive and emotional processes.

Shamanic Roots of Pilgrimage

A number of factors suggest that pilgrimage incorporates aspects of a shamanic past. The travel that is inevitably part of pilgrimage is a transition experience that may reflect the primordial and ever-present "shamanic journey," a travel to inner space and consciousness. Pilgrimage externalizes that sacred movement, bringing the pilgrimage into contact with the sacred other. Pilgrimage may constitute the basic training for shamanic roles, as exemplified in Peters' and Schaefer's chapters. Pilgrimage incorporates travel to the "exotic other," a process of ritual movement that imbues a rebirth and transformation, a renewal of self in the presence of sacred and social others, which is a hallmark of shamanism (Winkelman 2000). This rebirth experience is exemplified in Weibel's assessment of the religious creatives, whose focus on ecological issues and sacred places dovetails with their emphasis on spiritual self-development. The pilgrimage becomes a metaphor for life, a journey that mirrors their quest for personal enlightenment.

This shamanic interpretation is also supported in the chapters by Peters and Schaefer, who show that the processes of pilgrimage induce a shaman-like initiation and rebirth. Peters explicitly links the Nepalese initiate's pilgrimage to the processes of shamanic initiation. Similarities of pilgrimage to shamanism are found in their symbolic and actual incorporation of fundamental aspects of shamanism into pilgrimage, the ecstatic altered states of consciousness embodied in the "soul journey," the entry into communication with the spirit world, and the engagement with community.

However, the shamanic ASC exemplified in soul journey is quite different from that of the physical journey of pilgrimage, and the explicit altered states of the shaman are only mirrored in the less dramatic induction of altered states that can occur in pilgrimage. Moreover, the shaman's direct entry into the spirit world contrasts with the priest's mediation with the spirit world found in hierarchical religions. The tension and conflict over the hierarchical control exercised by the church that may occur in pilgrimage reflect the pilgrim's attempt to bypass such control and, like the shaman, to experience more direct entry into the spiritual world, embodied in the pilgrim's movement into the spiritual pilgrimage site.

While pilgrimage seems to reflect principles embodied in shamanistic healing worldwide (Winkelman 1992), pilgrimage is often incorporated into world religious systems with their priestly hierarchies and into cultural systems of meaning that are part of both local and global systems. Perhaps what remains as the most direct survival of shamanic roots in pilgrimage is the integration of disparate people into a symbolic, social, and physical community that can occur in the process and destination of the pilgrimage. This both connects pilgrimage to the healing practices of complex societies, and incorporates the universals of shamanistic practitioners.

Summary: Contemporary Pilgrimage

Cross-cultural comparisons such as those undertaken in this volume reveal similarities among pilgrimages in several respects. These include the symbolism of the physical journey, the developmental expectations for self linked to a special or holy place, establishing communication between the inner dynamics of self and the outer symbolic fields, and the structuring of experience provided by the associated rites. Pilgrimages can also provide a physical and symbolic return to a central source of religious belief and inspiration that constitutes an initiatory process. Many factors contribute to the transformation of consciousness and the induction of an altered state of consciousness, conditions that play many roles in healing (Winkelman 2000). Pilgrimage is a "multimedia therapy" that combines many different kinds of healing processes that are not normally found within a single healing tradition or activity. It is a form of "biopsychosocial" and spiritual healing that addresses many levels of the human need for healing and "wholing" the person.

Pilgrimage remains a vibrant activity in the contemporary world. The more traditional motives of pilgrimage—seeking a cure for physical ailments, finding resolution of family problems, enhancing the role of God's work in the world, and traveling to a devotional center of particular significance—continue to be important, along with more contemporary searches for identity and connection with others. What is common to all is the belief that a movement to a special place will facilitate a personal relationship with a spiritual world that is both sanctifying and healing.

While anthropologists may have turned their scholarly attention to pilgrimage relatively recently, pilgrims have been engaging in the practice for hundreds, even thousands, of years. That pilgrimage continues to exercise such a strong attraction in the contemporary world is testimony to its power and to its adaptive nature as a ritual and as a healing process.

Pilgrimage
and Healing

1

Pilgrimage Healing in Northeast Brazil

A Culturalbiological Explanation

Sidney M. Greenfield and Antonio Mourão Cavalcante

*T*his chapter begins with ethnographic data on a pilgrimage to the shrine of St. Francis in the northeastern Brazilian municipality of Canindé in the state of Ceará. The pilgrimage to this shrine is part of the Roman Catholic Cult of the Saints. Alleviation from the suffering associated with illness is shown to be the primary request made by *romeiros* (pilgrims) in the *promessas* (vows) they make with the saint. Pilgrimages are made after a romeiro is "cured" in partial fulfillment of the obligations incurred. To explain the large numbers of cures attributed to the saint and, by implication, to supernatural beings in other religions, as evidenced by the countless numbers of individuals making pilgrimages, we offer a theory in which studies of hypnosis and other altered states of consciousness (ASC) are articulated with culturally constructed views of the world as part of an alternative biomedical paradigm.

A Pilgrimage to the Shrine of St. Francis in Canindé

When the driver suddenly applied the brakes to the rickety old truck while making the sharp turn onto the traffic-congested road marked "Canindé," Maria da Fatima Batista[1] braced herself on the backless bench she had occupied for much of the previous four days. She was almost there. Her dream was about to be realized.

3

It all began some five years earlier when Fatima fell from a cart in the fields where she toiled as an agricultural worker. She had hurt her leg and, after several weeks of medical treatment, the swelling was still there and the pain even worse. Unable to work, she even had difficulty caring for her home, her spouse, and their children.

This thirty-year-old laborer from the small municipality of Regeneração in the interior of the northeastern Brazilian state of Piauí was not a religious person, although she had been raised as a Catholic and confirmed in her youth. It had been many years since Fatima had entered a church, or even thought about the supernatural. Now, desperate, she turned to St. Francis, the saint she had heard so much about, and with as much fervor she could muster, addressed the holy being. Fatima concentrated, focusing her attention completely on the saint whose help she was requesting, promising in a soft and deferential voice that if she received it, she would visit his shrine on the anniversary of his birth and light candles, attend mass, take confession, walk the stations of the cross, and dress in a *mortalha*, a brown habit similar to the one he wore. Fatima vowed, as an additional expression of her lowliness, dependence and humility in the face of this powerful heavenly figure, that if healed she would cut off her beautiful and much admired waist-length black hair at the shrine in Canindé.

In the weeks to follow, her leg improved and she gradually resumed her normal activities, even returning to work at the end of the month. Soon thereafter the pain disappeared completely.

When Fatima told her cousin what had happened, and of her vow and subsequent "miraculous" recovery, Maria Laura offered to accompany her when she went to Canindé. Laura's own visit there had been, in her words, "the high point of my life," and returning, though requiring great sacrifice, would give her untold pleasure.

Laura informed her cousin that Sr. Antonio, who freighted goods in the area, carried passengers to Canindé for the festival. Knowing the *pau-de-arara* (parrots' perch), as such trucks are called, would accommodate some sixty to seventy passengers, she volunteered to find out how much he charged and to compile an estimate of the amount of money they would need for food and other supplies to sustain them during the ten-day trip.[2] Realizing immediately that they had nowhere near the amount of money necessary, the women knew that St. Francis would understand the delay and wait patiently to receive his due. Four years later after saving small amounts periodically from their wages and selling several of the animals their families raised, they had accumulated sufficient money. Six months before the festival, Sr. Antonio was contacted and two places on his truck reserved.

The night before leaving, joined by family and friends who reminisced of their own experiences, the cousins carefully packed their food, a small stove, two hammocks, clothes and other necessities, including the wood carving of a leg that Fatima's spouse had made for her to present as a votive offering. Added to their belongings were gifts also to be deposited at the shrine from friends unable to make the trip themselves. Arriving at the designated place by mule cart before dawn, the cousins met the truck and were on their way.

For the next four days Fatima, Laura and the other faithful bounced uncomfortably across the dry, barren moonscape known as the *sertão*, a semi-desert the size of France and Spain. There had been no rain that year, or the previous one, and the riverbeds were dry. The plants that managed to sprout had withered quickly due to the lack of water and the livestock showed signs of being in danger, as carcasses were strewn along the roadside. The driver stopped the truck only when necessary, always at deserted roadsides, so the passengers could prepare and eat meals, relieve themselves, rest in the late afternoon heat and sleep at night. Four flat tires further complicated the journey and delayed their arrival at the shrine.

Although Fatima was not consciously aware of it, she had become part of a tradition that stretched back well over two millennia. The moment she boarded the truck, like countless others before her, she had separated herself from her normal, everyday social reality and entered what Victor Turner has called a "liminal state" (Turner 1969: 96). She was "betwixt and between" social worlds. Fatima had not been acquainted with her fellow passengers when they departed, did not interact much with any of them during the trip, and the same was true when they returned home. Those traveling on the truck formed no anti-structure and no *communitas*, as Turner maintained for pilgrims to the Marian shrines he studied (Turner and Turner 1978) and King reports in this volume.[3] Instead, each traveler focused almost exclusively on the primary reason for making the journey. They were going to celebrate St. Francis and to do what they had promised him when they requested his help.[4] Given the emotional weight of their undertaking, the demands of the journey, and their discomfort on the truck, there was little time or energy for engaging with others.

Christian Pilgrimage and the Cult of the Saints: A Magico-Religious Complex

A pilgrimage in Christian tradition is a visit to the shrine of a saint where a powerful and mystical religious intensity is believed to be present. The practice has its roots in both the Greco-Roman and Hebrew traditions.[5] Visiting sacred places did not become an important part of religious worship until after Constantine's conversion in the fourth century when Christianity became the religion of the Empire (Carroll 2001). From then on, when the faith was carried to other parts of the world, pilgrimage to the shrines of the saints was central to the complex of beliefs and practices to which the pagan peoples of northern and eastern Europe, Asia, and eventually the New World were, often forcibly, exposed.

The earliest Christian saints were martyrs who gave their lives for their faith. After Constantine, a new model of sainthood emerged: members of local communities would decide that one of their more admired fellows, who had healed, or performed other acts of wonder, had done so because God had so ordained it and was working his miracles through them. When that person died, those familiar with the exemplary activities would flock to the grave and request in death what had been given so freely in life. When it was received, a shrine was placed at the tomb and stories would circulate far and wide about the wondrous acts taking place there. On hearing the tales, others in need of help would visit the tomb and its shrine would become a holy place of worship.

The large and ever growing number of popular saints selected by the people created a dilemma for the church and its administrative hierarchy. Though veneration of saints undercut the emphasis the church wished to place on the divine trinity as the focus of the religion, the saints did serve as role models. The stories of these exceptional human beings, elaborated in myth, served to teach the virtues the church leadership wished to instill in its followers. Rather than downplay the cult of the saints, the church chose instead to take control of the saint-making process (Woodward 1990). Starting in 1234, the right to determine whom from among the once living had been chosen and elevated by God was reserved to the papacy alone.[6] However, Roman Catholics today still worship many more than the four hundred saints recognized by the Vatican.

The Reformation was especially harsh on the cult of the saints and pilgrimage for the "excesses and abuses result[ing] from an extreme familiarity with the holy" (Huizinga cited in Woodward 1990: 74). Though the Council of Trent (1545–1563) vigorously reaffirmed the cult of the saints, declaring, "only men of irreligious mentality deny that the saints enjoying eternal happiness in heaven are to be invoked," the papacy was able to use the criticism by Protestants both to prune many names from the list of those to be venerated and, more importantly, to increase its control over the saint-making process (Woodward 1990: 75).

Although the importance of the cult of the saints and pilgrimage declined in religious life after the Reformation, even among Catholics, both remained a vital element practiced by the inhabitants of the Iberian Peninsula when, in the late fifteenth and sixteenth centuries, they embarked on the conquest and colonization of the Western Hemisphere. Thus, the cult of the saints and pilgrimage were central features of the Christianity brought and imposed by the Portuguese upon Brazil.

Going on pilgrimage is not an independent activity, but rather an aspect of the cult of the saints (P. Brown 1981).[7] "Reborn" and elevated to everlasting life in heaven by an all-powerful creator God believed to have control over all aspects of the universe, including the destinies of those on earth, saints are considered "friends of God," able to act as intermediaries with him on behalf of supplicants on earth. As Wilson phrases (1983: 23) the position proclaimed in official church theology, "saint(s) might be seen as advocates pleading causes before a stern judge, as mediators, as go-betweens, as intriguers or wire-pullers, at the court of Heaven."

The faithful may invoke a saint's help with material as well as spiritual problems through prayer and petition. Attaining this supernatural intervention in our world is referred to as a miracle. Miracles, as Augustine of Hippo was so influential in maintaining, "were signs of God's power and proof of the sanctity of those in whose name they were wrought" (Woodward 1990: 62).

"The relationship between a saint and a devotee in Brazil," as Queiroz observes (1973: 86), "is one of reciprocity, or better of *dou ut des:* I give to receive something in exchange." For it to work, the petitioner must know what the saint likes or dislikes, how he wishes to be treated, and his ritual preferences, and he must include these in his vow. Furthermore, it must be done in a way that will entice the saint to accept the bargain. Vows are made conditionally and they do not have to be fulfilled (discharged) unless and until the petitioner obtains what has been requested. Christian—particularly Catholic—pilgrimage is part of the cult of the saints and, since the Reformation (and counter Reformation), is referred to as "popular"—as opposed to official—Catholicism.

The Cult of the Saints and Pilgrimage in Brazil

Representatives of the Portuguese Crown and the church brought Christianity to the territory that was to become Brazil when the New World colony was discovered and settled. It was to be its official religion until Brazil became a Republic at the end of the nineteenth century (1889), some six decades after national independence had been attained in 1822. Christian practice, institutionalization, and diffusion, as Freyre (1964) and others (e.g., Azzi 1978) have reminded us, were mostly a private matter. Many founders of the great family houses established around the production of sugar cane, the mining of gold and diamonds, or other economic boom activities had their own domestic shrines and chapels. Shrines also were built in out-of-the-way places, mostly in gratitude to a specific saint or the Virgin for some good fortune obtained there that was believed to have been the result of an intercession and a response to prayer.

Priests, always in short supply in Brazil, may have been brought in when available to say masses, perform baptisms, weddings, funerals, and to teach catechism to slaves and other dependents, but most of the "religious" activity practiced throughout Brazilian history was a personal dynamic between a "believer" and a saint at a private shrine. As Bastide (1951: 346) observed some time ago, popular religious worship in Brazil is turned more toward the saints and the Virgin than to God.

The saints venerated during the early years of the colonial period were those brought from the Old World and listed in the official church calendar. The pau-de-arara carrying Maria da Fatima and her fellow pilgrims was on its way to one of them, the shrine to St. Francis, which is located in the municipality of Canindé in the state of Ceará. St. Francis (of Assisi) is known by the inhabitants in this part of Brazil as São Francisco das Chagas, St. Francis of the Wounds. This is to differentiate him in the minds of his Brazilian worshippers from the Italian saint, thereby making him their own.

The shrine is said to have been founded in the late eighteenth century by Francisco Xavier de Madeiros, a Portuguese sergeant major traveling in the region who, for reasons not reported, wished to build a chapel on the banks of the Canindé river in honor of the saint after whom he had been named:

> He is said to have written to the three brothers who owned the land asking them to donate it as patrimony for a church. When they refused, the supernatural intervention that has come to be associated with the site is reported to have begun. One of the brothers took sick and died shortly thereafter. Then, following a brief illness, a second brother also died. When the third brother took ill, he immediately made the donation Madeiros had requested. He is reported to have recovered as mysteriously as he had become ill and his brothers had died. (Greenfield 1990: 3)

When construction was delayed due to one of the periodic droughts that plague this part of the country, a statue of the saint was brought to the site. Reports began to circulate about the sick or injured recovering "miraculously." People from surrounding neighborhoods started visiting the statue. Those "blessed" left gifts that were used to complete the first church, and donations made over the years were applied to build numerous additions.

Today a large basilica stands where Madeiros first planned his church. Public and commercial buildings are located to the north of it, across from the *praça*, or square. The streets spread out in all directions, with the more substantial homes of prosperous merchants and landowners located closest to the basilica, and the poorer ones stretching up an incline to the urban periphery where repair shops and marginal commercial and other establishments, including tire repair shops, Afro-Brazilian religious centers and brothels, can be found. The basilica, at the center, contains the holy activities. Just beyond it, along the river, is the grotto of Nossa Senhora de Lourdes. It is there pilgrims go to wash, drink the water and fill receptacles for friends and relatives unable to make the trip. Water from the grotto is believed to have miraculous curing properties (Cavalcante 1987: 6).

Located beyond the basilica is an area that houses a museum and a zoological garden owned and operated by the Franciscan brothers. Further on is a zone of religious commerce where one also finds food, beverages (including alcohol), and many manufactured items. Next come games of chance, pool, and an amusement park with a huge Ferris wheel, rides, and other forms of entertainment. Finally, at the outskirts, there are bars, dance halls, and "Vai Quem Quer" (Go Whoever Wishes), as the local houses of prostitution are picturesquely called. Preparations for the influx of pilgrims begin some six weeks before the official mass that opens the annual festival on September 24. The Franciscan brothers make ready the simple shelters called *abrigos* that will house those visitors unable to afford space in hotels and private dwellings. They will set up and clean makeshift lavatories, places to bathe, and facilities for the visitors to cook their food. Many residents who have family homes in the nearby rural hinterland, or relatives with whom they can stay, rent their primary houses to more affluent pilgrims. The merchants prepare their shops to make room for crosses; rosaries; pictures; statues of St. Francis, the Virgin, and other saints; foods; beverages; clothing; plastic toys; and other commercial items. Townspeople and residents of neighboring municipalities seeking to earn extra money set up stalls and booths, most often using poles, scraps of wood, and old pieces of cardboard brought in by truck from Fortaleza, the state capital and main commercial center some ninety kilometers distant. Those who live in or near Canindé depend on what they earn during the festival to sustain them throughout the year.

The municipality of nearly three thousand square kilometers is located at the edge of the sertão, about one hundred kilometers from the Atlantic coast and approximately four degrees south of the equator. The average temperature is seventy-five degrees Fahrenheit, but since there are few clouds and little rain, by late in the day it feels much hotter. In good years rains fall between January and June. In the 1980s, when we began this study, Canindé's official population was in the neighborhood of sixty thousand, with fewer than twenty thousand living in the town. Approximately one million people visit Canindé and its shrine annually, most of them during the ten days of the celebration at the end of September and beginning of October.

The Pilgrim's Round

When the vehicle from Regeneração turned off the pothole-filled, weather-beaten road on which it had crossed the backlands onto the new, paved highway that led into Canindé, it joined with the many other paus-de-arara bringing pilgrims from all over the Brazilian northeast. The slow-moving lanes contained buses rented especially for the occasion, private automobiles, and a number of horses and horse-drawn carriages. Some pilgrims came from great distances on bicycles, and others on foot.

Most of the visitors were from Ceará, while others came from neighboring states in northeastern Brazil. Pilgrims also traveled from as far away as São Paulo, Rio de Janeiro, and some even from Europe and North America.

Many of the travelers, like Maria da Fatima and her cousin, are agricultural laborers, domestic servants, or unemployed. One-third of some two thousand pilgrims interviewed fifteen years ago reported having neither land nor homes of their own, but lived on properties that belonged to large estates to which they paid a share of what they grew. Half reported migrating periodically, hoping to find better living conditions (Barreto 1986: 3). The number of men and women are approximately equal and although many of the pilgrims are poor, as are the vast majority of Brazilians, all social classes and racial and ethnic categories are represented in Canindé.

The truck carrying Maria da Fatima stopped at one of the abrigos located not far from the basilica. Finding space available there, the occupants strung their hammocks on hooks and stored the food, clothing, and various items they had brought with them. Then, although it was late in the day and they had not eaten since before noon, the two women left, walking along the street that led to the basilica. When they passed a *lame lame* (photographer), Fatima stopped to wait in line to have a picture taken of her wearing the brown habit of St. Francis and holding her votive offering while standing next to a life-sized cutout of the saint made of painted cardboard. A half hour later the two were again on their way to the basilica and the *casa dos milagres*, a large room on whose walls are hung thousands of pictures of pilgrims and the material representations of their miracles. Fatima placed one copy of the Polaroid snapshot on the wall. The other she would keep and put next to her bed at home. The next part of her vow was completed when she walked across the room to deposit her ex-voto. The huge receptacle was overflowing with thousands of carvings made mostly of pieces of balsa wood, local bamboo, clay, or cloth that had been crudely fashioned by devotees. Seen also were beautifully carved pieces made of fine wood, probably commissioned by people of means and made by professional craftsmen. The pile was so high that Fatima had to climb up on a ladder and then stretch to get her ex-voto to the top of the stack.

Fatima and Laura went next to a small room where a beautician stood shearing a woman's hair. The woman, Clarice Magalhães de Sousa, also wearing a brown habit that masked her middle-class status, had traveled with her husband, a lawyer who worked for a bank, by bus from the capital of the state of Rio Grande do Norte several hundred miles away. For their stay in Canindé, the de Sousas rented a room with bed and a bath and took their meals in restaurants where they ate eggs with their coffee for breakfast and meat and vegetables with the rice and beans served for lunch and dinner.

Dona Clarice had been diagnosed some years previously with breast cancer. Before undertaking the surgery and radiation treatment prescribed by her doctor, she had prayed to St. Francis, promising him that if he helped her she not only would make the pilgrimage to Canindé, attend mass, take confession, and light candles at his shrine, but if she were cured, she would cut off her shoulder-length hair. Certainly the educated and sophisticated de Sousas knew that her recovery could be attributed to modern medical science; but could it not also be that it had been the intercession by the saint? Like so many others, Dona Clarice had made a bargain with St. Francis before undertaking medical treatment. She had compensated her doctors as soon as she received their bill. Now she was paying what she owed to the saint.

Like Dona Clarice, most Brazilians seek doctors or other healers when they are hurt or take sick, but this does not stop them from also praying to saints. They believe that surgery and medications work, but more so when complemented by supernatural assistance.

Angela, a young lady from the state of Paraíba waited anxiously for the beautician to finish with Dona Clarice. She had sat in the same chair a year before, but had been unable to fulfill her vow at that time because she was "too vain" to face life without her beautiful hair. The nervous woman had suffered from severe headaches, and though a doctor had prescribed medicine, the pains worsened. She began to pray to St. Francis and when the symptoms disappeared, she knew a pilgrimage had to be made to discharge her obligations. Angela returned to Canindé, this time prepared to give the saint his due.

"Do you think that St. Francis will forgive you?" we asked her.

"Yes he will," she responded, "because he has forgiven more than this. I have faith, I believe that he will."

When Fatima's turn came, feelings of sadness and gratitude filed her. Certainly she would miss her beautiful hair, but she felt virtuous about losing it for such a special reason. Fatima took the bag in which the cuttings of her hair were placed and, like Dona Clarice and Angela before her, returned to the casa dos milagres to put it on top of the heap of ex-votos. Having completed this very personal and emotional part of her vow, Fatima joined her cousin, and the two returned to the abrigo to start the fire on which they would cook the rice and beans that would be their dinner. Several hours later, after cleaning up and storing their belongings, exhilarated, but exhausted, they climbed into their hammocks and tried to sleep.

At dawn, the city and the festival already were bursting with activities when Fatima and Laura joined a long line of pilgrims waiting for the lavatories and bathing facilities. Their breakfast, which consisted solely of coffee laced with ample sugar, was prepared as hastily as possible and then they were off to the basilica once again. As they entered the courtyard on their way to the church office where they would learn the schedule of masses and confession, they came upon Pedro, a young man from Fortaleza who made the trip to Canindé on his bicycle. He was circling the church on his knees. His mother had been sick, "it was her leg," he said, "the left one." She had gone to the doctor and had almost lost the limb. They had to graft parts from other places on her body to make the necessary repairs. She was in a cast for four months. "But now she is well, thanks to God and St. Francis." Pedro had prayed to the saint on her behalf, promising that if she recovered, he would make the pilgrimage and walk around the courtyard on his knees, not once, but twice. He was now completing his second turn. Though it was difficult and he was uncomfortable and sore, he was pleased that he had fulfilled his debt to the saint. He could return home satisfied and at peace.

At the small church office, a volunteer provided the women with the schedule of masses. When Fatima revealed that it had been more than ten years since she had last been to church, she was told that she would have to attend a preparation class before entering the confessional booth. Since the session was about to begin, the women hurried to the designated room. Forty-five minutes later they took their places in the line that stretched the length of the basilica to wait their turn at the confessional. Afterward they walked back to the abrigo to prepare, cook, and eat the rice and beans that would be their lunch. Several hours later they hurried to the basilica again, this time to attend mass. Joining other devotees, they walked the Stations of the Cross, the symbolic representation of the route taken by Jesus through Jerusalem to Calvary.

When Fatima picked up a stone that she would place on her head to increase the penance, she accidentally bumped into Sergio, a young man reaching for a rock at the same time. He had made the trip on foot from

Fortaleza where he attended the university. Twice failing the *vestibular*, a standardized examination all Brazilian students must pass to gain admission to the university, he made a vow to St. Francis before attempting the test for a third time. Now a freshman studying computer science, he was fulfilling his debt to the saint for the help he had received in surmounting the obstacle. As he, Fatima, and a score of others proceeded solemnly along the path, changing rocks at each station, the temperature exceeded ninety degrees Fahrenheit under a blazing sun. The women stopped to drink a cup of water, which they purchased from a girl sitting on the roadside with a bucket she had filled at a standpipe. Next they went to the museum to see some of the exquisite jewels and garments used in church services by the Franciscan brothers.

The two pilgrims wandered together through the stalls where they were tempted by both religious and secular items, few of which they could afford. Each did purchase one or two gifts commissioned by friends and relatives, and some small souvenirs for their families. By this time they were exhausted and returned to the abrigo to begin preparations for the evening meal. After cooking and eating some more rice and beans, they set out for the secular festival. As women traveling alone, they rejected visiting the bars and dancing establishments available to men, and for their entertainment concentrated on observing the games of chance. At about 9:00 P.M., when they returned to the abrigo, they were too excited to go to bed and instead sat for several hours talking and sharing with each other the joy they were experiencing. Each slept very little that night.

The following morning, after several long and tedious hours devoted to the same daily activities, the two women went to the grotto where they washed themselves in its curative waters. They drank and filled plastic containers that they would take back to Regeneração for friends and relatives.

Their next destination was the Franciscan monastery where they patiently stood with hundreds of others in the courtyard to observe and talk to a life-sized statue of the saint. When her turn came, after more than an hour of waiting, Fatima, like each of the others before her, quietly, but intensely conversed aloud with the saint. She thanked him, commenting to the statute about very personal matters, and petitioning help with other problems. Afterward, Laura excitedly led her into a small room near the entryway to the monastery. A group of pilgrims stood there trying to peek through the door of an inner room. A rumor was circulating that St. Francis was inside, alive and, in fact, had never died. The Franciscans were keeping him there, unwilling to share him with the pilgrims. When nothing further happened and the women concluded the report to be untrue, they left and returned to the abrigo to begin again the lengthy task of preparing their rice and beans. After a short rest, they visited the zoological gardens where they spent the next few hours looking at the animals, most of which they had never seen before. They giggled as they went from cage to cage, commenting on the magnificent colors of some of the birds and laughing at the strange postures assumed by other animals. Their favorite, and that of most of the visitors, were the monkeys, in front of whose cage they stood enthralled. Soon it was time to return to the abrigo, collect their belongings and place them aboard the waiting truck. By late afternoon they were on the road again headed for Regeneração. During the next four days as they bounced uncomfortably across the back roads of the sertão on the crowded truck, the women repeated aloud to each other, perhaps in a rehearsal of what they would tell their loved ones when they arrived home, the details of and their emotions about the experience they had shared.

Pilgrimage and Healing in Canindé

Research conducted in the late 1950s found that 80 percent of the visitors to the shrine of St. Francis in Canindé were there because they had been healed (Hooneart 1987: 5). Yet pilgrims rarely use such terms as illness or disease. Instead they speak of pains in the back, leg, head, or the inability to walk. Their assumption is that God has caused their suffering to punish them for the commission of a sin. The saint's intercession leads to the removal of the cause of their pain and, hence, they are "cured."

In another study, conducted over a five-year period between 1984 and 1988, Professor Adalberto Barreto and his students in the Department of Social Medicine of the Federal University of Ceará, collected, examined, and classified more than 80,000 ex-votos. In excess of 86 percent of them represented parts of the body the saint is believed to have "healed." Of these, almost 5,000 showed wounds, cuts, or other openings in the skin, 2,350 were protuberances indicating edemas or growths, 1,400 represented disfigurements of the skin or other dermatological problems, 800 were breaks and fractures, and another 325 were of deformities that had been corrected (Barreto n.d.). Fewer than 14 percent of the votive offerings were unrelated to illness and healing.

Pilgrimage and Modernity

The pilgrimage experience described is not a vestigial cultural practice from a less developed part of a contemporary national society that will disappear with its complete modernization. We stress that pilgrimages to shrines of saints continue in all parts of Brazil, from the northeast and distant Amazon basin to the industrialized urban centers of Rio de Janeiro and São Paulo and, furthermore, Brazilians are making vows and visiting more shrines to fulfill them than ever before. New saints are being created in a continuation of the ancient, but still vital, Catholic tradition of people venerating respected local figures, who when they die, are believed to be elevated to heaven where they are able to continue helping their brethren on earth (Cavalcante and Greenfield 2003). These "popular" saints, many of whom were medical doctors, may or may not eventually be recognized by the official Church (see Low 1988; Macklin 1974; Macklin and Crumrine 1973; Margolis 1984). That so many new saints were medical professionals in life reflects the continuing importance of healing as the predominant problem for which believers seek supernatural intervention, and the increasing acceptance of medical science in the lives of the faithful.

Culturalbiological Healing in Brazilian Pilgrimages

The numbers of people who make pilgrimages attesting to their conviction that a saint has cured them are sufficiently impressive to demand scholarly attention. In Brazil alone, millions of former sufferers visit shrines annually to fulfill vows for supernatural intervention. Tens of millions visit other Roman Catholic shrines worldwide. If hundreds of millions of cures are attributed to the saints—or other holy figures—how can these impressive numbers be explained? And what are the implications for medical science? Are faith and science to remain separate, independent, and competing realms of discourse?

We offer here, as a hypothesis, a model of healing based on recent developments in medical science, some at the fringes and others in the mainstream, that incorporates beliefs in the supernatural that might begin to account for the large number of cures attributed to the saints by believers in Brazil and throughout the world.

Hypnosis and Healing

In a 1989 paper on cures attributed to St. Francis, Greenfield summarized a number of studies establishing a relationship between stress and a broad range of illnesses. Pelletier's (1977: 7) generalization that most medical textbooks "attributed anywhere from 50 to 80 percent of all diseases to psychosomatic or stress related origins" was the starting point (Greenfield 1989: 5). Noting that large numbers of Brazilians, especially, but not only, those at the lower end of the socioeconomic hierarchy, have lives that subject them to considerable stress, and following Ley and Freeman (1984), Greenfield argued that "chronic depression and sense of helplessness may be affecting their immune systems, making them more susceptible to the ravages of illness-producing organisms" (Greenfield 1989: 17).

Based on T. X. Barber (1984), a review of the literature showed the reduction in, or elimination of, a number of illness conditions in response to hypnotic interventions. Pilgrims claiming to be cured by a saint, Greenfield argued, most probably had been in a hypnotic, trancelike, or altered state of consciousness (ASC) at the time they made their vow. This could lead to a reduction in stress and contribute positively to healing (Greenfield 1989). Recent studies have reinforced the hypothesis that hypnosis plays a significant part in stress-related healings such as those attributed to the saints, or other supernatural beings and forces (see Brown 1992; Brown and Fromm 1987; Goodman 1988; Holroyd 1992; Ruzalya-Smith et al. 1995).

A Mind-Body Model of Hypnosis and Healing

Building on this growing body of evidence supporting the role of hypnotherapy in the healing process, Ernest Rossi (1993) proposes an information/communications model of the healing process. Following Black (1969) and Bowers (1977), he suggests that information flow, to and within bodily systems, may be a way to rethink the relationship between mind and body (Rossi 1993: 26). Transduction, and the translation of its code, may enable information to be transmitted from one system (or level) to another and be integrated for use, thereby providing, as Bowers maintains, a "solution" to the mind-body problem.[8]

Rossi outlines how, and reviews the evidence for, the ways the major pathways of brain activity involved with memory, learning, and behavior are consistent with the view that the limbic-hypothalamus system is the primary mind-body transducer (1993: 47). He concludes that what is learned and remembered is "dependent on one's psychological state at the time of the experience."

An experimental study demonstrating the negative effect of stress experienced by medical students on their immune systems during academic examinations supports what has previously been said about the relationship between stress and reduced immune function (Glaser, Kennedy, et al. 1990; Glaser, Lafuse, et al. 1993). By measuring how "information transduction is modulated by stress throughout the main cellular-genetic loop," Glaser and his associates were able to demonstrate how psychosocial processes of mind and behavior can be related to genetic expression.[9]

The discovery of immediate-early genes, confirming Hebb's hypothesis of genetic plasticity, adds another dimension to Rossi's model (see LeDoux 2002: 135–37). Also known as primary response genes, these are a separate category of genes that "are actively turned on and off every second of our lives in response to messenger molecules that carry information.... Everything from sexual stimuli, temperature, food, psychological stress, physical trauma and toxins in the environment," Rossi notes, "can be signaled to the genes" (1998: 2; see also Merchant 1996). According to Trölle et al (1995: Preface), immediate-early genes "may function as third messengers in a stimulus transcription cascade transferring extracellular information into changes in target gene transcription, thereby changing the phenotype of neurons." These genes may turn out to be the specific mediators between learned behavior from the psychocultural domain and the genes.

The final piece in the model was recognition of the Basic Rest-Activity Cycle (BRAC). Half a century ago researchers observed that every 90 minutes throughout the night, sleep became a very "active process," and for about 10 to 30 minutes oxygen consumption increased and blood flowed freer to the brain. Breathing, heart rate, blood pressure, and gastrointestinal movements became more variable than when awake. In these periods of Rapid Eye Movement (REM) sleep brain wave patterns, as measured by electroencephalograph (EEG), became similar to the daytime activity pattern. Researchers confirmed that the 90-minute to 120-minute dream rhythm apparently continues during the day (see Rossi 2002: 209–10).

While early therapists using hypnosis were intuitively aware of this wave nature of human experience, it was Milton Erickson who first effectively applied it (Rossi and Rossi 1996: 124). Unlike his colleagues who saw patients for a fifty-minute session, Erickson preferred to meet for an hour and a half or more, claiming "that people in everyday life also naturally drifted between subtle but distinct mindbody states." By working with them for longer periods, he discovered that "they were almost certain to go through distinct changes in their consciousness and states of being," which he referred to as "common everyday trance" (Rossi and Rossi 1996: 129).

Culture and Information

Millions of bits of information flood through the human senses every second. Zimmermann estimates some 10 million bits per second entering through the eyes, another million through the skin, one hundred thousand each through the ears and nose, and still another thousand through the taste buds (1989: 172). Of these more than eleven million bits, human beings appear to be consciously aware of at most forty bits. The remainder either is discarded—lost for practical purposes—or organized and used without conscious (and reflexive) awareness.

Culture may be seen as a template through which the myriad of information individual members of a specific social group are exposed to through experiences is organized and stored in memory. Symbolically, in the category of religion, culture also provides frames of meaning and understanding to the members of a community or society.

The distinction made by psychoanalysts between conscious, or declarative and implicit learning and memory is useful here (Milner, Squire, and Kandel 1998),[10] as is the opposition between connectionist and serial or sentential logic as used by cognitive anthropologists (D'Andrade 1995; Bloch 1991; Strauss and Quinn 1994) that parallels it.[11] We hypothesize that the information stored in procedural memory, embedded in cultural codes that provide meaning and understanding, may be transduced under special circumstances, most often without the conscious (reflexive) awareness of the individual, to become part of the information flow that affects the physical body and its constituent systems by activating immediate-early genes.

Religious rituals, as Levi-Strauss (1963), Turner (1964, 1967, 1969), and others have emphasized, may be viewed as bodies of information that provide meaning, and also as forms of communication; perhaps, as Goodman observes, "the most exalted form" (1988: 33). In the course of their unfolding, the details about what she calls "the other reality," with its powerful forces and beings, is communicated to the participants. This stating "of the sacra," as Turner observed in his discussion of ritual initiation, "both teaches the neophytes how to think with some degree of abstraction about their cultural milieu (and the forces in it) and gives them ultimate standards of reference. At the same time, it is believed to change their nature, transforming them from one kind of a human being to another" (Turner 1964).

Traditional (shamanic and other) rituals and practices have as their end the destruction of

> "profane" sensibilities. The monotonous chants, the endless repeated refrains, the fatigue, the fasting, the dancing…create a sensory condition that is wide open to the "supernatural." This is not only…a matter of physiological techniques: traditional ideology directs and imparts values to all these efforts intended to break the frame of profane sensibility. What is above all indispensable is the absolute belief of the subject in the spiritual universe that he desires to enter. (Frecska and Kulcsar 1989: 70; see also Eliade 1976: 85).

Aijmer dramatically expresses the implications: "It seems to operate mentally more like visual pictures than formulations in words, and its semanticity hinges on the simultaneous presence of elements that are in themselves images.… If an actor constructs a great part of his scenarios as a resultant of his social review, he also calls on his social cognizance (for want of a better term) of cultural imagery, thereby drawing into his acts implications of morality, righteousness, correctness, order, and ultimately the force of blessing" (Aijmer 1995: 4–5).[12]

A cultural belief system then may contain symbolic images and understandings, whose view of the cosmos include information as to what exists and what has causal efficacy with respect to the lives of individuals. This is retained by its individual members in their procedural memories, executed by connectionist logic that affects them and their constituent subsystems when they participate in a religious ritual, without their being consciously aware of it. These beliefs are more than superstition. By focusing on the information they contain, and how it may be transduced under special circumstances into the codes of other bodily systems, most often without the conscious (reflexive) awareness of the individual, to become part of the information flow in cells and genes, we may discover the mechanisms by which cultural beliefs become part of a healing system. We may find, for example, how this information flow instructs the T-cells and killer cells of the immune system to attack the microorganisms that may be the immediate cause of a somatic illness. The effect may be like that of medicinal drugs whose information content is communicated more directly with the need for fewer translations of codes.

Altered States, Culturalbiology, and the Healing of Brazilian Pilgrims

Countless pilgrims, like Maria da Fatima Batista and her cousin Laura, visiting the shrine of St. Francis in Canindé to *pagar* (pay) their promessa to the saint for his help in their being healed, may have been in an ASC at the time they made their vow. Technically they were self-induced, most probably by the focused intensity of their prayer at the time they made their vow, bringing them into what Goodman refers to as "a religious ASC" (1988). Alternatively, they might simply have been experiencing what Erickson refers to as a common everyday trance, and Rossi maintains correlates with natural ultradian and other bodily rhythms like the BRAC (Rossi and Rossi 1996: 130).

Information stored in their procedural memories, ordered by connectionist logic, and relating to a symbolical view of the cosmos and a belief in the ability of saints to effect cures, was transduced, independent of their conscious awareness, through their various bodily systems perhaps activating their immune response. The result was the reduction of stress and/or the amelioration, and possible elimination, of the symptoms of their illness.

When participating in the sessions of spiritualist groups such as Umbanda, Candomblé, Xangô and other Afro-Indo-European syncretic groups, including Kardecist-Spiritism and popular Catholicism, David Akstein, one of Brazil's leading authorities on hypnosis, maintains that individuals enter trance states. When in this type of kinetic trance, "certain patients develop sudden and diffuse inhibition of the cerebral cortex" (Akstein 1977: 222).

In contrast with North Americans, Brazilians regularly engage in fantasy, one of the traits associated with hypnotizability. For this, they are socially rewarded and reinforced:

> Children (and adults) who claim to see the Virgin Mary, Saint Fran-
> cis, some other saint, or other supernatural being not only are not
> punished or taken to a therapist...but are rewarded and held up
> for praise. Those who claim to "receive" a spirit, whether a doctor
> from the past...or a deity from Africa...or the spirit of a former
> slave...or an Indian...not only are believed, but their help is sought
> by others who treat them deferentially and with respect. (Green-
> field 1991: 23)

Moreover, Brazil's traditional way of structuring interpersonal relations in terms of hierarchically ordered patron-client ties results in something not unlike the relationship between hypnotist and client/subject (Greenfield 1972, 1977, 1979; Hutchinson 1966; Roniger 1990). This leads us to suggest that Brazilians might more easily and regularly enter ASC than other populations that are the usual subjects in studies of hypnosis (and its effect on healing).[13] This does not mean that all Brazilians always enter altered, or trancelike states when they engage in prayer or other ritualized religious acts. Nor would that be necessary for our model. We maintain only that some do, and that they are the ones who experience this form of culturalbiological healing.

It would be impossible to estimate the number of Brazilians, or others worldwide, who make vows and whose prayers are *not* answered. One success in ten attempts would be a very conservative figure. Barber tells us that perhaps no more than five percent of the members of any population make good hypnotic subjects. For Brazil, we might arguably double that estimate. The resulting ten percent would keep us within the range of the conservative figure for easily hypnotized individuals who could enter an ASC while focusing and concentrating during intense prayer. While in that state, learned, deeply held, but not necessarily consciously recognized nor verbalizable, beliefs about the ability of saints to effect cures may be transduced, perhaps turning on immediate-early genes and activating the immune system. This may result in the reduction of (chronic) stress and the amelioration of and relief from the symptoms that first prompted the prayer and the making of the vow. "Cured" by means of culturalbiological transduction, those who successfully requested the saint's help then go on pilgrimages to repay the debt incurred for what they consciously believed he had done for them. While explaining why the many believers who make vows do go on pilgrimages to pay their part of the bargain, our model also accounts for why so many more who prayed, but did not enter a trance state may be skeptical and do not partake in the pilgrimage ritual.

By adding this view of culture to Rossi's framework, we may finally have "the common denominator between traditional Western medicine and the holistic, shamanistic, and spiritistic approaches to healing that depend on highly specialized cultural belief systems, world views, and frames of reference" (Rossi 1993: 68). Further research in culturalbiology may reveal that faith and science are not independent and competing realms of discourse, but interdependent and supporting analytic frameworks.

The Feminization of Healing in Pilgrimage to Fátima

Lena Gemzöe

O ne of the phenomena that has contributed to the growth of the cult of the Virgin Mary within contemporary Catholicism is the establishment of pilgrimage centers based on alleged apparitions of Mary. One such shrine is the sanctuary of Our Lady of Fátima (Nossa Senhora de Fátima), situated in central Portugal's Leiria region, outside the town of Fátima. The sanctuary is one of the Catholic world's greatest pilgrimage sites, visited by two million pilgrims a year. Pilgrimage to Fátima culminates each year on May 13, which is the date in 1917 when Our Lady allegedly appeared for the first time to three child shepherds, known as *os três pastorinhos* (the three little shepherds), on the outskirts of Fátima.

The first apparition was followed by a series of apparitions on the thirteenth of each month from May to October, during which Our Lady appeared to the children and spoke to them. Two of the children, Jacinta and Francisco, died a few years after the apparitions. As seers of Mary, they have since long been ascribed a saintly status at a popular level in Portugal, and in both cases formal processes of canonization are underway. The oldest girl, Lúcia, aged nine at the time, became a nun and had a unique position in Portuguese Catholicism as the sole surviving seer.

On October 13, the day of the last apparition in 1917, Our Lady performed the so-called "Miracle of the Sun" in the presence of twenty thousand people. The people who had gathered at Fátima after the story of the child seers of Mary had spread saw the sun spinning around its axis in the sky and felt the ground shaking under their feet.

25

The conversations between the children and Our Lady are known mainly through the writings of sister Lúcia, who as an adult nun was encouraged to write her memories by the bishop of Leiria. Mary's words to the children, known as the Message of Fátima or the Secrets of Fátima, contain many different details that the Catholic Church has interpreted and used to promote faith in different contexts. The most often cited detail (by the church and by devotees in general) is Mary's repeated pleas that the children (and people generally) say the rosary. In the last vision, Mary announced that she was "the Lady of the Rosary." Mary insisted on devotion to the Immaculate Heart of Mary, in order to save the souls of sinners, to stop the then ongoing World War I, and to bring peace to the world. She foretold "the conversion of Russia" and that the world would have a time of peace. She also showed Lúcia a vision of Hell. The vision of Hell is known as the "first Secret of Fátima," and the pleas for the conversion of Russia as the "second Secret." (Espírito Santo 1995).

Since the second half of the nineteenth century, Marian centers in Europe founded on apparitions have been powerful tools in the hands of the church to ward off the threat of antireligious forces and secularization. The apparitions at Fátima in 1917 took place during Portugal's First Republic (1911–1926), during which the church lost a large part of its properties, and anticlerical currents were strong. Later, during the dictatorship of António Salazar, the apparitions at Fátima came to be particularly associated with anticommunist politics. Little known outside Portugal until the 1940s, the Fátima story and reproductions of Our Lady of Fátima were spread by the church from Portugal throughout Catholic Europe during the cold war. Recently, the Catholic Church has ascribed new meanings to the apparitions at Fátima that represent a modern version of the "anticommunist" message of Fátima. The political upheaval in Russia in the late 1980s and the subsequent strengthened position of the Russian Orthodox Church have been interpreted by the Catholic Church as a fulfillment of one part of the secrets of Fátima: the conversion of Russia.

During the last decade of the twentieth century, the Vatican had thus put an increasing emphasis on the Fátima apparitions, an emphasis that culminated in May 2000 with Pope John Paul II's visit to Fátima. Renowned for his devotion to Mary, Pope John Paul II had a special relationship to Our Lady of Fátima. He ascribed the fact that he survived an attempted assassination on May 13, 1981, to the intervention of Our Lady of Fátima. One year after the assault, on May 13, 1982, the pope visited Fátima to thank Our Lady for saving his life, and on this occasion he also met sister Lúcia. The bullet that was fired at the pope was placed in the crown of the statue of Our Lady of Fátima. On May 13, 2000, the pope visited Fátima once again, and this time he revealed a part of the Fátima message that had been kept secret until then: that the so-called "third Secret of Fátima" was that Our Lady had foreseen the 1981 assassination attempt on the pope and had revealed this in her apparition to Lúcia in 1917.[1]

To the Catholic Church in Portugal, the site of Fátima, apart from being an important pilgrimage site, is a religious center. Frequent national and international conferences, seminars, and courses take place there. The image of Our Lady of Fátima is used in a range of different contexts, such as the campaign against abortion in 1998, in which the church's "No to abortion" was printed on posters alongside an image of the well-known statue of Our Lady of Fátima.

The shrine of Our Lady of Fátima offers a fascinating illustration of the early anthropological interpretation of pilgrimage sites, which sees them as vehicles for religious leadership to spread religious and ideological ideas to the masses (cf. Rabinow 1975, Wolf 1991, Redfield 1960). However, a more recent approach to the study of Christian pilgrimage points out that the official discourse of the church is not the only one present at a pilgrimage site (Eade and Sallnow 1991). Varied and possibly conflicting discourses are brought to a holy site by different categories of pilgrims, as well as by religious specialists, and even by residents of the site. The anthropological task, according to Eade and Sallnow, is to investigate how both the practice of pilgrimage and the sacred powers of a shrine are constructed through these different perceptions and meanings that are imposed upon it by pilgrims and others.

One feature that the shrine of Fátima seems to have in common with other Marian shrines is the presence of large numbers of female pilgrims. Writing about the Greek Orthodox tradition, Dubisch (1995) underscores the feminized character of pilgrimage to Mary on the island of Tinos. At Fátima one immediately notes the lines of women fulfilling vows by walking on their knees up to the shrine. I would like to stress that if women are prominent among the pilgrims at Marian shrines, as several studies suggest, women's interpretations of Marian pilgrimage sites form an essential part of the forces that create and perpetuate the sacred power of these sites.[2] Consequently, in order to understand the "sacredness" of Marian shrines, it is necessary to pay attention to gender-related perceptions and images of the shrines. In this chapter I discuss the meaning ascribed to the Fátima pilgrimage by mainly female pilgrims from Vila Branca, a small pseudonymous town with four thousand inhabitants on the northwestern coast of Portugal, where I conducted fieldwork in the 1990s.[3] In Vila Branca, the women's interpretation of the Fátima pilgrimage emphasizes healing as a key theme. What I concentrate on here is the link between healing, the figure of the Virgin Mary, and female pilgrims.

The Vow in Marian Devotion

In Vila Branca, as in so many other towns and villages in Portugal, there is a yearly popular feast of the patron saint of the town. The patron saint of Vila Branca is an invocation of Mary, Our Lady of "calm weather at sea," that reflects the fishermen's need for protection at sea. The feast of the patron saint is but one of the public celebrations of Mary. Another is the yearly candlelight procession to Our Lady of Fátima on May 13—the anniversary of Mary's first apparition at Fátima in 1917. Vila Branca residents can also worship Mary at different religious shrines and monuments in the town, such as the grotto of Our Lady of Lourdes, or a monument depicting Our Lady of Fátima's apparition to the three little shepherds.

In order to understand the outward manifestations of Marian devotion, such as candlelight processions or pilgrimage journeys, it is essential to comprehend the nature of the institution of the vow. The practice of making vows to Mary and the saints has been characterized by Sanchis (1983) as the essential institution that epitomizes popular religion itself.[4]

A vow is a conditional prayer, with a common form known throughout the Roman Catholic and Eastern Orthodox world (Christian 1989; Dubisch 1995; Sanchis 1983). When making a vow, the devotee directs her/himself to Mary or any other holy figure and asks for something, promising that if the request is fulfilled s/he will perform a certain act in honor of the holy personage. A vow can be made in any situation in which a person feels the need to seek spiritual aid, but typical situations in which vows are made are situations involving acute danger or risks. Writing about Portugal, Sanchis states that a vow is made when one's existential safety, whether individual, familial or social, is in danger (1983: 47).[5]

Vila Branca residents say that one can promise to do almost anything in a vow, but a certain repertoire of devotional acts exists from which it is common to choose. Common vows are to visit the shrine of the saint in question (often in connection with the saint's feast) and perform, at the shrine, an additional act such as saying prayers or walking around the shrine a number of times, participating in the procession of the saint, carrying an *andor* (the stand on which statues of saints are carried), or paying for the decoration of such a stand. Transporting oneself to the shrine can in and of itself be part of the vow. In more heavily invested vows, the vow can be to walk on one's knees, to walk barefoot, or to crawl to the shrine. The vow can also include the promise to offer a votive gift at the shrine. In Vila Branca, the most common votive gifts are wax models of the part of the body that has been cured as a result of the vow, candles, photographs, and little slips of paper on which the vow is described, or money.

Vows can be made for the sake of others, such as when a mother vows to go to Fátima if a sick child gets cured. One can also make a vow that another person should fulfill. During my fieldwork many people mentioned to me that during the colonial wars in Africa (which only ended in 1974), mothers whose sons were serving as soldiers vowed that if their sons survived, the sons would go to the sanctuary at Fátima and crawl all the way up to the church.

During my fieldwork in Vila Branca, Our Lady of Fátima was the divine figure that was mentioned most frequently in discussions about vows, particularly by women. In addition, the devotional act that was mentioned most frequently was "to go to Fátima." However, the undertaking of journeys to Fátima is a relatively recent religious practice among Vila Branca residents. The first organized bus tour, like the one I describe below, took place in the mid-1970s, and was arranged by the local priest. Although the central position of Our Lady of Fátima in Marian devotion among Vila Branca residents might be relatively recently established, the kind of vows that are made in her cult are deeply rooted in local religious tradition.

In the history of the cult of Mary and the saints, vows for the curing of illnesses and healing of parts of the body have been a constant theme. These kinds of vows predominate in the devotional practices connected to Our Lady of Fátima. Furthermore, the practice of making vows has a clearly gendered character. This is not surprising if we consider that vows originate in the everyday life of the devotees and therefore are shaped in a gendered social context (cf. Dubisch 1995; Christian 1989). The largest category of vows— in which the theme of healing is elaborated—includes vows concerned with the life and health of oneself or one's family, particularly the children. These vows are made predominantly by women. Women also make vows at child-birth or when they have difficulties getting pregnant. Men also occasionally make vows if they themselves are ill or if a child is seriously ill, but the pre-dominance of women in vows for health is clear. Examples of vows made by men, on the other hand, are the vows of soldiers or fishermen facing death, or vows for protection in the military service. Another category of vows, made by both women and men, concerns employment, exams, and success at school. Male informants in Vila Branca told me about vows concerning employment, and mothers mentioned vows for their children's success at school.

It is worth noticing both the differences and the similarities between women's and men's vows. The most typical occasion when both men and women make vows is in a situation when life and health is put at risk. As mothers and housewives, women seek to maintain the health and lives of their families, and thus make vows for the whole group. Men risk their lives as fishermen, and sometimes as soldiers, and make vows when their own lives are in danger. It could be maintained that women make more vows than men do because their responsibilities as mothers and housewives provide daily opportunities both to positively secure, as well as worry about, the well-being and health of others. Healing, in the broad sense of promoting health and life, is a central theme in women's religious experiences.

The Vow as a Healing Ritual

Several authors writing on Catholic women's relationship to Mary have understood the impact of the cult of Mary on women in negative terms. Feminist writers have pointed out that Mary represents an unattainable ideal for women: chastity and fruitfulness at the same time (Warner 1990, Ruether 1993). Davis (1984) asserts that Marian devotion dwells most on the aspects of Mary that make her *least* like real women. However, a perspective that focuses on women's own thoughts and practices within the Marian cult offers another picture. In my conversations with Vila Branca women about proces-sions to Our Lady of Fátima or the site of Fátima itself, women never spoke of Mary as a model for themselves, nor did they refer to the theological image of Mary as obedient, passive, and humble. Instead, in order to make me under-stand the meaning of their devotion to Mary, Vila Branca women chose to tell me stories of vows.

Women's stories of vows are embedded in those stories that women refer to as *contar a sua vida* (to tell one's life). As vows are often made in dramatic situations, the vow and the circumstances that occasioned it are among the events a woman remembers in her life. These stories would tell about dramatic situations when a child's well-being had been put at risk: at childbirth, when a daughter had had an inflammation of the ear that would not heal, or when a son had been shot in the foot during a hunt. These stories included all the details and concrete experiences of mothering: the constant worry for a sick child, the sense of guilt if a child would not recover (reflecting the mother's sense of responsibility for the child's life), and the practical arrangements for being able to accompany a child to the hospital in town.

Women's vows can be said to be spiritual expressions of what philosopher Sara Ruddick (1980) sees as two primary goals of mothering practices: the preservation of lives of children and physical and mental growth of children. When the mother's ordinary measures to accomplish these goals are not enough, she turns to Mary. However, women have a responsibility not only for the health and growth of children, but for the general well-being of their extended families. One woman pointed out women's responsibility for health, saying that women are much more aware of everything concerning health, whereas men do not bother even about their own health.

Mothering and caring activities ultimately aim to promote health and life. These activities can be said to have a religious dimension in themselves, since the concept of *saúde* (health) is directly linked to the religious sphere. Health is understood as given by God in a very concrete sense. As I have already noted, health and illness are central concerns in the cult of the saints and Mary. Human health is a fundamental value to Vila Branca residents and to have one's health is seen as the basis of everything else in life. The time when most health problems were taken care of in the home or when a visit to a doctor was an expense that many could not afford is not a feature of the distant past. The fear of being sick with no one to help is very real, and many people still prefer to be taken care of by their own kin if they become ill, instead of going to the hospital.

Prayers and vows are thus embedded in concrete activities of mothering and caring, activities that "sustain intimate, domestic and personal relations, and tend to the comfort and nurturance, bodily safety, nourishment and cleanliness of others" (Walker 1998: 52). These activities are all deeply concerned with physicality. The theme of physicality is expressed in women's stories of vows, not only verbally, but also by means of the narrative style, by gestures and metaphors. One woman's fear that her daughter's face would become disfigured after an ear operation was transmitted physically, in grimaces. On one occasion I was talking with a group of women in a seamstress' shop about the repeated vows of a woman suffering from cancer. Suddenly, the seamstress took the chalk used for marking cloth and drew circles on a piece of cloth to illustrate the way she assumed that the tumors of the sick woman had developed. This kind of graphic description of the body is constantly repeated in stories of vows. Another woman had been covered with sores when struck by chicken pox. She showed to me with gestures the part of her face that had been covered with sores. However, she continued, as a result of a vow she had ended up without scars. When she had finished her story she invited me to look at her face to verify that there were no marks. These stories all communicate that the healed body is a sign of divine interference, just like the healthy body reveals the presence of God.

In Vila Branca women's understanding, body and spirit are not dichotomized. This is perhaps most clearly illustrated in a story told by Maria, age 29, of the vows she made when giving birth to a daughter, her second child:

> Something very funny was that I—it was the same thing with my son—I started to pray. When I did not have pains I prayed. Then I had the pains, I breathed like I was blowing out a candle, then I started praying again, I went on praying. I prayed all the time, all the time, all the time. And I promised on the occasion, on the occasion I also made a vow, I promised that I would…I think it was that I should walk up the stairs of the Calvary, those of the Grotto (of Our Lady of Lourdes) and that I would say the rosary there, it seems to me that it was that. And thank God, everything went well.

In her story, the physicality of the experience is not obscured. When telling the story of her own birth-giving, labor pains, breathing exercises (like blowing out a candle), and vows to Mary are equally important parts. Maria describes her childbirth in religious terms as both physical and spiritual and thus links her real, physical parturition to the figure of Mary.

While Vila Branca women's participation in the Marian cult in no way explicitly opposes the church's teachings on Mary, neither can it be said to confirm the image of Mary in theology. Women introduce their experiences of lived motherhood into the cult of Mary, experiences that include the joyful, life-affirming sides of motherhood, and the very concrete and physical care of children. By doing this, Vila Branca women ignore or pay little attention to aspects such as Mary's purity, chastity or "silence, obedience and modesty" emphasized in the official teachings of the church (McLaughlin 1974). In fact, women's invocation of Mary in their own lives stretches her womanly sides so far that the connections with purity and modesty are eclipsed.

Furthermore, many of women's religious activities in Vila Branca are not conducted according to guidelines from church authorities. When Maria, in fulfillment of her vows to Our Lady after giving birth to a daughter, visits the Grotto of Our Lady of Lourdes, it could be assumed that she honors the purity and chastity of Our Lady. However, the meaning of Maria's ritual act is connected to an image of Mary as midwife and protectress of women's real and physical child delivery, a ritual not mentioned, much less promoted, by priests. Maria's ritual activity thus creates and acts out meanings and images distinct from the official tradition.

The Anthropocentric View of Mary

Mary's role as a divine protectress of human health is reflected in the invocation "Our Lady of the Health" (Nossa Senhora da Saúde). In his study of the cult of the saints and Mary in Portugal, Sanchis (1983) points out that this invocation of Mary is common in northern Portugal, and particularly so in the Minho province (where Vila Branca is located). Sanchis documents not less than seven manifestations of Our Lady of the Health and two of Our Lady of the Remedies in Minho. He points out that these invocations represent anthropocentric manifestations of Mary—manifestations that refer to aspects of Mary that are also parts of the lives of humans.

Such a characterization of the invocations of Mary in Minho fits well into the mode of approaching Mary elaborated by Vila Branca residents, particularly the women. The tendency to give attention to aspects of Mary that make her similar to ordinary women is demonstrated in various ways at a popular level, perhaps most significantly through the emphasis on her motherhood. In the popular tradition, Mary is almost exclusively called "Nossa Senhora" (Our Lady). Mary is seldom talked about as the Virgin, although the expression *a Virgem Maria* might be used occasionally. That the epithet "a virgem" is relatively rare in ways of talking about Mary reflects the fact that her virginity is not emphasized in the popular image of her, or in religious practice. A common appellation given to Mary is "Mother of all" (Mãe de todos). As the patron saint of Vila Branca, Mary appears as the omnipotent mother and protectress of all humankind, an image embraced by both women and men. In women's direct, personal relationship to Mary, the public "Mother of all" becomes the more intimate *nossa mãe* (our mother) or *minha mãe* (my mother). Relating to Mary as minha mãe allows a woman to construct a direct, intimate, and spiritual relationship to Mary.

Moreover, Mary, the divine mother, is the figure who has the power to give health and to heal. The features of the Marian cult in Vila Branca that I have discussed above are clearly reflected in the practice of going on pilgrimage to Fátima. Whereas popular/female and official religious forms many times coexist more or less peacefully at the local level, at Fátima the tension between folk and official religion is accentuated.

Going on Pilgrimage

Dubisch (1995: 38) states that "pilgrimage depends on (1) the association created within a particular religious tradition of certain events and/or sacred figures with a particular field of space, and (2) the notion that the material world can make manifest the invisible spiritual world at such places." Similarly, Eade and Sallnow (1991) underscore that pilgrimage depends on the notion of localization of divine power in a place. At Fátima, the localization and materialization of divine power has been realized through the apparition of Our Lady to the three little shepherds.

At a popular level, the notion of pilgrimage is intimately connected to the traditional religious feast. The Portuguese word *romaria* refers to the traditional feast but is also a word for pilgrimage. Feasts involve a "pilgrimage"—a journey to the chapel where the statue of the devoted saint is kept. The aspect of pilgrimage can be more or less elaborated in feasts to the saints, but it is common in Portugal that the sanctuaries where a feast is held are situated on the outskirts of a community or even in an isolated place at a distance of several kilometers from the closest community. In these cases, the feast involves the exodus of the village to the sanctuary (Sanchis 1983: 39f).

If they have not vowed to go on foot, modern pilgrims travel to holy sites by bus, car, or air (cf. Sered 1992; Taylor 1995). In Vila Branca, a layman organizes trips by bus to Fátima and other places several times a year. Excursions to Fátima are organized when the major ceremonies are held there, that is, on

May 13 (marking the first apparition) and on October 13 (marking the last apparition in 1917). Another popular date is June 10, when thousands of children gather at Fátima to celebrate the Peregrinacão das Criançinhas, "the Pilgrimage of the Little Children." Similarly, the Hope and Life movement (a national association of widows) gather at Fátima every April 24. People do not use the more formal word *peregrinacão* (pilgrimage) when talking about these journeys, but say simply *excursão* (excursion) or *passeio* (trip).

Although people often travel together in family groups (as people seem to do in other parts of Europe as well; cf. Eade and Sallnow 1991; Taylor 1995), on the whole, women take the opportunity to go to Fátima more often than men or whole families. When larger family groups go to Fátima, the initiative and the planning is very much in the hands of the women. The motives for going on a tour to Fátima that were mentioned most often, apart from the primary motive of fulfilling vows, were that the tours offer recreation, beautiful sights, and a good time together with family and friends or with new acquaintances. In the bus, one tells others the story of one's life, one woman explained. These recreational aspects are not seen as conflicting with the devotional dimension or with the fulfillment of vows; both dimensions—recreation and devotion—are seen as equally important (cf. Taylor 1995).

The priest of Vila Branca has tried to diminish the festive dimensions—*o arraial*—of the local religious feast to Mary, even as he simultaneously has promoted pilgrimage to Fátima, in line with the view of the church establishment. The priest's effort to make Vila Branca residents go to Fátima can be interpreted as a strategy to channel their devotion to Mary into a more orthodox form of Marian devotion. The celebrations at Fátima do not include any arraial, only processions to Our Lady of Fátima and masses in the church at Fátima. However, as I discuss below, Vila Branca residents resist the strategy of their priest in various ways. They go to Fátima, but they model the pilgrimage on the traditional romaria.

A Trip to Fátima

On the morning of October 12, a hired bus set off from Vila Branca to Fátima. The passengers traveled together with family and neighbors, and there were slightly more women than men. Aside from myself, only one elderly woman traveled on her own. The organizer, who tried to make sure that everybody was happy on the tour, had given me a seat next to Judith, a young woman in her early twenties. Judith was traveling together with her five-year-old daughter, her sister, and other relatives.

The bus stopped frequently for coffee pauses, and one woman said to me jokingly, "This is what we do, when we go to Fátima, we eat and drink!" The stop for lunch was at a beautiful site above Nazaré with a view over the town and the sea. Before lunch there was time for sightseeing, we visited a monument of Nossa Senhora de Nazaré and some also visited the church of Nazaré. Stops for sightseeing were made also on our way back home. We visited a site with natural caves and also a bakery, famous for a special kind of cake. In other words, the tour offered both sights of a miraculous place and other unusual or beautiful sights and experiences.

For the lunch at Nazaré, everybody sat down on the grass at the site with the view and unpacked the enormous quantities of food and drinks they had brought with them. People offered each other food to taste, and bottles of wine and *bagaço* (the local liquor) circulated. The organizer strolled around between the groups of people with a bottle of wine in his hand, making jokes and having a bite of food here and there. After lunch, when the bus was on its way and everybody was more relaxed, the organizer made everybody sing popular folk songs and the atmosphere in the bus became more and more holiday-like. We arrived at Fátima late in the afternoon.

Bringing and displaying to others an abundance of food and drinks, including wine and liquor, is one way in which the pilgrims spontaneously create the festivities that otherwise are lacking in the Fátima pilgrimage. Senhora Laura, a neighbor of my landlady in Vila Branca, made a lot out of the holiday aspect of the trip. During the whole stay at Fátima she made jokes and comments that contributed to the atmosphere of being on vacation and having fun. She would take small dance steps in the street and then say, "Oh, no, now we are not going to dance, we are going to pray!" Before going to bed, in the rented basement at Fátima, where I, Senhora Laura, and a group of neighbors from Vila Branca all shared the same room, Senhora Laura made everybody laugh with her comments, and she and her neighbor, Carla, told jokes and laughed hysterically for several hours. During the day, Senhora Laura spent most of her time eating in restaurants or resting.

At Fátima one sees people barbecuing and eating and drinking wherever they can find a place to do so. The organizer of our tour was seen most of the time with the large bottle of wine in a basket he had brought from home. The church establishment tries to stop this kind of behavior by regulating where people are allowed to eat and sleep. This disagreement regarding the recreational aspect of religious feasts illustrates what Brettell (1990: 56) calls a structural opposition between church and people concerning "the uneasy balance between the sacred and the profane" in Portuguese Catholicism.

The Vows to Our Lady of Fátima

The religious shrine at Fátima consists of several buildings and monuments. There is the Basilica of the Rosary located in front of a large square where the pilgrims gather to attend the major ceremonies. In the shrine square there is the Capelinha das Aparições (Chapel of Apparitions) built on the spot where Our Lady supposedly appeared to the shepherd children. The shrine at Fátima also includes the surroundings, where the little shepherds tended their flocks of sheep. About two kilometers from the shrine square, is the house of the little shepherds.

In the town center of Fátima, there are hotels, restaurants, cafés, and dozens of stores selling religious artifacts of all imaginable kinds: statuettes, paintings, rosaries, crucifixes, memory plates with the inscription "Fátima" and the apparition scene reproduced in a range of different materials, as well as wax models of different parts of the body to be used as votive offerings. The Vila Branca pilgrims talked about the activities in the town centre as *"o comercio"* (the commerce), and some pilgrims made negative remarks, regarding it as antithetical to the devotional activities.

When we arrived at Fátima in the late afternoon, some pilgrims started to talk about visiting the sanctuary right away because they had vows to fulfill. Several pilgrims (on the bus tour and later) told me that they preferred to carry out their vows immediately upon arrival. Judith, the young mother I was sitting next to, told me that she and her sister had vows to fulfill and would therefore go up to the sanctuary together and rejoin the rest of the family in the bus afterward. Judith and her family were all going to spend the night in the bus. As we were talking, Judith changed her blue jeans into a pair of black tights (as a preparation for the fulfillment of her vow). At this point, I left the bus with Senhora Laura and the group of neighbors with whom I shared a room for the night at Fátima.

When we came back to the bus, many of the other pilgrims had returned from the sanctuary. Soon Judith and her sister showed up. Judith hurried to her seat and changed her now very dirty black tights into a pair of jogging trousers. She looked exhausted. Suddenly, she turned to me with an expression of pride on her face and said, "I did it on my knees." As I did not understand at first, she repeated what she had said in a loud voice and bent down and touched her knees. "My vow—I did it on my knees," she said once again. Judith wanted me to know that she had come to Fátima to carry out the kind of vow that Vila Branca residents speak about with admiration and respect.

The following day, I visited the shrine square with a couple in their thirties, Carla and Rui. Large numbers of people were in motion in the square, and among them were lines of women who walked on their knees across the square to the Chapel of Apparitions. Some carried children on their backs. Some prayed as they walk, others cried, still others were silent. The sight of these women on their knees made an impression not only on a foreigner like me, but on the Portuguese pilgrims as well. When Rui, Carla, and I approached such a line of women on their knees, we stopped and watched them for a while. Carla said to me, "It is faith. It can only be explained by faith."

I learned later that Judith's vow concerned the recovery of her husband, who had been hurt in an accident while he was working at sea. The injury would not heal properly and it affected the life of the young family profoundly, as the husband had not been able to resume his work as a fisherman or sailor. Judith's husband had not yet recovered and her vow was one of many prayers and vows that she had repeated, in the hope that her husband's condition would improve. She told me that her husband had not wanted her to go because he did not want her to be uncomfortable in the bus and tired when she came home. The trip was also tiresome for her daughter, but Judith had not wanted to leave her behind. Judith was sad because of the difficulties of their situation, but also proud of the vow she had fulfilled. This pilgrimage journey to Fátima took place in the beginning of my fieldwork and only later, when I had talked to many different women about vows, did I understand more fully the reason for Judith's pride: she had done what a Vila Branca woman must do in a situation when the "existential safety" of herself or her family is in danger.

A Female Link to Mary

One set of competing discourses that has been noted at Christian shrines, and that can be noted at Fátima as well, is the tension between the "this-worldly" concerns of the pilgrims and the discourse of the church that is more concerned with the otherworld (Eade and Sallnow 1991). Given the predominance of women at Fátima, it is clear that the tension between popular and official interpretations of the shrine has a gendered dimension; popular/female perceptions of the sacred stand in contrast to the interpretations offered by the male hierarchy of the Catholic Church. At Fátima, the large numbers of women make visible a female link to Mary. Although both male and female pilgrims come to the site, and the pilgrims turn to Our Lady of Fátima for many reasons, it is clear that a large number of female pilgrims turn to Mary primarily in their roles as mothers, healers, and caretakers of families. The this-worldly character of the cult of Our Lady of Fátima is thus particularly elaborated by women. Healing is in itself feminized. Most vows related to healing are carried out by women and healing is mainly ritually expressed in the context of the female activities of mothering and caring.

The cult of Our Lady of Fátima can be compared with the findings presented by Sered in her study (1994) of what she calls "female-dominated" religions, religions in which women predominate not only as participants but also as leaders. To a large extent, these religions are centered on the ritual elaboration of the maternal role, and stress women's social roles as nurturers and healers. Furthermore, there is a particular emphasis placed on illness and curing, manifested, for example, in the centrality of healing rituals. This characterization is also pertinent regarding Vila Branca women's cult of Our Lady of Fátima. Health and illness is of central focus in the cult of Our Lady of Fátima, and the vows made by Vila Branca women can be seen as mainly healing rituals.

Sered underscores that many of these patterns can also be found in women's religious activities in male-dominated religions. In such a context, however, these themes tend to be categorized as marginal or deviant to the official religion.

To the clergy and other representatives of the Catholic Church, the female/popular forms of Marian devotion displayed at Fátima do not represent proper ways of honoring Mary. The women's acts of devotion, such as walking on one's knees, are tolerated, but many priests seek to combat these forms of religious expression, and urge the pilgrims to offer monetary donations instead. The local priest of Vila Branca discouraged all women from making physically arduous vows.

I mentioned earlier that Vila Branca women's invocations of Mary in their own lives emphasize the human, womanly aspects of Mary. The lived motherhood of Vila Branca women is not identical with Mary's motherhood in the theological image. There are occasions when these more human aspects of the cult of Mary can bring women in direct confrontation with the standpoints of the clergy. An urban, intellectual Catholic woman told me that while she was working as a volunteer to support pilgrims on their way to Fátima, she heard the following story of one woman's vow. The pilgrim had vowed to walk to Fátima if the illegal abortion she had would turn out well—a prayer that, according to the woman, had been granted. To the urban Catholic this case showed the alienation of popular religion from the official positions of the church. While I heard of no similar case in Vila Branca, the logic fits in with the general context of vows. Mary is seen, at a popular level, as a divine figure to whom women can turn, especially with all problems relating to the physical aspects of motherhood. Taken together with the fact that the prohibition against abortion by the church and the laws of Portugal is not supported by the whole population, such a vow might well have been made.

Mary's Materialization and Its Reenactment

The feminization of healing, as I have described it above, accentuates the gendered character of the tension between folk and official interpretations of Fátima. Another feature of female/popular discourses at Fátima, one that distinguishes them from churchly discourse, is the emphasis on Mary's materialization at the site. According to popular belief, the healing power of Mary is particularly strong at Fátima because the divine figure has appeared at the site. This belief, and the way of perceiving the divine that it represents, is related to the anthropocentric image of Mary that I mentioned earlier.

When I asked my informants in Vila Branca to tell me the story of the apparitions at Fátima, it struck me that they never paid any particular attention to the Message of Fátima. Since I had read about the mysterious secrets of Fátima, I was eager to hear what Our Lady had *said* to the shepherd children. However, my informants did not share my interest in the verbal content of the Fátima message. Instead, they talked about the miracles that Our Lady had performed and the fate of the three little shepherds. To learn more about Mary's apparition at Fátima, I was directed to Senhor João. Senhor João had several elder sisters, who were now deceased. His eldest sister had been present at Fátima on October 17, 1917, the day when Our Lady performed the so-called Miracle of the Sun in the presence of the three children and the thousands of people gathered there. In his childhood, Senhor João's sisters had told him the Fátima story over and over again, and hearing the story from him was considered to be almost like hearing it from an eyewitness. Senhor João told me the story of Mary's first apparition in the following words:

> There was nothing at Fátima at the time, only olive trees and bushes.... The three little shepherds were strolling in the bushes, when they saw a beaming light. It came towards them, from the east. The light stopped and was transformed into a woman. It was this white woman. The children asked her who she was and she answered that she came from heaven.
>
> "What do you want"? the children asked.
>
> And she answered: "I want you to say the rosary every day and I want you to come here every month on the thirteenth."

Senhor João went on to tell how the children were called liars when they told the people in the village that they had seen "a very white woman." He concluded the story by telling how the children were finally believed when Our Lady, on the occasion of her last apparition, performed the Miracle of the Sun, to which his eldest sister had been a witness.

Mary's Materialization

When Mary materializes in Senhor João's story, she appears as *uma senhora*, which is the appellation used for adult women (that is, married women, not young girls). She emerges from light and appears to the children as "very white," but the children cannot know who she is from her mere appearance. The apparition story emphasizes that Our Lady when she materializes looks almost like an ordinary woman. It is only the light that surrounds her that distinguishes her. In the apparition story, the divine figure known only through images and words takes an earthly form, the form of a woman who can be seen and spoken to by human beings.

I argued above that women construct a direct and personal relationship to Mary and that they give attention to aspects of Mary that make her similar to ordinary women, thus elaborating an anthropocentric view of Mary. Through such an approach, women strive to bring Mary "down to earth," to make her more accessible for their requests to her.

The appeal of apparition stories at a popular level is that they apply the same strategy in constructing an image of Mary. In apparition stories, the popular religious imagination, so to speak, makes Mary materialize as a strategy to bring her closer to humans. When Mary is material, people can direct prayers to her and partake of her healing power. When people experience difficult moments, they want Mary to be as *present* and as *accessible* as possible. It is the desire to experience Mary's physical presence and to see her face-to-face that makes stories of her apparition so appealing. Such an approach to the divine also underlies the way the pilgrims model their participation in the official ceremonies.

The Reenactment of the Apparition

The localization and materialization of divine power at Fátima is vividly experienced by the pilgrims. The area where the three little shepherds tended their sheep is still wilderness, a flat piece of land where the only things growing are grass, small bushes, and single trees. This landscape is in itself imbued with divine power to the pilgrims. Fátima is clearly an example of what Eade and Sallnow (1991) call a place-centered, or spatial, sacredness. At Fátima the landscape owes its sacredness to Mary's apparition, which turned the trees, bushes, and water holy.

Most of the Vila Branca pilgrims visited the house of the little shepherds. There, the pilgrims looked at Lúcia's little bed and the simple furniture of the house and commented on the humble conditions in which she lived. The Vila Branca pilgrims clearly identify with the little shepherds, who came from the same kind of humble, rural conditions as many of them do. In this way they emphasize that the Mother of God chose to talk to three children of humble origin like themselves in a rural periphery, far away from religious or secular centers.

Following in the footsteps of the child shepherds, seeing their house, and meditating on the apparition story served to prepare the Vila Branca pilgrims for the so-called Farewell ceremony. In this ceremony, a statue of Our Lady of Fátima is carried by priests around the large square in front of the basilica. The square is filled with thousands of pilgrims and as the statue passes them, the pilgrims take up white handkerchiefs they have brought especially for the occasion and wave "goodbye" to Our Lady.

When I arrived to attend the Farewell ceremony, together with a group of pilgrims, the square was already full and it was almost impossible to move towards its center. Everybody wanted to move forward to get a place with a good view and people behind us shouted, "Oh, here one does not see anything, move ahead!" The crowding and the burning sun made everyone tense and irritated. People pushed and insulted each other. Finally, the pilgrims around us calmed down and accepted the places they had managed to obtain. Carla pulled out some white handkerchiefs from her handbag and gave one to her husband and one to me. Estefánia and Iría also clutched white handkerchiefs. We were all waiting eagerly for the statue of Our Lady to appear. Iría tried to push her way a bit further to be able to see better, but the wall of people in front of us was dense.

Then, suddenly, we got a glimpse of the statue, which had slowly started its journey through the crowd about two hundred meters away. "There she is!" Carla exclaimed, radiant with joy. "Can you see her? There, there!"

She pushed me exaltedly, but I could only see the back of the statue, far away. Iría stretched her neck to see better and blew kisses toward the statue, which was approaching slowly. "Oh, there she is, my loved one!" Iría exclaimed. I heard other pilgrims shouting *"Que linda, que bonita!"* (How sweet, how beautiful). The statue of Our Lady was carried around the square and passed us on its way back. One saw nothing of the priests who were carrying the statue, only the figure of Our Lady floating above the crowd.

Finally, Our Lady passed us, and her mild face framed by the blue cloak was turned toward us. At this moment the women around me sobbed and everybody, both men and women, waved their handkerchiefs to the statue. Then Our Lady was carried away through the crowd surrounded by white handkerchiefs as if thousands of doves were following her.

A procession with a statue of Mary is a familiar ritual to the Vila Branca pilgrims and probably to many of the other pilgrims present as well. But in the ceremonies at Fátima, the pilgrims relive the experience of the shepherd children who saw "a white woman" appear out of the blue sky. The appearance of the statue of Our Lady takes on the meaning of a "real" apparition, as implied in Carla's exclamation: *"There she is! Can you see her?"* The pilgrims' visual experience of the Farewell ceremony is captured in one of the many different kinds of religious souvenirs that are sold at Fátima. In an ordinary ballpoint pen, for example, there is a small picture of the statue of Our Lady of Fátima with beams of light around her figure standing above a crowd of people. When one moves the pen up and down, the picture moves slowly from one side of the pen to the other, as though the radiant figure of Our Lady was floating along above the people.

I suggest that the Vila Branca pilgrims construct their participation in the Farewell ceremony as a meeting with Mary, a meeting in which she appears to be physically present, and where it is possible to interact with and talk to her. The concreteness of the encounter is expressed in various ways: waving with handkerchiefs to the statue, shouting to it, and the intensification of feelings when the face of the statue is seen. The notion of a materialized divinity is linked to sensory rituals. At Fátima, the pilgrim's rituals are elaborated through sight. In Senhor João's story of the apparition, he stresses the apparition itself, when Mary emerges from light and appears as very white, and the Miracle of the Sun. These are both visual phenomena and this visuality is elaborated by the pilgrims at Fátima. The climax of the Farewell ceremony is the *sight* of Our Lady materialized in the statue. The pilgrims also create additional visual effects at the major ceremonies, such as the thousands of white handkerchiefs waving in the air at the Farewell ceremony. When a national association of widows gathers at Fátima, the participants wave with scarves of different colors. At the "Pilgrimage of the little children," the children carry balloons in different colors that they all let go at a given moment. In candlelight processions, the visual effects are created by the thousands of candles carried by the pilgrims.

The materiality and visuality of religious experience are linked to the role of religious artifacts. As caretakers of houses, women are particularly involved with religious objects, such as rosaries, statuettes of Mary and the saints, and religious paintings. These kinds of artifacts are kept in the homes for devotional as well as decorative purposes.

Apart from water and branches that pilgrims bring home from Fátima, the Vila Branca pilgrims also visited one or more of the stores selling religious artifacts, and all of them bought some kind of artifact. Many of the artifacts represent the scene of the original apparition to the shepherd children. Others play on the visual theme, like lamps in the form of statues of Our Lady, which are illuminated from the inside. Still others allude to the miracle theme, like statuettes that change color depending on the temperature of the air (these can be found in all Vila Branca homes). The ballpoint pen that shows Mary "appearing" during the ceremonies refers directly to the pilgrims' own experiences at Fátima. By bringing home artifacts, the pilgrims seek to bring something of the healing and benevolent power of Our Lady of Fátima back with them into their homes.

Fátima of the People and Fátima of the Church

An important feature of the pilgrims' activities at Fátima is their independence in relationship to the authority of the church. Vows are made and fulfilled without the knowledge of any priest. The Vila Branca pilgrims come to Fátima on a bus tour, organized by one of their neighbors. Whereas the ceremonies outdoors that the Vila Branca pilgrims did attend are organized by the church, the Vila Branca pilgrims denied the church its role of leadership in different ways. One incident on the eve of October 13, when a candlelight procession to Our Lady of Fátima was arranged, illustrates clearly the pilgrims' attitude.

I was waiting together with the group of Vila Branca pilgrims in front of the Basilica of the Rosary for the procession to start. On a stage, quite close to us, a priest with a microphone in his hand was trying energetically to make the crowd sing. But the crowd was silent. Not a single tone was heard. The priest went on for a long time, singing about four or five hymns in the same energetic way.

Then suddenly, as if by magic, the crowd started to sing. It was the familiar hymn of Fátima that I had already heard in the candlelight procession to Our Lady of Fátima in Vila Branca. Although I could not see much in the midst of the crowd, I realized that the statue had started to move. In a minute my guess was confirmed: the statue of Our Lady had been carried down from the stage and was moving slowly in the dark night surrounded by the flames of thousands of candles.

To place a priest in front of the crowd of pilgrims at Fátima is the church's way of trying to impose a religious style on the pilgrims that it finds appropriate, presenting priests as the leaders of the ceremonies. The pilgrims resist these efforts on the part of the church and interpret the procession differently: they focus on the sight of the statue of Our Lady surrounded by candlelight.

The incident at the candlelight procession manifests the way the pilgrims construct the meaning of the Fátima shrine, as discussed earlier. In telling the apparition story, Senhor João focused on the apparition itself, the direct encounter between Our Lady and the children. As I discussed above, the processions at Fátima, in particular the Farewell ceremony, are interpreted as such an encounter between the pilgrims (identifying with the shepherd children) and Our Lady. This encounter does not need any intermediary church, and such an attitude characterized all the ritual activities of the Vila Branca pilgrims at Fátima.

Shortly after the pilgrimage to Fátima in October, the Vila Branca priest distributed a text to his parishioners that explained the official theological interpretation of the message of Fátima. Some of the people who had been to Fátima read the text; many did not (many in the older generation, like Senhora Laura, are illiterate). The interpretation holds that the message of Fátima calls for a true encounter with Jesus Christ in Holy Communion. It emphasizes that Christ is represented on earth by the pope and the bishops. Mary, or Our Lady, is mentioned only once and not by name; she is referred to only as "the heavenly messenger."

The theological interpretation of Fátima offered by this text reveals one of the dimensions of the gulf between orthodox and popular conceptions of Fátima. The church establishment emphasizes that the message of Fátima reveals the centrality of Christ and of the sacrament of communion, and underscores the intermediary role of the bishops and the priests. To Vila Branca pilgrims, however, the Fátima story signifies that Mary can manifest herself directly to the poor without any intermediary church, and that her healing power is accessible at Fátima. One common characteristic of pilgrimage sites is that they offer experiences of the sacred *outside* the physical boundaries of the church (although the church, when asserting control over pilgrimage sites, also asserts its presence at the site). The church text seeks to promote the view that true encounters with God can only take place within the physical boundaries of the church, in the sacrament that is distributed by the priests. Such a view seeks to undermine what is actually going on at Fátima, where pilgrims experience true encounters with the divine by focusing on Mary and avoiding the church structures as much as possible.

In addition, there is another kind of tension inherent in this situation. The pilgrims do not see Mary in relationship to Christ but as a divine figure in her own right. As *Mother* of God (Mãe de Deus), Mary is on par with, or even symbolically above, God and Christ in popular devotion. Mary was proclaimed Theotokos "Bearer of God" at the council of Ephesus in 431 (and she is still referred to by this term, among others, in the contemporary Greek Orthodox context). The proclamation at Ephesus constitutes the beginning of the cult of Mary as Mother of God (Warner 1976: 66). Ever since, Mary's place in the divine hierarchy has presented a problem to the church. The church encourages devotion to Mary, but only as a secondary, subordinate figure in the divine hierarchy (cf. Davis 1984). In 1974, the pope proclaimed that Mary is accorded special veneration, but that devotional practices should never lose sight "of the unique and sole mediation of Christ" (McBrien 1995: 814).

Healed by the Mother of God

The church's strategy at Fátima clearly aims at placing the apparition phenomenon and the Marian devotion within the boundaries of the church and under its leadership. The church promotes pilgrimage to Fátima, but seeks at the same time to impose its interpretations of the shrine on the pilgrims. The message of Fátima is used to spread the orthodox teachings of the church in multiple ways, as I have exemplified above. However, although the interpretations of the Fátima message made by the church generally seem to contradict the meanings ascribed to Fátima by the pilgrims, the Vatican does not distance itself completely from popular discourse. When Pope John Paul II declared that Our Lady of Fátima had rescued his life, and then revealed, as he did on May 13, 2000, that the "third Secret of Fátima" was that Our Lady had foreseen the assassination attempt on him, it is on the one hand an interpretation of the Fátima message that underscores Mary's historical role as protectress of the church. On the other hand, it is evident that the pope here speaks the same language as the pilgrims. In fact, the pope declared to the thousands of pilgrims who had gathered at the site that he had come to Fátima for the same reason as so many of them: when he was severely injured and feared for his life, he was healed by the Mother of God.

The Feminization of Healing

The main ritual activities of many of the pilgrims at Fátima, such as fulfilling vows and experiencing encounters with the sacred, are modeled on traditional practices and understandings that characterize local cults of Mary. These practices and understandings are, to a large extent, feminized, particularly elaborated by women in the context of mothering and caring practices. At Fátima, the connection between women and the theme of healing is conspicuous. It is manifested, for example, in the presence of large numbers of female pilgrims performing bodily acts, such as walking on their knees, in fulfillment of vows for the health of their families. The apparition mode of viewing the divine is another variant of the strategy to bring Mary down to earth, to make her present and accessible. This strategy and mode of relating to the divine is connected to an anthropocentric image of Mary, which is characteristic of local cults of Mary. Whereas such an image of Mary is embraced by both women and men, women's invocation of Mary in their own lives, as well as women's use of appellations of Mary such as "my mother," elaborate further the human/womanly sides of Mary.

These feminized religious themes stand in sharp contrast to the official discourse of the Catholic Church at Fátima. The church encourages pilgrimage to Fátima, but seeks at the same time to impose its interpretations of the shrine on the pilgrims. The message of Fátima is used to spread the orthodox teachings of the church. However, the official position is somewhat ambiguous. The Vatican's increased attention to Marian apparitions during the twentieth century might also be interpreted as recognition of the importance of female/popular strands within contemporary Catholicism. Within these strands, healing is a key ritual and divine power materializes in the form of an ordinary woman.

3

Pilgrimage, Promises, and Ex-Votos

Ingredients for Healing in Northeast Brazil

C. Lindsey King

*F*or people living in the *sertão*, the harsh and infertile backlands of northeast Brazil, every day is a situation of one political negotiation after another. With a binary social system comprised of the elites and the masses that has changed little in over four hundred years, most *sertanejos* serve as members of a marginalized labor force of sharecroppers and migrant workers who must continue working under socially manipulated conditions that insure a system of dependency for the subaltern of this region. Due to a paucity of water, subsistence agriculture can barely be maintained. Roughly 75 percent of the population suffers from malnutrition and related diseases, and 52 percent of the infant mortality in Brazil occurs in this region (Nations and Rebhun 1988). Covering an area comparable to the Australian outback, the sertão encompasses the largest area of poverty in South America (Pang 1989; Robock 1963, 1975).

Living in a world full of uncertainties due to governmental corruption and neglect as well as an inhospitable environment, the majority of the population must assume a position of submission to survive. One method of ensuring continued survival is by negotiating advantageous religious relationships by repaying divine favors with an *ex-voto*.

Popularly called *milagres* (miracles), ex-votos are part of the material culture of pilgrimage. This religious tradition is based upon a reciprocal spiritual contract called a *promessa* (promise), which is made between a supplicant and his or her favorite saint and functions much like the secular contracts between patron and client. In this ritual, the supplicant promises to repay the saint after the saint has fulfilled the supplicant's request, most often a physical healing. Many of these spiritual contracts involve making a pilgrimage to the shrine of a particular saint and in most cases the spiritual payment is made with an ex-voto.

In Canindé the favored saint is St. Francis of Assisi, called "São Francisco das Chagas" (St. Francis of Wounds) by his followers, and the ex-votos are one-of-a-kind mimetic artifacts. This unique practice is found in shrines throughout Brazil's Northeast. The more typical offering, such as the small, pressed-tin, mass-produced *milagro* found in other parts of Latin America, the United States, and Europe, and the *tamata* utilized by practitioners of the Greek Orthodox religion, are not found at this shrine. Instead, in Canindé, most milagres are handcrafted, usually carved in wood, but also fashioned from clay, wax, cloth and, more recently, Styrofoam. These offerings are three-dimensional and are extremely personal, as they are made to repay St. Francis for a specific physical or social problem.

The ex-voto tradition has roots in pre-Christian beliefs and can be traced through the archaeological record to civilizations predating that of the Greeks and Romans (Cassar 1964; Davidson 1998; Deyts 1988; R. Jackson 1988; Lanciani 1893; Rouse 1902; Sambon 1895). This pagan tradition was syncretized into early Christian practices, and with the movement of the Roman Empire, spread throughout Europe where it continues to be practiced.[1] This tradition was brought to the New World by Spanish and Portuguese explorers where it blended with compatible indigenous practices and is today a vital part of folk Catholicism from the North American Southwest to the southern tip of South America.[2]

This chapter discusses the lives of the sertanejos, their strategies for survival, and the healing role that their belief systems in general and pilgrimage in particular play in their survival. I argue that this votive tradition, which precludes intercession from a priest, serves as a form of silent rebellion against the religious hierarchy and instills in the practitioner a sense of empowerment. I also feel that the therapeutic value of making a tangible symbol of disease and then giving it away in the form of the ex-voto further empowers practitioners by giving them a direct input into their healing.

The Pilgrim Population

Today, the population of the sertão accounts for 46 percent of the total population of the Northeast (Mitchell 1981: 3). The *fazenda*, the large-scale, privately owned plantation or ranch, is the predominant form of landholding in northeast Brazil, with a few *sitios*, small subsistence farms, scattered throughout. Owners of the fazendas contract with landless farmers in a variety of tenure arrangements and harsh negotiations whose outcome is always in the owners' favor. The smallest percentage of peasant farmers are tenant farmers. They pay money for the land upon which they live and work. Sharecropping accounts for about 15 percent of the small farming operations. These sharecroppers are in a sense salaried employees who receive land and a percentage of the crop in exchange for labor. In the 1950s and 1960s, many of these sharecroppers and tenant farmers were dislocated, prompting a growth of organized peasant leagues. The growth of these leagues allowed the angry farmers strength to vent their feelings. As a result, this was a time of many violent actions between the league members and the hired gunmen of the landowners. Today, most agricultural workers are working for a daily wage. A few are given a small piece of land to work in their spare time (which is a rare commodity), and some are given lodging. This new system of wage work instead of tenancy has broken down the social system of patronage, leaving the peasant in an even worse situation than before. It is reckoned that 81 percent of the people whose lives depend upon agriculture are landless laborers (Forman 1975: 42). In a 1970 study by the Instituto Brasileiro de Geografia e Estatistica (IBGE), it was reported that 20.7 percent of the rural workforce earned no cash income at all, that 72.1 percent earned less than minimum wage, and only 7.8 percent of the rural workforce earned higher than minimum wage (Dias 1978: 176). Since the landowners still control the land, but have no real investment in their workers, they are less likely to provide the security that the patronage system supplied. This has created a situation of despair for vast numbers of people. In an area where there is often a critical shortage of water, subsistence existence is precarious, resulting in a large population who have no resources to fall back on during times of "catastrophic crisis," such as drought-induced famine, or to help endure the more serious "endemic hunger," the chronic famine caused by the poverty that plagues the people of the sertão. It is this endemic hunger that is the greater villain (Reis 1981: 42).

The diet of the typical backlander consists primarily of manioc, beans, and *rapadura*, a hard block of coarse brown sugar; all are staples that can be purchased inexpensively. This menu has not varied significantly in over one hundred years. While this diet is adequate in vitamins A and C and carbohydrates when eaten in sufficient quantities, the basic caloric intake and levels of nutrients such as protein, iron, riboflavin, and niacin are questionable. Reis states that insufficient caloric intake will cause the body to burn its existing protein for energy, diverting it from its nutritional function. Under these conditions many people will become emaciated and apathetic, and tend to be small in stature. Chronic deficiencies can cause hormonal problems, which lead to debilitating diarrhea, delayed puberty, and menstrual irregularity. Niacin, thiamine, and riboflavin deficiencies can cause dermal problems, depression, and irritability. Deficiencies of vitamins A and C can cause even more severe conditions. Inadequate ingestion of Vitamin A will cause night blindness and can lead to permanent blindness. An insufficient amount of vitamin C causes scurvy. While an adult can more or less maintain on this diet, the consequences that a child can suffer are quite serious. Because of the important developmental stages occurring during childhood, insufficient caloric intake and nutrients often lead to mental and physical retardation, and even to death (Reis 1981).

The conditions that Reis discusses aptly describe the physical appearance of many people I saw in Canindé. The fact that many people suffered from wounds that would not heal properly, skin problems, and brittle bones also illustrates the consequences of chronic malnutrition. These dietary insufficiencies could also account for the high number of stillbirths, weak and sickly infants, and the high rate of infant mortality. The average woman in the Northeast has about ten pregnancies during her reproductive years. Averages indicate that out of these pregnancies she will experience 1.4 miscarriages, abortions, or stillbirths; have 3.5 of her children die; and have 4.5 living children. Seventy percent of the deaths occur between birth and six months, and 82 percent by the end of the first year (Scheper-Hughes 1986).

To some extent, this nutritional deficiency also may account for the high rate of illiteracy, which is well over 50 percent in the Northeast and often 100 percent in rural areas. In the same 1970 study by the IBGE, it was found that only 13.5 percent of the rural workforce had attended school at all, and only 3.4 percent attended for more than three years (Dias 1978: 176). In many cases these rural schools are taught by people only semiliterate themselves and who have no instructional materials with which to work (Forman 1975: 84). Under the best of conditions, children who are hungry cannot concentrate. If they do not have the right foods to eat they can suffer from apathy, anxiety, and depression, none of which is conducive to learning. These conditions also apply to parents. If the parents are full of apathy, anxiety, and depression and haven't the strength to work, they will not encourage their children. It is a vicious circle that has been misdiagnosed by the Brazilian government, which blames ignorance and resistance to change as the primary reasons for the sertanejos' continued existence in poverty.

This situation of poverty and governmental neglect is not new. According to Mitchell (1981: 4), there has never been a government administration that has "attempted with serious and honest concern to come to grips" with the chronic poverty in the Brazilian Northeast. Because of the land monopoly it is almost impossible for the poor to acquire land, even if it is lying fallow. In many cases, the farm workers have lost their position on a fazenda and literally have nowhere to go. In this northeast region many people migrate to shrine towns, such as Canindé, where the Catholic Church will often supply basic physical necessities. While it is not uncommon that in desperate situations people turn to religion for help, Brazilian anthropologist Thales de Azevedo suggests that religion for the oppressed poor is used for "therapeutic value rather than a path to salvation" (Forman 1975: 275). By this he means that these people turn to religion as a means of satisfying worldly concerns rather than spiritual concerns. My conversations with pilgrims reinforced this thesis. Over and over I heard pilgrims say, *"vida e luta,"* life is struggle. No one I spoke with mentioned concern with an afterlife or his or her immortal soul. They were concerned with the here and now. One hundred percent of the people I spoke with had come to St. Francis with concerns of physical or social "dis-ease": illness, pain, homelessness, or anxiety about their situation here on earth. They had vowed to make a pilgrimage to Canindé to pay their part of the contract when St. Francis helped them with the suffering they were experiencing. I spoke with a woman who had brought an ex-voto that was a shoe box that she had fashioned into a house. On the shoe box/house she had written her own house number and the words "Vila da Paz" (House of Peace). I asked her what this signified. She told me that her husband was out of work and drank too much *cachaça*, a locally produced rum made from sugar cane. When he got drunk he would beat her. She had appealed to St. Francis to help her. Soon afterward her husband had quit drinking, quit beating her, and had found a job. She said that, *"graças a Deus e São Francisco,"* now she lived in a house of peace.

Many times I have heard the *freis*, the Franciscan lay brothers who facilitate the shrine, speak about how the pilgrims go to the House of Miracles to repay their promises but do not necessarily attend Mass. In some cases, it seems the pilgrims view priests in a service role to the church but as doing nothing for them. One of the most significant aspects of the ex-voto tradition is that the spiritual contract is between the pilgrim and the saint, circumventing clerical intercession (see also Dubisch 1995). In the case of pilgrims in Canindé, St. Francis rather than a priest acts as their emissary to God, making this tradition unpopular with many clergy. The ex-voto ritual is not recognized by Roman Catholic liturgy as an official sacred rite of the church, yet my observations suggest it is the most practiced ritual in Brazilian folk Catholicism. Many times priests are not present in remote rural areas to perform baptisms, marriage ceremonies, or give last rites. Instead, the families do without these rituals or must perform these rites themselves. Because many people have never been indoctrinated into the officiated traditions of the formal church, these have no place in their lives. There are usually two priests in the confession booths in the House of Miracles, yet they are seldom busy. People come to Canindé to repay or renew a contract with St. Francis. Church dogma in many instances just does not enter into their equation. Instead, what is important to them is fulfilling their *promessa*.

Pilgrims rely on St. Francis to ameliorate difficulties in their lives, and he gives them what they need. He heals their physical and mental aches and pains, and as a result it is to him that people turn for help. In fact, Brazilian anthropologist and professor at the Department of Community Health at the Universidade Federal do Ceará, Adalberto Barreto, who has worked in Canindé for many years, says that because the people of the Northeast are so disenfranchised, they are more than just followers of the saint; they can be thought of as "residents of the nation of St. Francis," not Brazil. He says that since they are so poor, they pay no taxes, have no driver's licenses, or any legal identification as Brazilians. In addition, they receive no institutional benefits from the government. Instead, they pay all their tribute to St. Francis and turn to him for the types of institutional aid they should receive from the government. It is to St. Francis that they give their surplus money and it is to him they go for food, shelter, and medical problems (Barreto personal correspondence).

There is a Latin American folk saying, "A saint who is not seen is not worshipped" (Toor 1947: 541). This saying certainly applies to St. Francis. To the pilgrims, St. Francis is a living entity. They "see" St. Francis walking in the Basilica and they sit outside the monastery hoping to catch a glimpse of him. Across the front of the monastery is painted, "Casa de São Francisco." Many a time, I left the gates of the monastery and was asked by those waiting, *"São Francisco esta en casa?"* (Is St. Francis home?). At first, I assumed that I had not understood the question. However, I soon came to expect such questions and usually replied that *"Não, São Francisco não esta en casa hoje"* (No, St. Francis is not home today). As my Portuguese improved, I would occasionally hear pilgrims talking together, asking if one had seen St. Francis. The other might reply, "Oh, no, I'm not good enough to see him, but I know someone who has." Most people had a type of dualistic view of St. Francis walking here among them and residing in heaven as well. They were very territorial about his being located in Canindé while on earth. Even though there were pictures of the shrine in Assisi, Italy, in the House of Miracles, and the freis instructed about St. Francis of Assisi being the "original" St. Francis, the people would have none of that. São Francisco das Chagas do Canindé was THE only St. Francis that they were interested in. The word *chagas* means wounds. This name refers to St. Francis after his receiving the stigmata. At the shrine, pilgrims see images depicting these stigmata and strongly identify with his suffering from wounds to the hands and feet.

Many ex-votos offered to St. Francis represent injuries to the hands and feet. Almost all of the people living in this part of the Northeast wear only rubber thongs on their feet. Without gloves and in this type of footwear, they must work the fields with sharp machetes and hoes, work construction lifting heavy bricks and avoiding sharp nails, or work around animals avoiding heavy hoofs and piles of excrement. In this region, full of pricking cactus thorns and biting insects, even the natural environment is hazardous. These conditions combined with polluted water and poor sanitation create infections that are hard to heal. Children walk around with running sores left on the arms and legs by mosquito bites. Walking is, for most sertanejos, the only mode of transportation. Traveling the hard packed dirt roads dries the skin on the feet to such an extent that they simply split open, creating another prime location for infection. Ex-votos with missing fingers and toes, misshapen

hands, feet, and ankles; gaping wounds; infected insect bites; and dermatological problems reflect the poverty and hazardous working conditions in
which most people of the Northeast toil.

The idea that body knowledge and manifestation of illness can be socially
constructed has been cross-culturally explored by many researchers (Jackson
1989; Lock 1993; Martin 1987; Ngokwey 1995; Rebhun 1993; Scheper-
Hughes 1992). In *Death without Weeping*, Scheper-Hughes discusses how
pressures from the social and political system faced by the typical Nordes-
tino (Northeasterner) influence and are revealed in their physical afflictions.
Basing her discussion on Marcel Mauss's idea of "habitus," a term later made
popular by Pierre Bourdieu, as the way people "inhabit" their bodies, Scheper-
Hughes looks at the somatization of the typical Northeasterner. This investi-
gation brings into consideration the activities of "working, eating, grooming,
resting and sleeping, having sex, getting sick and getting well." She maintains
that these are all "forms of body praxis and expressive of dynamic social, cultural, and political relations" (Scheper-Hughes 1992: 185). In other words,
everything we do, even mundane activities, has been consciously or unconsciously influenced by culture and the way these activities are manifested in
the body reveals socially encoded statements about that culture.

Taking this line of thinking a step farther, Scheper-Hughes turns to French
phenomenologist Luc Boltanski, who proposed that because the poor and
working classes spend their days doing physical labor, they communicate primarily with and through the body. On the other hand, the upper classes are more
disassociated from their bodies because their work is more of the mind. As a
result, they express personal and social "dis-ease" psychologically rather than in
the physically manifested way of the poor (Scheper-Hughes 1992: 185).

Looking over questionnaires given to pilgrims and also interviews with
pilgrims, I notice time and time again where people describe afflictions that
have manifested in the body, with symptoms that could be interpreted as
socially mandated. Tremors, loss of voice, spontaneous blindness, pain in arms,
paralysis, a hand curled into a fist, and the catch-all *nervos* (nerves) can all
reflect the internal manifestation of rage and frustration that must be endured
by a subordinated people. This rage and frustration springs from what Brazilian philosopher Paulo Freire has defined as the "culture of silence" that exists
between the "subordinate and superordinate sectors of the social system."
He says that in the culture of silence "[t]o exist is only to live. The body carries out orders from above. Thinking is difficult, speaking the word is forbid-

den" (Forman 1975: 207). In this sort of situation, where thinking will only bring on more frustration, where speaking out is forbidden, where does rage, or for that matter any emotion, have to go but to turn inward? You want to talk back but you cannot, so the voice disappears. You cannot look at instances of injustice anymore, so your vision spontaneously disappears. When you long to raise your arms against your employer but cannot, paralysis sets in. The list goes on and on.

Out of three hundred questionnaires, there were only fifty-five people who had cuts or broken bones. While the situation in which these people were injured might be indirectly related to a social problem, these were physical problems with inarguable physical causation. In addition to these fifty-five, two men had been shot in alcohol-related fights, and one woman said that she was crazy and, when pressed further, said that she drank too much. These alcohol-related problems could also be indirectly tied to social "disease." The two hundred and forty-two other people who responded to the questionnaires all had problems that might be directly construed as socially related. Thirty-two people said they had the vague affliction of tumors, fifty people said they had rashes, thirty-nine people complained of headaches, twenty-four people had recovered from temporary paralysis, twenty-five people had problems with their heart or other internal organs, ten people complained of nervos, and the sixty-two remaining suffered from female reproductive problems and other disabilities.

Other demographics gleaned from the questionnaires were that the largest percentage of pilgrims was female. Two hundred and twelve women and eighty-eight men were interviewed. While this finding might reflect a greater willingness of women to answer questions, the margin of difference reflects that more women enter into contracts with St. Francis than do men. I can verify this percentage from my own experience. I spent nearly every day for six months at the shrine, and on a daily basis saw more women there than men. Within a subordinate population, no one has a voice against the dominant population. But within the subordinate population everyone is still not equal. Brazil is a patriarchy. Men hold title to property, and tenancy and sharecropping are negotiated through the males of the family. I spoke with at least two women whose husbands had died and who had been told that they must move off the owners' lands. Both women had nowhere else to go and faced homelessness. In both cases they appealed to St. Francis, and they were able to find other accommodations.

Brazilian men are dominant in their households, especially in the rural backlands. Women who repeatedly voice their opinions are often beaten or even abandoned. Men living in or near a community get to release frustration in bars and by playing and watching *futebol* (soccer). Women have no such outlet. Women who work outside the home are almost always in domestic service in someone else's home. This occupational category had the largest representation for women on the questionnaire. The typical woman gets up very early to take care of the needs of those in her household and then spends the day taking care of the needs of another woman's household. When she goes home, there is still her own work to complete. Most domestics have only one afternoon off a week. Because of this, the childhood of females ends early. Older sisters often are charged with the care of younger siblings. It is not unusual to see a girl the age of seven or eight carrying a younger sister or brother on her hip walking through Canindé. When families live in rural areas, labor is hard for everyone and the stresses are even more intense. However, urban or rural, women are still subordinate to their husbands. With so little autonomy, it stands to reason that they are likely to have more physically manifested symptoms than men. It also makes sense that they would turn to St. Francis to hear their plea. Here in the spiritual realm they can get the relief of voicing their problems without fearing any sort of repercussion.

With respect to the category of age, one third of the pilgrims who responded to the questionnaires were over fifty. This number is not surprising. In most cultures older generations adhere most closely to religious practices. When this age category is compared to the occupational category, some interesting facts can be learned. Even though unemployment rates are very high in this region of Brazil, only twenty-six of these people stated that they were retired. While sixty-two people did say they were unemployed, many of them were women who did not work outside the home. Many of the women who were fifty and over were employed as domestics. Fifty of the eighty-eight men who responded were working in agriculture. Ten of the twenty-nine people under the age of twenty stated that they were students. The remaining seventy-five people came from other occupations. The largest portion of these were carpenters, although there were a few people with white collar occupations, such as teachers, a nurse, several waiters, two municipal officials, and a policeman.

Half of the people had come to Canindé to repay St. Francis more than four times. When asked why they appealed to St. Francis for help, some of the responses were: "He is my protector," "He can work miracles," "I believe in his miracles," "Because I love him," "To obtain a cure," and "God gave him power to make miracles."

Even though the followers of St. Francis pray directly to him, they do not forget the hierarchical power of God. It is just that God is so powerful, and according to their worldview, he does not have time to listen to those as small and insignificant as they are. St. Francis, however, does listen and does love them, and acts as their emissary. They believe that with God's will, he can perform the miracles they ask. Many times people will say *"Graças a Deus e São Francisco"* when depositing their ex-voto. Reference to the Holy Trinity used in the formal Church liturgy is missing from all the conversations I had with pilgrims. In fact there is a joke in the sertão that the Holy Trinity is not the Father, the Son, and the Holy Spirit, but instead is São Francisco, Deus, e Padre Cicero (Padre Cicero is a very popular folk saint who has a shrine devoted to him in Joazeiro del Norte, also in the state of Ceará).

The Politics of Marginalization

The tradition of ex-votos, while tangential to the cult of saints, is outside orthodox praxis of the Roman Catholic Church. To reinforce this marginalization, many shrine sites have a designated area for the deposition of ex-votos outside the "sacred" areas of the sanctuary and the main altars. In many places it is a niche off to the side of the sanctuary, as in San Xavier del Bac in Tucson, Arizona. Sometimes it is a small room off the sanctuary, as in the Santuario de Chimayo in Chimayo, New Mexico. In Canindé, votives are placed in the House of Miracles, a building within the Basilica compound, but physically separate. The paying of the promise appears to be the paramount activity for the pilgrims who come to Canindé. This is reflected in the huge numbers that visit the House of Miracles as compared to the smaller numbers who attend Mass or go to confession. Yet, the church places more sacred importance on the Basilica.

In an article on "empowering place," Margaret Rodman (1992) discusses the importance of "multilocality." She states that much research has been written about the importance of multivocality and suggests that the concept of place should also be examined. She goes on to say that "place, like voice and time, is a politicized social and cultural construct" and by giving it attention it can "encourage the understanding of the complex social construction of spatial meaning" (640).

The physical separation of the practice of the ex-voto tradition from the "sacred" area of the church is just one example of ways in which the hegemonic views of the Catholic Church in Canindé are not the same as those of the subordinate population it serves. Though there are many church officials who are trying to bridge the gap, their work is often thwarted by the hierarchical authorities, who have no direct contact with the people. For this reason, and probably several others, the followers of St. Francis of Wounds have additional allegiances outside the Catholic mainstream to which they turn for spiritual and physical healing. This overlapping of treatment is to ensure a reasonable chance of survival in their precarious existence. The pilgrims with whom I spoke revealed that they had received treatment from western medical doctors, *rezadeiras/rezadores* (prayer healers), *curandeiras/curandores* (healers who use herbs and magical practices), and priests and priestesses of Afro-Brazilian religions. However, in all instances, credit for healing was ultimately given to St. Francis.

The generic ideologies of syncretized Afro-Brazilian-based religions and the folk form of Catholicism practiced in northeast Brazil are not so divergent as one might assume. Both are focused on life on earth rather than an afterlife. Both employ a pantheon of intermediaries in the form of saints or spirits to act on humanity's behalf to a hierarchical power. Both of these pantheons focus on the belief of miraculous powers that can cure illness and answer petitions. And both of these religious movements are located or had their beginnings in rural areas, and cater to a subordinate population. Additionally, as is found in many cultures of the African Diaspora, the same iconography is used to represent both Roman Catholic saints and Afro-Brazilian spirits (Brown and Bick 1987). Perhaps these compatibilities are the reason that these Brazilians often blend practices of what an outsider might view as more than one religion at a time into their ideal form of worship.

Pilgrimage to the Sanctuary of St. Francis of Wounds

In Canindé when pilgrims come to the shrine, they say they have come to pay the promise. There are several methods pilgrims use to pay this promise. One writer categorizes them as animate, inanimate, exuvial, and replicative (Finucane 1977). The replicative milagres are by far the most common and are the main focus of this research. These typically depict affliction of the human body but occasionally illustrate other subjects such as animals, houses, or occupational equipment. Each milagre is a one-of-a-kind artifact created by the pilgrim or commissioned from a neighbor or relative. The range of artistic ability is vast, but each milagre is a tangible symbol of physical or psychological pain.

Animate votive offerings most often are displayed through physical actions of the pilgrim, such as walking a great distance to reach the shrine; the wearing of a *batina*, the pilgrimage costume that resembles the brown monk's habit worn by St. Francis and the Franciscan order that he founded; or creating a situation that causes mortification of the flesh, for example, traversing the concrete steps to the shrine on one's knees.

Inanimate offerings range from lighting candles to monetary tithes, while exuvial offerings are basically anything that comes from the human body, be it hair or nail clippings, dried umbilical cords, kidney stones, and the like.

Periodically, a pilgrim will pay his promessa by walking to Canindé carrying a cross. These pilgrims are attributed celebrity status. One such pilgrim arrived in Canindé on June 8, 1996, after much anticipation by the townspeople. He had begun his pilgrimage about fifteen months earlier in the state of Sergipe and had received quite a lot of press coverage during the length of his journey. He was called "Homen do Crux" (Man of the Cross) by the pilgrim population and had achieved almost legendary folk hero status as stories about him spread through the region. His cross was placed in the House of Miracles after his arrival and was treated as a holy relic. When the cross arrived in Canindé it was covered with photographs and small ex-votos that people along his route had attached to it. After it was brought into the House of Miracles, people would lay prostrate before it, touch it, and tie *fitas* and locks of hair to it as if through contagious magic, they would be imbued with his grace. Though his cross had been made a bit more mobile by the addition of wheels, it was so heavy that I could not even lift it to my shoulder. He had carried the cross for so long that there was a worn, indented place in the wood where his shoulder had been. This is a translation of his story as told to one of the freis:

> I was born nearly blind, deaf, mute, and paralyzed. After ten years I received a gift from the family of a child that died in a bus accident. The family gave me her eyes. My mother made a promessa with St. Lúcia, and from that day, I could see better. At eleven years of age, on September 4, 1977, at the Festival for Padroeira de Aquidabám, in

Sergipe, a wagon loaded with dried meat had bad brakes and killed seventeen people. It crashed into our house causing the roof to fall down. Part of the roof fell on me and crushed my leg. I was in the hospital for nine months, and my mother was afraid I would die. My mother had hope in St. Francis of Wounds and over the course of two years and six days made one hundred and nineteen promessas with him to make me well. The payment of the promise would not be valid unless I walked to Canindé on foot. I hope I have another chance to walk here again.

The cross of the Homen do Crux eventually was taken to the shrine museum where it joined five crosses that had been collected from previous pilgrims who had walked from the northeastern states of Alagoas, Paraíba, Pernambuco, and Piauí. Just like the new one, each of these crosses is completely covered with names, cuttings of hair, small wooden anatomical ex-votos, and photographs, among other items, which are applied to the cross by people all along the route traveled by the pilgrim to Canindé. As the pilgrim travels through the countryside, people turn out to see him, much as people do in the United States with the passing of the Olympic Torch. As the pilgrim travels, his cross becomes emblematic of the regional faith in the miraculous power of St. Francis. As the cross passes through the countryside and is laden with more and more offerings, it is transformed from the symbol of one man's devotion into one representing the devotion of the whole Northeast. As this cross is carried across the country, people become directly linked with other pilgrims, creating a spiritual chain that reaches all the way to the shrine at Canindé. Since these types of pilgrimages often occur after a terrific drought, a time of devastation shared by everyone, they serve as a revitalization and healing agent for the entire region. These pilgrimages enable even those who cannot make the pilgrimage themselves to pay their promessas by proxy. The crosses in the museum can literally be read as lasting "metasocial commentaries," because they chronicle the miracles shared by the "forgotten" people of the Northeast through time and space (Geertz 1973: 448).

In cultures where there are high rates of illiteracy, such as is found in the Northeast of Brazil, storytelling and the oral narrative are cohesive agents that connect people through space and time. A bulk of oral information dealing with "miracle stories" is shared by pilgrims coming to Canindé from all over this vast region (Slater 1986). This shared knowledge crosses generational boundaries and acts as information of membership into the community of

St. Francis. While these stories are based upon factual events, over time they are transformed into stories of mythic proportions that glorify the healing power of St. Francis and reinforce the benefit of being counted as one of his followers. They are, to paraphrase Geertz's words, stories they tell themselves about themselves. Many of these stories have been repeated for generations. This is a revealing testament to the efficacy of the miracles of St. Francis and the vitality of this tradition.

One such narrative, a famous miracle story that has been transformed into legend, was repeated to me by several pilgrims. I was given a factual account of this story by Dr. Barreto, who was in the House of Miracles when the event occurred and captured it on film. The popular miracle story, as it was told to me, goes as follows:

> Many, many years ago there was a very devout man. He was very, very sick and the doctors could not diagnose what was the matter with him. He appealed to St. Francis to help him and promised to make a pilgrimage when he was well. He did get a bit better, but he was too weak, and died before St. Francis could heal him. Before he died, he asked that he be taken to Canindé in his casket to pay his promise to St. Francis. He was a very religious and good man and wanted to pay his promise even after his death. When his family brought him to the shrine at Canindé, and set his casket before the statue of St. Francis, they heard knocking coming from within the casket. They removed the casket lid, and the dead man sat up—alive. St. Francis had been so moved by the faith of the man that he decided to bring him back from the dead. The man and his family walked away from the shrine, leaving his casket as an ex-voto.

Several times, I heard pilgrims ask where they could view this casket. However, it was destroyed along with other ex-votos brought to the shrine that year by the annual burning occurring at the end of each year's pilgrimage season.

Dr. Barreto, who in addition to being an anthropologist is a practicing psychiatrist, supplied the background of the story. While it is true that the man came to Canindé in his casket, he was not dead. However, no one knew this but Dr. Barreto, a frei, the man, and his family. The actual story unfolded in this way: Dr. Barreto received a telephone call from a frei who was disturbed by a letter he had received from this man. In the letter, the man told the priest that he had been told by St. Francis himself that in order to be healed of the emotional problems that he was having, he must make a pilgrimage to Canindé in a sealed coffin. And, once he arrived in Canindé the coffin could only be opened by a priest. The priest, wanting to help the man, but unsure how to deal with such a bizarre request, turned to Dr. Barreto for his professional opinion. Dr. Barreto spoke with this man and discovered that his problems stemmed from a childhood incident. As a child the man had gone to church with his mother. She had told him to go to confession, but he had not. When it came time to receive Communion from the priest, the boy was afraid to tell his mother that he had not gone to confession. He knew from religious teaching that it was a sin to take Communion if one had not been to confession, so when the host was laid upon his tongue, he spit it out. Horrified by this act, and learning of his lie about going to Communion, the boy's mother told him he was doubly damned. Apparently, the man was truly traumatized by this, because as he grew older, he began to have psychological problems relating to this incident and even had tried suicide. In desperation, he appealed to St. Francis for forgiveness, who then told him that he must go to Canindé in a casket and have it opened by a priest. Then, St. Francis said, he would have forgiveness. Dr. Barreto thought that this request was very profound, as it was the perfect metaphor for the man's emotional problems. His spiritual death had occurred when he spit out the host. As a result, his resurrection could only be accomplished by forgiveness by the church, the authority that damned him. Dr. Barreto encouraged the frei to cooperate and suggested that tiny airholes be bored into the lid of the casket to ensure that suffocation would not occur. The man was brought to the House of Miracles in his casket, which was then opened by the priest. To all effects, it appeared to onlookers that a dead man was brought to life, and it created quite a stir. To this day, no one knows that this was a staged "miracle," and the resurrection story is repeated to each new generation of pilgrims. It is truly a wonderful story of the redemptive qualities of faith, and I doubt at this point that even if people were told the facts, they would believe them.

A more recent addition to the miracle stories, "A Criança con Cruzeiro" (the Child with the Coin) relates an event that happened during the 1996 Romaria in honor of St. Francis. During the ten-day festival, the shrine is literally packed with people, and the town is transformed into a human camp. City streets are closed off, and hammocks are tied to anything vertical, be that a tree, a lamppost, or a gate. At this time, the House of Miracles is continually a swarming mass of bodies, pushing and shoving to get to the bin in order to view the milagres. It was into this mass of people that a man appeared one afternoon with a crudely made ex-voto representing his daughter. The milagre immediately attracted attention because it was very grotesque. It was about two feet tall and crudely hewn from wood. What made it so grotesque was the fact that it was dressed in a baby's diaper, it had a Brazilian coin in its mouth, and its head was covered with human hair. Fellow pilgrims surrounded the man after he had deposited the offering and demanded to hear of the miracle it represented. The man, a local resident, was more than willing to repeat the story over and over to all who wanted to hear it. The story spread throughout the pilgrim community and for the next several days people came to the House of Miracles just to see this milagre and to recount the story behind it. It was interesting to watch this dynamic process in action as it became obvious that with this new milagre, a new legend had been added to the oral literature surrounding the miracles of St. Francis. This is what he said about his miracle:

> Earlier that day I had been at home, taking a break from the festivities, when I saw out of the corner of my eye, Tonia, my little girl, a toddler, put something into her mouth. Before I could grab her and see what was in her mouth, she swallowed it and began to choke. I turned her upside down and smacked her on the back, but whatever it was lodged in her throat. I could see that she could not breathe and that she was beginning to turn blue. I did everything I could to dislodge the object; finally my little girl stopped moving and I feared that she had died. I screamed, *"Não, não, São Francisco, ajuda me"* (No, no, St. Francis, help me). At that exact moment, my little girl coughed and the object, a coin, was magically expelled from her throat. Within a few minutes she was back to crawling around and playing as if nothing had happened.

The father, overcome with gratitude to St. Francis for saving the life of his daughter, decided to immediately make an ex-voto for payment. He found the wood and measured the height of his daughter. He then took the clothes that she was wearing and dressed the milagre in them. When he was carving the facial features, he opened the mouth enough to wedge the same coin she had swallowed into the opening. Finally, he cut the curls of hair from the head of his child and glued them onto the milagre, making it as representative as possible. The father, still visibly shaken by the recounting of the events, and so full of gratitude toward St. Francis for coming to the rescue, made a compelling storyteller. This, in combination with the uniqueness of the votive offering, resulted in a sort of instant celebrity status for the ex-voto. For the rest of the festival, crowds of people pushed to examine and discuss the "Criança con Cruzeiro." Because of its notoriety, this ex-voto was removed from the bin to be placed in the museum. I am sure that in years to come, the Criança will be a popular attraction for pilgrims coming to the shrine in Canindé.

Healing and the Ideology of St. Francis

The ideology of the pilgrimage in the "nation of St. Francis" is replete with its own heroes and legends, which are separate from institutional Catholic liturgy. Pilgrims' insistence on calling the saint "St. Francis of Wounds," rather than by his ecclesiastical name of St. Francis of Assisi, further reinforces their autonomy from clerical authority. In the same vein, while the followers of St. Francis do revere the holy icons of the Church, they also create icons of their own, such as the crosses that are carried by Homens do Crux. In many ways, these crosses and certain notable ex-votos, such as the "Criança," are more important icons to the people because they are of their own making. These are objects that are approachable and available to them, unlike the ornate emblems of the church, which are kept behind protective barriers and brought out to the people once a year. This cadre of symbols, because it is created by the practitioners, can be added to spontaneously. In this way they serve as objects of revitalization that can stimulate the vitality of their faith. All of these factors, when combined with the ex-voto tradition, serve to create a religion of the people that effectively bypasses clerical intervention and satisfies their needs.

Besides the social and psychological healing that is facilitated through the actual divine healing received, there are many other therapeutic benefits that can be obtained through this pilgrimage and the ex-voto ritual. During the Romaria there are community Masses held nightly in an outdoor amphitheater. These Masses are far more exuberant than traditional Masses that I have attended elsewhere, and were in fact more akin to a Pentecostal revival in the southern Appalachian region of the United States than to a Catholic Mass. Many times the service sounded almost like a political rally, as the officiating priest would stir the congregation's emotion by encouraging them to scream over and over, *"Viva São Francisco"* until there was a tangible electric current running through the crowd. This ecstatic display of emotional voice allowed the people to release tension and stress through physical catharsis. This is of much therapeutic value to a people whose normal behavior is inhibited to meet a standard set by the dominant class.

There are also therapeutic benefits to be found in the creation of an ex-voto to St. Francis. The autonomous contract negotiated between a pilgrim and St. Francis is in itself beneficial for the reassurance it gives that s/he has a benefactor upon whom to call in times of need. The payment of the promise with the ex-voto reinforces a sense of self-worth in being able to fulfill a contract, if only a spiritual one. Additionally, the crafting of the actual artifact itself may have the most therapeutic potential. In the crafting of an image of one's affliction, the pouring of emotion into that object, time is allowed for pondering the problem, celebrating its resolution, and the cathartic releasing of it into a tangible symbol that literally then can be cast away. The people I spoke with who made their own ex-voto reinforced this sentiment.

Many of the diseases and afflictions from which the pilgrims in Canindé suffer are the result of the cycle of poverty and frustration in which they live. Conditions of malnutrition and chronic gastrointestinal problems can be traced directly to lack of sufficient nutrients, potable water, and sanitation facilities. These situations could be corrected by the governmental services to which all Brazilian citizens have a right. However, the rights of these people have been neglected. In addition to those physical symptoms manifested by cultural neglect, many people also suffer from culturally based conditions such as *susto* (shock sickness) and nervos, which are limited for the most part to members of the subordinate class. These conditions are a result of the prolonged periods of fear, frustration, and anxiety in which most of the subaltern of the Northeast live, and are somatized by lack of energy, chronic headaches and bodily pains, and fragile nervous states to which medical personnel can find no basis. This in turn reinforces the anxiety of the sufferer, who feels further negated by the dominant culture through the doctor's inability to see and recognize her/his pain. In my opinion, it is for this reason that people who are members of the culture of poverty in the Northeast "constructed" St. Francis of Wounds to heal their diseases. It is their belief that St. Francis can bring forth an easing of their condition because he listens to their problems and can see their pain. By finally being seen, the pilgrim's suffering is validated, and through a milagre their affliction disappears. The ex-votos that pilgrims create to fulfill their contract with St. Francis are encoded with symbols depicting conditions of disease caused by the culturally created environment of neglect in which they exist. These symbols can be read by like individuals, and the messages they send provide visual proof of St. Francis' devotion and, as such, reinforce group solidarity and reciprocity. In this manner, the ex-votos serve the therapeutic function of allowing these unfortunate people a way to vent their anger and "voice" their frustration without fear of recrimination by the dominant class.

Exile, Illness, and Gender in Israeli Pilgrimage Narratives

Susan Sered

Contemporary Israeli-Jewish understandings of illness and healing echo biblical themes that are kept alive through the sequential reading of the Five Books of Moses (the Torah) in synagogues over the annual liturgical cycle, through the biblical stories and midrashim (exegetical embellishments of biblical stories) that are taught to children in nursery and primary schools throughout the country, and through awareness of the proximity of geographical landmarks related to biblical characters. For many Jewish Israelis, Torah heroes and heroines are understood to be biologically and culturally linked to all Jews, and are referred to as "Our Fathers" and "Our Mothers."

In Israel today, pilgrims visit the tombs of dozens of biblical figures and other saints associated with a variety of periods in Jewish history, a range of ethnic groups, diverse parts of the country, and numerous mythic charters (see Ben-Ari and Bilu 1987; Weingrod 1990). One of the few traits shared by most Israeli saints is their gender. Like mortal Israeli religious leaders, almost all saints are men. Men's near-monopoly on sainthood highlights the curious fact that the only three women saints who are foci of broad-based Jewish cults in Israel today are all named Rachel. Despite differences in period of mythic origin, the three Rachel cults share important ritual and mythic features. Indeed, each of the two later Rachels is understood, in some way, to be a reincarnation *(gilgul)* of the biblical Matriarch Rachel. The grave of each of the Rachels is an object of pilgrimage primarily (though not solely) for women, and each of the three Rachels is popularly believed to be especially gifted at understanding the suffering of her pilgrims.

This article grows out of my ongoing interest in the cult of the biblical Matriarch Rachel, who in biblical and midrashic texts is deeply associated with illness (particularly infertility and death in childbirth) and exile. I shall show that the root paradigm represented by the biblical Rachel has expanded in recent years to encompass cults of two other Rachels—Rachel the Poetess and Rachel the Wife of Rabbi Akiva. All three of these cults tie together themes of illness and exile with another closely associated theme—the connection between female gender and illness. These themes are mediated through the notion of "understanding": each of these women saints is believed to excel at "understanding" the primarily women pilgrims who visit their tombs. After exploring the development of these three converging cults (or, perhaps more accurately, these three variations on one root cult), I offer some reflections on the experience of illness for Israeli women, and why it may be that women more than men are associated with, and in need of, "understanding," and why "being understood" is construed as a healing experience by many Israeli women.

Illness, exile, healing, and female gender constitute a cultural constellation that comes to ritual fruition in the cults of the three Rachels. It is important to understand that this constellation draws upon the mythic material of Jewish foundational texts, not all of which are ritually enacted yet which serve as a sort of cultural reservoir into which the cults tap. To my mind, the most concise traditional assertion of the illness-gender-exile mythic constellation concerns another biblical heroine: Miriam, the sister of Moses.

In a well-known story related in Numbers 12:1–15, Miriam and Aharon (Moses's brother) speak out against Moses, yet God punishes only Miriam with leprosy. Aharon then begs Moses to help and Moses cries to the Lord with words that have become the template for Jewish healing prayers: "Heal her now, O God, I pray thee."

The gendered themes in this family drama have been interpreted throughout Jewish exegetical writings as indicative of universal gender characteristics. Thus Miriam's sin of gossiping about her brother and his wife has been seen as paradigmatic of the penchant of ALL women to gossip. Especially relevant here, the gender of the one who is sick and the one who has the power to heal are also prototypical. The first clearly sick person in the Torah is a woman (although both Miriam and Aharon complain about Moses's wife, only Miriam is punished through illness); the holy person who prays to God on her behalf is male; and the liturgical formulaic healing prayer adopted by the Jewish people casts the patient in feminine grammar and God in masculine grammar: "Heal her!" *(rf'a na la)*.

The conceptualizations of illness and healing that emerge in this story continue to resonate strongly for many Israeli Jews. The notion that illness is a punishment for inappropriate behavior seems to be particularly compelling. In the biblical anecdote, the implication of illness for Miriam was isolation—exile from the community—and the meaning of healing was the return to community life. Exile and the return from exile are, of course, ongoing themes in Jewish cultural history and of particular importance to the generations involved in building the Jewish State. The Jewish prototype of intercessory prayer is laid out in this passage as well: Aharon asks Moses to pray to God on Miriam's behalf, a pattern well known to Middle Eastern and Hassidic Jews, who ask a variety of rabbis and holy men—alive or dead—for their blessings. Even Moses's cry, "Heal her now, O God, I pray thee" remains the conventional liturgical formulaic healing prayer.

Saints and Their Cults

At this juncture, I wish to clarify my use of the term *cult*. What I call cults are situations of mutual engagement of mythic and ritual activity; a cult (whether of a saint, hero, god, spirit, founder, or leader) occurs at the point of convergence of myth and ritual. As part of the process of cult crystallization, devotees and patrons may consciously or unconsciously adopt a mythic charter that imparts rituals with an aura of tradition, or conversely, adapt ritual acts to the myth of a particular person, hero, place, or object. I am not claiming that myths precede ritual activity or that rituals precede myth. Rather, what interests me are the specific situations in which both myth and ritual are actively and concurrently called upon, and the processes by which certain myths and rituals drawn from a larger cultural repertoire coalesce into an active cult.

In this article, I look at cults of saints. I use the English word *saint* as translations of two overlapping and somewhat interchangeable Hebrew words: *tsaddik* (righteous or pious person) and *kadosh* (holy person).[1] Jewish culture does not include a formal process for declaring an individual to be a saint, nor are there explicit criteria for what constitutes sainthood. Rather, these terms are popularly used to describe individuals distinguished for their piety or good deeds. The contemporary Israeli Jewish understanding seems to be that pious people are somehow closer to God and that receiving their blessing or coming into contact with something that they have touched may, in a not clearly articulated way, elicit divine concessions.

The Three Rachels

In terms of this conceptual framework, the Matriarch Rachel is the only biblical woman around whom an Israeli-Jewish cult has formed. The cult of the Matriarch Rachel took form during the nineteenth century when the rather ordinary ritual activity surrounding her tomb, documented for over a millennium, began to incorporate symbols and images associated with her unique biblical and midrashic myth—when her particular myth began to be translated into ritual activity. Today, the Matriarch Rachel's cult is comprised of distinctive themes (fertility, Zionism, and the Holocaust), a place (her tomb in Bethlehem), an object (red thread), occasions (the day before the Festival of the New Moon and the anniversary of her death), an honorific title (Rachel Imenu—"Our Mother Rachel"), and miracle stories, all of which reveal elements of her unique mythic configuration.

The cult of Rachel the Poetess, with a far more modern mythic charter, began to emerge within the first week after her death in 1931. Her cult is associated with particular themes (death, youth, suffering, the Land of Israel, pioneering, romantic love, and nature), a place (her tomb on the shore of Lake Kinneret), texts (her poems and other writings), occasion (the anniversary of her death), ritual (reciting her poems next to her grave), a title (Rachel is often called the "National Poetess" although there is no official status of national poetess of Israel; her title is a cultic one), and apocryphal stories of her life and death.

The cult of Rachel the Wife of Rabbi Akiva is still in the early stages of development (although the figure of this Rachel has been known in Jewish texts for nearly two thousand years); therefore, the testimony is less profuse. Still, her cult is associated with a particular theme (*shalom bayit*—marital harmony), a title (Rachel the Zaddeket—the Righteous One), a site (her grave near Tiberius), an occasion (the anniversary of the day on which the building that houses her tomb was opened), and apocryphal stories of her life and of miracles that occurred in her merit.

The convergence of cults of women saints around figures named Rachel is far from coincidental. All three cults are offshoots of a root icon deeply embedded within Jewish cultural imagination, and that comes to the surface in different ways at different times. In its oldest and most comprehensive design, that root icon takes form as the cult of Our Mother Rachel. Later cultic versions pick up on and expand certain elements of the root Rachel icon and gloss over other elements. Still, these variations, whether ostensibly identified with Jewish folk religion or with Zionist civil religion, leave intact a cultic constellation comprised of themes of suffering, self-sacrifice, self-abnegation, exile, domesticity, illness, and the unique ability to understand the needs of their primarily female pilgrims.

Rachel the Biblical Matriarch

The Matriarch Rachel's biography, which is related primarily in Genesis 29ff, is well known in the Jewish world: Jacob's parents had sent him to Haran so that he could find a wife from among the women of his mother's family. Falling in love with Laban's beautiful daughter Rachel, Jacob served Laban for seven years in exchange for the right to marry Rachel. At the wedding, Laban tricked Jacob, giving him Leah, his elder daughter, instead of the beloved Rachel. When Jacob learned that he had married the wrong sister, Laban consented to Jacob's marrying Rachel in addition to Leah, in exchange for another seven years' labor.

The Genesis story continues with a rather detailed account of Leah's fertility and Rachel's fruitless efforts to conceive. Rachel's sorrow leads her to experiment with herbal cures and to exclaim to Jacob that without children she is as one who is dead. (Significantly, in light of the Miriam and Moses anecdote, Jacob interprets her cry as a request to him that he—a mortal man—answer her prayer for children). After years of barrenness, Rachel bore Joseph, conceived once again and then died while giving birth to Benjamin. The story ends with dramatic understatement: "And Rachel died and was buried on the way to Ephrat, which is Bethlehem. And Jacob set a pillar upon her grave; that is the pillar of Rachel's grave to this day" (Genesis 35:20).

Jeremiah uses the imagery of Rachel's death from Genesis 35 as a metaphor for God's promise to return the people of Israel from exile in Babylonia to the land of Zion: "Thus says the Lord: A voice is heard in Ramah, lamentation and bitter weeping. Rachel is weeping for her children. She refused to be comforted for her children, because they are not [here]. Thus says the Lord: Keep your voice from weeping and your eyes from tears, for your acts shall be rewarded, says the Lord; and they shall come back again from the land of the enemy. And there is hope for your future, says the Lord, and your children shall come back again to their own border" (Jeremiah 31:14).

The sparse biblical Rachel stories are fleshed out in the midrashic literature. Perhaps the best-known midrashic tradition is recounted twice in the Babylonian Talmud (Megilla 13b and Baba Bathra 123a). Before the wedding, Rachel warned Jacob that her father would not allow the younger sister to marry first, and to expect that Laban would try to pull a switch at the ceremony. Jacob and Rachel thus exchanged signs with which she could identify herself to him. Rachel however realized that it would embarrass Leah to be exposed as an imposter, gave the signs to Leah, and allowed Jacob to marry the wrong sister. This story is developed further in later sources where Rachel is portrayed as uniquely able to intercede on Israel's behalf because of her personal history. Still, until the nineteenth century there is little evidence of cultic activity specifically associated with Rachel.

From the mid-nineteenth century through the late twentieth century, a series of social and political changes gave rise to themes that have resonated (in the popular cultural imagination) with aspects of the Rachel myth. These themes are exile and nationhood, and infertility and female corporeal failure.

The late 1930s and 1940s were a time of especially vigorous cultic growth at Rachel's Tomb. This period was marked by intense cultural upheaval—World War II, the Holocaust, and the struggle for the establishment of the State of Israel. This period, in which the cult of Rachel flowered, was characterized by a kind of societal liminality. The Jewish people stood in between extinction and redemption, and whereas old symbols and cultural metaphors had become insufficient, new ones had not yet crystallized. The acceleration of Rachel's cult at this time reflected a communal attempt to make sense out of a turbulent current reality by linking it to sacred history.

Pilgrims' Day Books were kept at Rachel's Tomb from sometime in the 1920s until 1948, when the site (along with Bethlehem and Hebron) was captured by the Jordanians (see Sered 1995). These books lay open on a table inside the building, and numerous pilgrims signed their names, some adding from where they came or a short petition or prayer. Although several volumes have disappeared, we do have the books kept at the tomb in the 1930s and 1940s, and since the pages of the Day Books are dated, we can trace the development of certain themes at the tomb. In the Day Books of the 1930s there were very few references to political or broad societal themes. In the volume covering those years there are a handful of prayers in which Rachel is asked to help the exiles return to Israel, but these supplications are either nonspecific or messianic, not blatantly political like the supplications in the 1940s. In contrast, in the 1940s Rachel's Tomb became explicitly identified with the return to Zion, Jewish statehood, and Allied victory. During the early 1940s the Day Books are full of messages written by soldiers and members of the Jewish Underground crying at the grave, praying before going off to war, or lighting oil candles for an Allies' victory.

As the resting place of the mother of her people and the matriarch most connected with exile and the return to Zion, Rachel's Tomb had special significance for European Jewish refugees during and after the Holocaust. Whereas in the 1930s there were a few scattered prayers to Rachel to intercede for her children in exile, in the 1940s there are hundreds of references to and prayers for the Jews of Europe. The title "Mother of the Nation" (Em HaUma) became more popular at about this time, as did petitioners referring to themselves as "your child" and to the Jews in Europe as "your children in exile." In several entries Rachel is called upon to witness the bloodshed in Europe. One entry in the Day Books from early 1945 reads: "Rachel, Rachel, Mother of the Israeli nation, for how much longer will the tears of Israel be shed in vain? Arise, arise from your sleep." In August 1944 this passage was written: "Rachel Rachel Mother of the Nation. We received the news about the Holocaust and everyone's sufferings. They should all be able to come here [to the Land of Israel]." Holocaust survivors were among those who came to pray at the Tomb of Rachel, Mother of the Exiles. On March 16, 1943, thirty-six immigrant Polish children who had escaped Nazi Europe via Teheran came to the tomb and lit candles. On April 2, 1944, the Tomb was visited by children who had recently escaped from Hungary. According to the caretaker at the tomb, "They cried out loud and so did everyone else at the Tomb." Again on August 7, 1945, approximately thirty children who had survived Buchenwald concentration camp came to Rachel's Tomb.

The late nineteenth century produced the first evidence that Rachel's Tomb had become a place to which people, and especially women, would go to cry. Increasingly, Rachel's specific mythic image—weeping mother—merged into ritual performance. In an early twentieth century discussion of Jewish tombs all over the land, the Christian John Fulleylove wrote that, "None of them, however, is at all so impressive as the tomb of Rachel, where a modern house and dome cover a rough block of stone worn smooth with the kisses of centuries of Jewish women. The wailing, as we saw it there, is a memorable custom." (Fulleylove and Kilman 1912: 230). Jewish observers made similar comments. In 1909 Yitzhak Ben-Zvi wrote how, "They come everyday of the year for trips and prayer. Women stream to the tomb of Our Mother Rachel to spill out their bitter words of the sorrows of their heart, especially sick women and barren ones who come to light candles and throw notes into the cracks of the tomb" (Ben-Zvi 1960: 39–40).

In 1948 Rachel's Tomb passed into Jordanian hands. When the tomb returned to Israeli control in 1967, the themes of exile and return were no longer as salient in the Israeli cultural ethos. Fertility, however, had become a sacred national goal. Israel has the highest birth rate of any developed country, the government ideologically and economically promotes natality, and women are encouraged to begin giving birth immediately after marriage. The ideology behind Israel's pro-natality culture combines a desire to replace the Jews lost in the Holocaust with the need to provide a new generation to build the land and defend its borders. The social demand for children is even greater. For women to bear and raise children is considered a national duty equivalent to men serving in the army or, in the ultra-Orthodox community, to men devoting their life to studying Torah.

In the post-1967 years, Rachel's Tomb came to be associated in the popular imagination almost exclusively with fertility. The custom of winding a red string seven times around the tomb and then wearing the string as a charm for pregnancy and childbirth increased in popularity; during the 1970s and early 1980s red string was explicitly and uniquely associated with Rachel's Tomb. Women who had difficulty conceiving, or who had suffered from miscarriages, would go to Rachel's Tomb—to the tomb of the one who "understands" because she also suffered from infertility—to ask for her help. According to a report in the *Jerusalem Post* (November 2, 1990), one hundred thousand women came to the tomb during the week of the anniversary of Rachel's death. The *Jerusalem Post* report quotes a conversation between a visitor from abroad and a local woman at the tomb. The visitor from abroad asked whether it wasn't idolatrous to pray to the dead Rachel rather than directly to God. The woman replied, "What does God know about the grief of not being able to have a baby?! Mother Rachel knows, and she can tell him in exactly the right words."

With the intensification of the Palestinian Uprising (Intifada) and then the establishment of Palestinian autonomy in Bethlehem, Rachel's Tomb has declined as a focus for women's fertility rituals, although the association between fertility and Rachel continues to exist in the popular imagination and some women do continue to visit the tomb to enlist help with pregnancy and childbirth. Women do, however, still visit Rachel's tomb to cry with Rachel, like Rachel, and for Rachel. Her tears are understood to have redemptive value, and her crying is understood to resonate both in cosmic spheres (for all Jewish exiled from the land of Israel) and in earthly spheres (for all women suffering from problems of fertility and maternity). This combination is a potent one, linking personal suffering to the greatest meta-narratives of the Jewish people, elevating one's personal sorrow to the status of national mourning, and allowing the individual to participate in the grieving of the biblical Matriarch.

Healing in the case of the cult of Rachel the Matriarch is a boon granted in the merit of the saint who, within her own lifetime, did not find health or consolation. Rachel heals because she is a devoted mother, never abandoning her children even in their exile, always ready to intercede on their behalf. Rachel's healing powers are rooted in her own exile—exile from her own children because of her death in childbirth, exile from her natal family because she left to follow Jacob, exile from her husband's family buried in Hebron because she is buried in Bethlehem. The flip side of the exiled Rachel is her proximity to the Jewish people; buried on the road she accompanies them wherever they go, ultimately welcoming them when they return from exile.

Rachel the Wife of Rabbi Akiva

In the words of a woman pilgrim in April 1997, "Rachel's Tomb in Bethlehem is dangerous. When they gave it to the PLO this one [the tomb of Rachel the Wife of Rabbi Akiva] got going. God [HaShem] closed one place and opened another for us. This Rachel is a *gilgul* (reincarnation) of the other. Both were good wives. This is a place for women, women come and can speak to Rachel who is the re-incarnation of the other one—a wife."

The story of the wife of Rabbi Akiva, as told in Babylonian Talmud (Nedariam 50a and Ketubot 62b–63a), goes as follows. Rabbi Akiva was a shepherd who worked for the wealthy ben Kalba Savua. The daughter of ben Kalba Savua perceived Akiva's wonderful and modest qualities and asked him whether, if she were to marry him, he would go and learn Torah. He answered that he would, and they married. When her father heard of the marriage he made a vow to cut her off without a penny, and Akiva went away to learn in a religious academy. He was gone for twelve years, at the end of which he returned with twelve thousand pairs of disciples. Before he met his wife again, however, he overheard her say that if she had her way Akiva would go and study for another twelve years. He went back to the academy. At the end of the second twelve years he returned with twenty-four thousand pairs of disciples. When the townspeople came out to greet him, his wife came to show herself to him, looking like an impoverished beggar woman after twenty-four years of supporting her children without any help from her father or husband. His disciples pushed her aside, not realizing her identity. Rabbi Akiva raised her up and reprimanded them, telling them "That which is mine and which is yours is really hers." Her father then asked to be relieved of his vow. In a separate incident, related in the Jerusalem Talmud, Shabbat 7:1, we learn an additional detail about Rabbi Akiva's wife. She cut off the braids from her head and sold them and gave him the money so that he could learn Torah.

The basic story has received very little elaboration in early Jewish sources, yet one embellishment has proven particularly relevant to the contemporary cult. In *Avot de Rabbi Natan*, nusach a, chapter 6 (an eighth- or ninth-century text, well after the redaction of the Talmud), Akiva's wife is, for the first time, given the name "Rachel."

A newly produced booklet sold at her tomb provides the longest version of the myth of Rachel the Wife of Rabbi Akiva. This booklet weaves together the various Talmudic versions and incidents, expands and embellishes them, and presents a cohesive story in which the themes of Rachel's continuous self-sacrifice and the love and harmony in Rachel and Akiva's marriage intertwine. Among the details underscored in this booklet are Rachel's pleasant voice (never whining or complaining), her ability to make do with what she has, her reluctance to make demands of any kind on her husband, and her role as his helper even after he becomes a famous rabbi. In this booklet, the story of Rachel ends (apocryphally) with her death: "As in her life, also in her death, Rachel left this world quietly and humbly. At her funeral Rabbi Akiva was overcome with tears, and at her grave he said these verses that so suited her: 'A woman of valor, Who will find? Strength and splendor she wears and she laughs to the last day.'" The literary technique of ending the myth of Rachel with these verses from the biblical book of Proverbs that are recited in every observant Jewish home on Friday night strengthens the image of Rachel as a role model for contemporary Jewish women.

The cult of Rachel the Wife of Rabbi Akiva seems to have emerged out of three somewhat separate social forces. First, in recent years there has been a profuse flowering of new holy graves both in the north of Israel and on the coast (Sasson 1997). A second catalyst to the cult of Rachel has been the increasing pressure in ultraorthodox communities for men to spend their lives as full-time Torah scholars. Except for cases of a few exceptionally wealthy families, the absence of a husband's income sentences the wife to a life of poverty and unending work. The story of Rachel the Wife of Rabbi Akiva is one of the most common stories taught, especially to girls in religiously obser-vant schools, and a song about Rachel and Akiva is fashionable in Orthodox kindergartens and elementary schools. And third, as already noted, the increasing difficulty of reaching the Bethlehem tomb of the Matriarch Rachel has encouraged some women to look for, or at least happily embrace, a "branch" tomb—a sort of "Mother Rachel in exile" if you will.

As I discuss in the following section, Rachel the Poetess saw herself as a spiritual and physical link to Our Mother Rachel. In the case of Rachel the Wife of Rabbi Akiva, the link to Our Mother Rachel has been explicated and nourished by others. Until a few years ago, the small sign leading up to the tomb had written on it "The grave of Rachel the Wife of the Tana Rabbi Akiva." Recently, a new and much more visible sign has replaced the old one. On the new sign the words "RACHEL'S TOMB" are written in big letters, followed by "wife of the Tana Rabbi Akiva" in small print. I was told by a local tour guide that because of the sign, "some people get confused" between this tomb and the tomb of Our Mother Rachel. One local devotee told me that she once saw a woman measuring red string around the tomb and asked her why. She answered, "They do it at the other Rachel's Tomb."

Women pilgrims often stress Rachel's self-sacrifice *(mesirut nefesh)* and her devotion to her family. *Shalom bayit* (petitions for a peaceful married life) seems to be the specialty of the tomb. The booklet sold at her tomb includes five stories of recent miracles that have occurred in the wake of prayer at the tomb. Of the five, two have to do with recovery from illness, and three have to do with finding a mate (connecting to the marital theme in the Rachel and Akiva story)—in itself a matter of "healing" the individual from the unhealthy and unnatural state of being single.

Rachel, the Wife of Rabbi Akiva, is less dramatically associated with heal-ing of physical ailments than the biblical Rachel the Matriarch. The ills that Rachel the Wife helps heal are social ills, such as difficulty finding a mate and marital problems. Yet the gap between the two is not large—a mate, a reasonably harmonious marriage, and a properly functioning reproductive system all are prerequisites for filling the culturally mandated female gender role that both of these mythic women suffered in order to achieve.

Rachel the Poetess

Rachel Blubstein (1890–1931), who published her poems under the name "Rachel" (without her last name), came to Palestine as a pioneer in 1909. Rachel expressed her sense of identity with Our Mother Rachel in a number of poems, and most explicitly in this poem entitled simply "Rachel."

> *Lo her blood flows in my blood,*
> *Her voice sings in me Rachel who herds Laban's flock,*
> *Rachel—the mother of my mother.*
> *Therefore my house cramps me, And the city, foreign*
> *For her shawl would flap, In the desert winds.*
> *And therefore I take to the trail, With such assurance*
> *For my feet keep the memories, Of that time, of that time.*[2]

Rachel is the most famous Israeli poetess. Many versions of Rachel's life story have been written in the almost seventy years since her death. One of the best-known biographies was published by her sister's grandson. Because of his privileged access to his grandmother's memories, Uri Milstein's writings about Rachel have their own special aura of authenticity.

The first chapter of Milstein's book is entitled "My Aunt Rachel." In a manner reminiscent of the opening scene of the Broadway hit *Evita*, Milstein begins Rachel's life-story with her death and her funeral. The opening paragraph of the biography describes the last days of Rachel's life: "She was confined to bed and suffered, suffered terribly" (Milstein 1985: 25). Rachel's painful last journey—from a sanitarium (she died of tuberculosis) in Gedera to a hospital in Tel Aviv—is recounted in graphic detail. At the hospital, her friends who had accompanied her left, and Rachel spent her last hours alone, in terrible pain. Although her poems were already quite famous, the hospital staff did not recognize her: "Rachel gasped with pain. The duty nurse came over to the anonymous dying woman to give her a shot of pain killer. 'I don't need it. I want to feel,' said Rachel" (Milstein 1985: 27). Once she was dead, the friends and relatives who had abandoned her in her last days came to her funeral and, in accordance to the request she had written in her poem "If Destiny Ordains," they buried her on the shores of the Kinneret.

Milstein then takes the reader back almost one hundred years and describes the difficult youth of Rachel's father in Czarist Russia. We learn that Rachel's mother's family traces itself to the Jewish sage Rashi, who is believed to be descended from the family of King David. The emphasis upon this detail provides a mythic lineage to Rachel's story and serves to contextualize her story in Jewish mythic time. Rachel herself, according to Milstein, was beautiful: white skin, blue eyes, tall, a composed demeanor, and she usually "looked sad." Even when she acted happy "it looked more like she only wanted to be happy" (1985: 32).

Rachel grew up in Russia and then as a young woman came to Palestine with her sister. Their trip coincided with the years of Zionist fervor. Although her father sent her enough money to live, she wanted to work the land, and after one year joined Hannah Meisel's educational farm. The farm work was physically demanding but Rachel never complained. According to Hannah Meisel, "It was not easy for her soft hands and thin fingers to hoe, but it filled her with happiness to try to farm the land" (Milstein 1985: 32).

Following this brief happy period, Rachel was sent to France to study agriculture. In the meantime, her gentle and refined mother had died and her father had come to Tel Aviv with his third wife, a classic wicked stepmother. At school in France, Rachel was both the only woman and the only Jew. With the outbreak of World War I, passage to Palestine was blocked, and so she spent years in exile, first in France and then back in Russia, where she taught refugee children. From the children, she contracted tuberculosis. In 1919 she returned to Palestine on the first boat from Odessa. She arrived pale and coughing but denied to her friends and relatives that she was sick. Her community from Kinneret had moved to Degania where she rejoined them and tried to work on the farm, but she was too sick. She then worked with children, which was less physically demanding, but when her medical diagnosis was made known, her comrades at Degania forced her to leave. The night she was told to leave was the worst night of Rachel's life, and is depicted often and in great detail.

Penniless—when her father died his money went to his sons and various religious institutions—Rachel then taught children in Petach Tikvah and Jerusalem, moving many times from one apartment to another. Finally, too sick to teach, she turned to her brother for help but his wife wouldn't let her live with them because she feared that Rachel would infect their five-year-old daughter.

During these years of exile from the Kinneret, Rachel wrote almost all of her poems. A great number of her poems blend themes of death, unfulfilled love, and longing for the Kinneret to which she could not return. One of her most famous poems, "The Barren One," expresses her yearning for a son (whom she names "Uri" in the poem), but her fate was to die childless. By the time of her death, Rachel was already a well-known and much-published poet. According to Milstein, Rachel's fans loved her poetry but didn't care that she was suffering: "It was as if they said: 'Go on suffering and writing your beautiful poems for us'" (1985: 50).

Dan Miron (1991) has traced the development of the cult of Rachel the Poetess. Miron, like all of her biographers, describes her final days of suffering and loneliness, neglected and betrayed by all. Even her funeral was only attended by a handful of friends. However, according to Miron, "In a short time the handful became masses. Rachel's loneliness ended with her death, and the modest funeral at the Kinneret became a mass funeral in print, rallies and conferences.... Rachel literature [anecdotes about her life, obscure letters written by Rachel, lamentations written for Rachel] grew and grew each year as the anniversary of her death approached, a date that became a cultic occasion in every way" (1991: 114–15).

For younger generations in Israel today, one of the best-known facts about Rachel is the location of her grave. Referred to simply as "Rachel's Tomb" by her devotees, it is visited daily both by organized groups of schoolchildren and tourists, and by individuals seeking to communicate with, or find comfort in, Rachel's presence. Visitors to her tomb include both religious and secular Israelis. Tour guides who lead groups to the grave have a crucial role in propagating her cult, and different tour guides choose to elaborate upon different mythic aspects.

Rachel's grave, in the old cemetery outside of Tiberius, is just one grave among dozens of Zionist leaders of her era. Yet, one typically finds that only her grave is covered with stones left by visitors (a Jewish custom) and by candles. A copy of Rachel's poems is kept at the grave, and pilgrims come to recite her poems, sometimes to cry, and occasionally to leave notes for Rachel at the grave.

Some of these notes have been saved in the archives of Kvutsat Kinneret, and offer extraordinary insight into the meaning of the cult of Rachel the Poetess. Healing through identification with the saint is the overwhelmingly dominant theme in many of the notes. Here is one example: "How wonderful your poems are in my eyes! You and God are witnesses that only here I found comfort, drew strength and left rewarded.... I pray that I can again visit and go up to your grave to share with you the sufferings of my soul, and to draw strength to continue to march to the not distant bitter end" (August 15, 1982). Another example reads,

> Rachel! I sit here at your side and try to muster all my spiritual strength in order to express...to express...Rachel! Rachel! I am already almost grown up and in a half a year I will go into the army, Rachel! Rachel give me the strength to face the difficulties and stumbling blocks that will be in my way, Rachel, give me the strength to love and to be torn down and to build up anew, the strength to glue together the cracks and to breathe the air, of my country and your country Rachel, give me the strength to build and to accept and to suffer.... Rachel, my mother! my sister! I am here at your feet, a young woman who wants your soul, who wants you to recognize me. (April 6, 1978)

A theme in quite a few of the notes is that the writer's life and sufferings parallel those of Rachel, or that Rachel is the only one who understands what the writer is going through. Some of the notes clearly invoke the cult of Rachel the Matriarch: "Rachel, in your merit I will become pregnant and give birth" (March 31, 1976); or, "Rachel. Not only your name do I carry but also your fate. If only God will allow that my end will not be like yours and that my yearning for a child will bear fruit and your Uri [the son about whose existence Rachel fantasized in one of her best-known poems] will also be mine" (1991).

Israeli Women and Illness

Israeli women frequent the tombs and pay tribute to the life-stories of healing saints as part of a much larger cultural script that associates women with illness. As I point out in the story of Moses' sister Miriam, this script is deeply embedded in ancient Jewish myths. It has taken new life in contemporary Israel where dichotomized gender roles are organized around axes of military prowess, strength, hardness, and health for men, and vulnerability, weakness, worry, grief and illness for women (see Sered 2000). If the prototypical

Israeli man is a farmer and a fighter, the prototypical Israeli woman is a consumer or service provider in need of support and protection. If the prototypical Israeli man is fearless and strong, the prototypical Israeli woman is filled with fear and anxiety for the safety of her soldier son or husband, or grief for the son and husband who died making the supreme sacrifice for their country. If the prototypical male body is solid and reliable, standing ready to protect the collective, the prototypical female body is erratic and undependable, mired in private projects of sexuality and motherhood, defenseless, penetrable, and exposed.

In the mid-1980s I carried out fieldwork among Jewish women who had come to Israel from Kurdistan and other parts of Asia and North Africa (Sered 1992). It was at that time that I first began to understand the focal role of illness in the life experiences and personal narratives of many Israeli women. As I listened to these women, I noted that their conversations almost always had to do with illness: aching legs and backs, fertility problems of daughters and daughters-in-law, illnesses of grandchildren, neighborhood clinics, visits to the hospital, wonders and miracles performed by zaddikim (holy men), trips to tombs of saints rumored to specialize in one or another health problem, and folk remedies and modern medicine. In subsequent years, as I have carried out fieldwork among postpartum women in Jerusalem, at the ritual baths used by Jewish women for purification after menstruation and childbirth, among Israeli women who have been treated for breast cancer, and at a variety of holy tombs visited by Israeli women, I have come to see illness as a constitutive part of the cultural and corporeal experiences of Jewish Israeli women.

Israeli women are sicker and die younger than their counterparts in other western societies. Over the past decade the life expectancy of Israeli women has ranked in the vicinity of thirteenth to seventeenth in the world—after Greece and Ireland—while the life expectancy of Israeli men has remained among the highest in the world—ranked second or third, following only Japan and Sweden (Israel Center for Disease Control 1997: 55–57). As is the case throughout the developed world, women in Israel outlive men, yet Israel's "gender gap"—what is called women's "survival advantage" (3.6 years)—is only half the gap characteristic of contemporary European societies (approximately 7 years).

Gendered patterns of sickness among Israelis start young. Among sixth- and seventh-grade Israeli pupils, 30.6 percent of boys and 41.3 percent of girls report suffering from dizziness, or head, stomach, or back aches more than once a week. By tenth and eleventh grade, the percentage of boys with these symptoms drops to 29.1 percent while the percentage of girls increases to 48.1 percent—close to half of all girls (Harel, Kaneh, and Rahav 1997: 219). As Israeli men and women age, the health disparity increases, with women reporting a higher rate than Israeli men of many debilitating chronic diseases (Avorva et al. 1996).

Of the one thousand women who returned a health questionnaire published in the popular Israeli women's magazine *At*, one in three women reported having suffered at least one miscarriage, one in four had at least one abortion, and almost one in eight of the married women had undergone some kind of fertility treatment. Seventy-five percent of the women reported that they suffer from headaches, one third reported suffering from backaches, 28 percent from chronic tiredness, and 25 percent of the women reported using some kind of pain killer on a regular basis (Avgar and Gordon 1997). In another survey, Eshed (1991) found that close to 40 percent of Israeli women between the ages of twenty and sixty reported feeling stress, anxiety, or depression.

On Suffering, Healing, and Women Saints

It is within this context of the gendering of health and illness both in mythical formulations and in epidemiological reality that the cult of the three Rachels has taken shape in contemporary Israel. The most prominent theme in the cultic stories of the Rachels is suffering. Suffering, of course, characterizes the life-stories of many saints, both male and female; indeed, suffering and affliction are the classic road to sainthood in many cultures. Suffering, however, can take myriad forms. All three Rachels embody what I see as particularly gendered forms of suffering: corporeal vulnerability, self-abnegation, self-sacrifice, and self-denigration. The wife of the Talmudic Rabbi Akiva calls herself a "beast" to his "master." The Poetess tells the world that her learning and literary repertoire are very limited: "Only about myself I know to tell"—an easily recognizable contrast to the best-known male Hebrew poets of her day who wrote about broad cultural and political matters and whose poetry is replete with references to classic literary works.

All three Rachels are said to have suffered for their men and for their children or for their community, rather than for their own spiritual progress or enlightenment (as male saints in Israel and elsewhere typically do). In cultic versions, all three Rachels renounce their own needs in order to further the needs and desires of others. The biblical Matriarch Rachel sacrifices herself for her sister by giving her the signs that make Jacob think he was marrying his true love, for her son whom she dies giving birth to, and then for the Jewish people by being buried alone and on the road so that she can pray for them and accompany them in exile. Rachel the Wife of Rabbi Akiva sacrifices herself for her husband—but in broader terms for Torah, the study of which excluded women. Rachel the Poetess sacrifices herself for love of children (from whom she contracted tuberculosis) and for the land of Israel (in popular culture her illness is often attributed to the hard work she did in the fields). I emphasize that, in the biblical story, Rachel did not give her life for others and even in midrashic texts her volitional sacrifice was limited to where she died and was buried; no hint is given that she chose to die. It is in cultic tellings that we hear her, like the Wife of Rabbi Akiva, described as a "martyr." Similarly, the Poetess is only made into a martyr after her funeral— she certainly did not choose tuberculosis, exile, or death—and her devotees need to be rather creative to find in her writings and life-story hooks on which they can hang the placard of self-sacrifice.

All three Rachel myths tell stories of women whose exemplary lives were limited to very domestic arenas. In male-dominated "warrior societies" like Israel, women are identified with the domestic realm of individual, affective relationships, rather than with the public realm of the society-wide associations that institutionalize and sustain male dominance (M. Rosaldo 1974). The three Rachels (to varying extents) fill this structurally "feminine" role within their stories. All are associated with the private rather than the public realm, and with relationships rather than rules. The Rachels share expertise at dealing with immediate, personal, and interpersonal suffering, and it is around this expertise that their cults have flourished. Even Rachel the Poetess, active in a literary domain that cannot be depicted as entirely domestic, earns praise for her folk simplicity and the intimate and familiar themes of her poems (Kritz 1976).

In the pilgrimage discourse of all three cults, the word "understand" is reiterated with particular fervor and frequency. Rachel, according to devotees, is the one who "really understands us" or "really understands my suffering." While compassion and assistance with life's problems also characterize certain male saints in contemporary Israel, the theme of understanding—and more specifically understanding as the sole or most celebrated public trait of the saint—is particularly associated with the Rachels. The distinction that I am making here is between male saints who in one-on-one interactions (such as visitational dreams) express sympathy, and the three Rachels who are widely and publicly known as the "one who understands." Most male saints in Israel today are considered holy because of asceticism, leadership abilities, miracle working (while alive), or vast learning—all of which are high-status traits. While tombs of biblical figures such as the Patriarchs, of Talmudic figures such as Rabbi Meir baal HaNess, and of contemporary national figures such as Theodore Herzl are popular shrines in Israel, none of these figures—and indeed no male saint—is associated with or celebrated for "understanding" to the extent that the Rachels are. Women pilgrims are clear in their statements; they go to Rachel's Tomb because "she understands," and specifically, "because she is a woman and she understands women's problems." The closeness that pilgrims feel for Rachel has important implications. From a cosmic perspective, the role of "understander" is of relatively low status. The woman saint "understands" mortals because she is not very far above them, she is not transcendent, learned, powerful, or especially exalted; she is—by virtue of her female identity—confined to the domestic realm.

Striking features in the biographies of the Rachels are the common human situations confronted by each: death of parents and children, romantic love and marital discord, difficulty conceiving and bearing children, illness, poverty, conflict with siblings and parents, and illness. These are situations that resonate with the actual life experiences of most human beings. The specialty of Rachel is that she translates personal matters into universal symbols, and universal symbols into personal matters. Rachel shows her women devotees that their seemingly individual problems and anguish cosmically reverberate with the eternal suffering and self-abnegation of the saint; that their individual difficulties are reflections of deeply rooted prototypes of femininity. As Geertz (1973), among others, has argued, through linkage to mythic suffering one's own suffering acquires meaning as part of the cosmic scheme of things.

For the women who come to pour out their hearts at the graves of Rachels, the subordinate status of the "understanding saint" is balanced by the cognitive reinforcement that women obtain through the cultic sacralization of their own individual perceptions and experiences.[3] Put in broader terms, just as the ability to understand is characteristic of those whose role is subordinate, so the need to be understood is an expression of the desire for legitimacy. Marginalized or subordinate individuals—and members of marginalized or subordinate groups—lead a double cognitive life.[4] On the one hand, they are taught—and to a greater or lesser extent also internalize—the world-view of the dominant group. On the other hand, their own experiences and perceptions often deviate—sometimes secretly and sometimes publicly—from that world-view.

In patriarchal cultures, the dominant model of reality is one that reflects and expresses men's perceptions. Women may develop their own alternative models of reality, but these models receive far less social confirmation than men's models receive for the simple reason that in patriarchal societies the principal public social institutions rest upon men's models. As members of the culturally dominant group, men—and more thoroughly, elite men—experience congruity between their own perceptions and the perceptions that are formalized and sanctified through schools, rules, laws, jokes, theology, symbols, and customs. Women—as members of a culturally subordinate group—experience disjunction between what they are told is true and what they may feel to be true. This disjunction is the impetus for the need to be understood. The cult of the "understanding Rachel" offers a model of reality that fits women's experiences and so affords consolation, empathy, and, above all, the comfort that comes from knowing that you are not alone, that your own experiences and feelings are shared by others. Rachel does not need to work great miracles, possess great learning, or exhibit great powers. That she understands, that she provides cognitive reinforcement, is often enough to generate a sense of healing that, in the final analysis, is what brings pilgrims to the graves of saints. If in Jewish culture illness is equated with exile and healing with reincorporation into the community, visiting an understanding saint can be enormously health enhancing for women.

Rachel the Poetess was exiled from her beloved Kinneret (which for her was the symbol of the Land of Israel). Rachel the Wife of Rabbi Akiva was exiled from her father, from the prosperous community and conventional feminine role into which she was born, and in essence from her husband (and by extension from the centers of Jewish learning). Rachel the Matriarch was exiled from her natal family (as are many women in patrilineal and patrilocal societies) and her children (through death), and she is the symbol of the exile of the Jewish people from their homeland. Exile is, of course, a paradigmatically Jewish theme, and association with exile is absolutely appropriate for saints whose myths and cults are embedded within the unique Jewish cultural experience. The metaphor of exile is not only Jewish but also gendered. Women in patriarchal societies are exiled from the centers of political power, from the resources to create mainstream cultural patterns, and—in a deep sense—from their own souls. For some contemporary Israeli women, awareness that their exile is understood and shared by a saint can be a tremendously empowering and healing experience.

At the beginning of this article, I proposed that Miriam, the sister of Moses who is afflicted with a skin condition and then sent out of the community encampment, should be seen as the prototypically gendered sick person in Jewish culture, and I offered the idea that exile is the prototypical condition from which Jewish culture seeks to be healed. The high morbidity and mortality rates of Israeli women suggest that this paradigm continues to be operative in contemporary Jewish culture. Israeli women never fully "returned" from exile in the Diaspora. They never fully appropriated the post-exilic Zionist traits of autonomy, aggression, strength, courage, military prowess, and good health. The cognitive, corporeal, and personal alienation experienced as illness by Israeli women, rooted both in ancient cultural metaphors and in modern social realities, allows some women to experience a sense of healing through identification with the "understanding" (and ill) female saint. Stuck in perpetual exile, a visit to the tomb of a saint ameliorates the sense of disconnection that characterizes the life experiences of many women. Put differently, the healing that occurs at the shrines of the Rachels has to do with bringing one's own sorrow into a meaningful cultural narrative—a process that is far from commonplace and never taken for granted in a society where women rarely have the power to tell the national story. Still, I would argue, as each additional woman pilgrim adds her own pains and sorrows to the cosmic tears of Rachel, understandings of women's corporeal weakness as built into the very structure of the world are continually reenergized and reinscribed into a cultural script that perpetuates the gender inequalities that make women seem sick to themselves as well as to others.

Putting It All Together Again

Pilgrimage, Healing, and Incarnation at Walsingham

Simon Coleman

Engagement and Ambiguity

Some years ago, I went with my friend Marianne, her husband David, and one of David's brothers to the Christian pilgrimage site of Walsingham.[1] A medical doctor, Marianne had recently completed a postgraduate degree in anthropology and was now several months pregnant. I had told her and David—also a doctor—that I was thinking of carrying out fieldwork at Walsingham, and they were curious to see the place. We drove from Cambridge toward the North Norfolk coast, gradually exchanging freeways for smaller roads and then narrow, winding lanes that led us to the outskirts of the village. Our initial stop was at the Roman Catholic pilgrimage shrine, situated a mile from Walsingham itself.

My first surprise came as we got out of the car to have a look around the chapel that is the focal point of the shrine. David's brother refused to move from his seat. In common with Marianne and David, he was a lapsed Catholic; but unlike them he felt deeply uneasy about entering such an overtly "religious" place. He stayed in the car while the rest of us took a quick tour of the chapel and its grounds.

My second surprise occurred when we drove to the Anglican shrine, located much closer to the center of the village itself. Marianne, David, and I entered the front of the shrine church, and were confronted, as all visitors are, with a mass of images, scents, candles, and altars. Directly in front of us was a large tableau of the Annunciation, a biblical event with which Walsingham is particularly associated. However, Marianne was more interested in the holy well that we could see just to our left as we came in. We read the sign by the well, which states: "This well of 11th century stonework is the one which was discovered when the Shrine was re-built in 1931. Through these waters many have been healed of diseases and other pilgrims who have come here all through the ages have drunk the water and been sprinkled with it. This indeed forms part of the Pilgrimage to England's Nazareth."

Instead of moving on as I had expected, Marianne paused. Then she persuaded David to take a ladle of water from a container by the well and, somewhat self-consciously, to pour some "holy" water over her rounded stomach. She made little subsequent comment about the event, and we made our tour of the shrine and its garden before going to one of the many cafés that line the main street of the village.

This particular trip to Walsingham took place a little before I started extended fieldwork at the site in the mid-1990s, and it has stayed in my memory because it encapsulates much of my subsequent experience of the shrine and its visitors. Walsingham, a tiny village in a remote part of the English countryside, is visited each year by perhaps a quarter of a million people, mostly but not exclusively from the United Kingdom (Williams 1996: vii). Many of these people explicitly define themselves as pilgrims, and may even come to the village with fellow parish members and a priest at the same time each year. Others, like the informal group of friends I have just described, are more loosely organized and ambivalent in their intentions and affiliations.[2]

It is this element of ambivalence, or at least ambiguity, in visiting Walsingham that I want to highlight here. What was the significance of my early trip to Walsingham with friends? Were Marianne, David, and I pilgrims, tourists, or fieldworkers? Were we perhaps transformed from tourists *into* pilgrims by Marianne and David's act of "pre-baptizing" their unborn child? And were my friends merely playing with the paraphernalia provided by the shrine, or did Marianne really "believe" that she was ensuring the safety of herself and her baby? Although I did not ask my friends subsequently to explain their actions, I suspect that they would not have been able, or perhaps willing, to give me a firm reply. Marianne and David became the proud parents of a healthy child a few months later, but I have no reason to believe that they attributed their good fortune to their visit to the Norfolk shrine.

I am obviously posing questions with no definite answers, but my point is that the ambiguous actions I have just described gain significance and resonance when juxtaposed with the behavior of the many other visitors to Walsingham whom I have observed in later years. Note for instance that Marianne and David's act of physical engagement was counterbalanced by David's brother's act of rejection. Walsingham has indeed tended to polarize opinions over the years, even the centuries, and to this day it is the target not only of Protestant evangelical Christians who accuse the shrines of peddling idolatrous and magical ideas about the divine, but also of many mainstream Anglicans who feel uneasy with their shrine's "High" liturgy and apparently reactionary opposition to the ministry of women priests.[3] What these opinions have in common is a sense that the site somehow matters, and may even have some kind of power; after all, David's brother did not feel apathy but rather a sense of threat in relation to what Walsingham represented about his past experiences and present attitudes.

The individual, private responses of my friends also display intriguing parallels with wider frameworks of liturgy and theological interpretation. David and Marianne were marking, perhaps for the first time, the presence of three people rather than two within their family. Besides the bonds of close kinship, however, their action also evoked the sacrament of baptism, and could be seen as gaining implicit spiritual significance because it took place in a shrine so closely identified with the Annunciation and subsequent birth of Christ. I am not suggesting that Marianne and David necessarily took these issues into conscious consideration when they approached the well; nor am I suggesting that they suddenly forgot their medical training and trust in the powers of, say, antenatal scans and folic acid. However, I do recognize in their spontaneous act a much broader pattern that is evident among visitors of many backgrounds: a desire to physically engage with the site that is partially prompted by the organization and arrangement of the place itself. Their engagement, slight as it was, might have been "about" spiritual rebirth, concerns over health, a celebration of family, or all or none of these things. The ambiguity of the act was compounded by the fact that it involved nominal Roman Catholics visiting an Anglo-Catholic shrine, in a context where the two have been in sharp competition for at least some of the past hundred years or so. Yet, Marianne and David's impulse cannot be regarded as less ethnographically significant than more "official" performances of healing during "formal" pilgrimages to Walsingham. In fact, it reveals much that is common to many forms of material and embodied involvement with the village's shrines.

Numerous pilgrimage sites offer means through which physically to "snare" pilgrims who come to visit. Within Catholic contexts, the kissing and touching of images, the sprinkling of water, the performance of the Eucharist, and so on are common, tangible components of repertoires of engagement. The particular flavor—one might even say efficacy—of Walsingham as a site emerges from the specific combination of symbolically loaded ideological and material resources that it makes available to its varied visitors. Recall that the notice at the well referred to a site that was both ancient (early medieval) in foundation and more recent (twentieth century) in its restoration. It also claimed that the taking of waters was part of pilgrimage to "England's Nazareth," suggesting the juxtaposition of national identity with a biblical reference to the place of the Annunciation and Jesus' early life. A quasi-biblical landscape has been created in a distinctly rural setting and, moreover, one associated not only with human birth but also with material reconstruction. At the same time, something rather interesting has happened in the rebuilding of the place, since England's Nazareth now appears to have at least two focal points: one Roman Catholic, the other Anglo-Catholic.

These features of the Walsingham pilgrimage form the background to my argument in this chapter. I show how contemporary "healing" at a pilgrimage site such as Walsingham occasionally involves claims of miraculous physical cures, but that in practice it usually implies a much more multivalent set of associations and effects. By this I mean more than that the site plays host to competing miraculous and sacrificial discourses, although such a statement would contain an important element of truth (cf. Dahlberg 1991; Eade 1991: 62–63). The "healing" that is offered and sought by pilgrims includes but goes beyond the physical, into realms of social, psychological, spiritual, and even material "well-being." Indeed, although contemporary Walsingham has been associated with miraculous cures of illness and disease, it does not particularly specialize in these. So my exploration of healing certainly does not exclude consideration of the physical body, but it locates such consideration in a much broader appreciation of possible locations for the healing process.

What is most significant about Walsingham is the way it provides a complex context for multiple modes of physical and emotional engagement that allow pilgrims to participate in social as well as liturgical dramas. Such practices often involve developing an experiential relationship to sacralized architecture (Ousterhout 1990: 109). The bodily idioms enacted at the shrines tend therefore to partake in a specific cultural world—that of English Catholic Christianity, with its rich aesthetic heritage and overt focus on such related somatic themes as Annunciation and Incarnation (cf. Kleinman 1988: xiii). There is a reasonably widely held, if debated, assumption among the more pious visitors that the holy can infuse material existence, involving places as well as bodies (see Frank 2000: 14). Thus, Dahlberg (1991: 46–48) is correct to highlight the Catholic emphasis on the body, with its associated notions that the Host can regenerate the communicant, and that saints' relics contain sacred power. Yet, ideas about the body are connected with ideas about the possibility of the divine permeating other aspects of the physical environment.[4]

Ousterhout has noted (1990: 108) that medieval pilgrims sought physical contact—seeing, touching, holding, kissing—with holy sites and objects that were perceived to be prophylactic. Smaller objects had frequently come into contact with other holy places, while buildings possibly replicated (and translated into local architectural idioms) the shape and form of paradigmatic sites. In turn, the physical senses were themselves regarded as able to perceive divine presence (Frank 2000: 29). Variations on such mimetic, metonymic, and contagious means of accessing what is perceived to be the sacred are evident at modern Walsingham.

I also show how forms of engagement with pilgrimage experience must be viewed in the light of contemporary concepts of the self, spirituality, and well-being. What kinds of contact with "the sacred" might be viewed as therapeutic or "healing" by modern pilgrims, and should we assume that numinous experience need be confined to conventional, theologically defined conceptions of the holy? In practice, many of the experiences that are considered to be both powerful and personally beneficial by pilgrims involve forms of contact or engagement that go far beyond the touching of relics. Often, a more active sense of engagement with the narratives of the site is cultivated—one that invokes the agency of the pilgrim alongside the apparent power of the place.

Walsingham has been marked by a period of destruction and fragmentation (associated with the Reformation), and the effects of this painful history are still evident and highly visible in the fabric of the village and the shrines. A root metaphor runs through many pilgrimage practices in the village, deriving some of its meaning from this period of destruction and simultaneously recalling many of the associations of a deeply Catholic, sacramental view of the world. I gloss the metaphor (in common with some pilgrims) as "restoration"—the sense of bringing back, putting back together again, even reenacting that which has been lost, destroyed, or misplaced. In one sense, it echoes Taussig's (1993) depiction of mimesis as both imitation and appropriation of the Other, with the Other contained here within an idealized vision of the past. At the same time, in the specific context of a Catholic religious sensibility, it evokes parallels between the body as powerful "natural symbol" and the physical environment as reflection and container of such power (see Douglas 1970; Strathern 1996: 13). If the bodies of Christ and Mary are associated with a physical environment that is visibly fragmented—indeed partially ruined—then the actions of the pilgrim in recalling and re-embodying a past before the ruination occurred take on deep sacramental significance.

I therefore use the "condensed" term of *restoration* because it can refer to aspects of the body (health, memory, and so on), to spiritual well-being (faith, belief) and, more broadly, to the material world.[5] It implies both a set of ideas and a series of physical actions that have certain consequences. Most importantly, the idea of restoring something prompts us to ask questions about how people identify anew the "presence" of what had been lost—an inquiry that is at the heart of many sacramental, "healing" experiences of pilgrimage. As in the case of Marianne and David, the possible links to orthodox theological discourse in such matters can be attenuated, ambiguous, and possibly even unconscious. Whatever the connections with conventional theology or human consciousness, however, bodies in the pilgrimage site can be seen as "mindful" in the sense described by Strathern (1996: 28; drawing on Lock and Scheper-Hughes 1987), inextricably fusing the physical and the moral.

A broader than normal focus on the notion of healing should not move us away from appreciating the embodied dimension of moving through Walsingham. As Desjarlais has suggested (1992), in considering healing practices it can be fruitful to locate them within the wider metaphysics of space evident within the culture in question, so that bodily movement can be shown to take on particular meanings in the context of local understandings of topography, architecture, and aesthetics. What, then, might have been "restored" when David sprinkled water over his wife's pregnant stomach? We should not succumb to the dangers of overinterpretation—and we must of course remember the brother who remained aloof from all proceedings. Yet, perhaps the Anglican shrine provided a stage for a minidrama of reconciliation. No priests were on hand to tell the couple what to do, or to construct a formal liturgy for their arrival. They nevertheless chose to regard the holy water as a beneficial medium rather than a sign of irrational superstition or unfounded authority. A material expression of their rejected religious pasts became, for a brief moment, salient in the articulation of hope for their joint future. In a minor and personal way, they enacted a theme that recurs again and again, albeit in very different ways, as we consider the historical and contemporary fate of the shrines of Walsingham.

Foundation and Fragmentation

The story of Walsingham's origins as a site of pilgrimage combines myth and history in a manner that still colors contemporary interpretations and uses of its shrines. The main written "source" for the origins of the site is the so-called *Pynson Ballad*, a fifteenth century document of dubious reliability (see Morrison 2000: 17). The text tells of how, in 1061, a pious widow named Richeldis was granted three visions of the Virgin. Wishing to perform some task for Our Lady, Richeldis was led in spirit to the Holy Land by Mary and shown the exact dimensions of the Holy House where the Annunciation had taken place. She was also instructed to build a copy of the Holy House in her home village of Walsingham. Richeldis wished to locate the replica in a meadow, where heavy dew lay on the ground. Overnight, however, angels moved the house some two hundred feet within the field. A pilgrimage site was born, and from its early days, according to the *Pynson Ballad*, Walsingham proved a rich source of miraculous cures, answering many prayers won by Our Lady's intercession: the lame were made whole, the blind restored to sight, lepers cleansed, and even the dead restored to life.

Whatever the historical truth of the story, certain of its symbolic implications are worth mentioning. The Holy House is seen as an exact copy of an original, not the original itself, but still a powerful focus of divine intercession. The idea of a House is reminiscent of the Virgin as vessel, as womb, as "God-bearing"—indeed, the Virgin's body was used to represent the church in medieval Catholicism (Dubisch 1995: 234). Sacralized forms of bodily and material translation are evoked not only by the transportation of Richeldis to Nazareth and the dimensions of the house to Norfolk, but also by the angelic movement of its foundations from one part of the field to another. Water is present in the story in the form of dew (a medieval sign of the Virgin) and the two wells. Finally, although it actually seems unlikely that Walsingham was established as a pilgrimage site before the twelfth century (McDonald 1997: 15), the claimed date of 1061 conveniently places the foundation of the shrine just before the "foreign" Norman invasion of 1066.

Walsingham became for a time the premier focus of Marian pilgrimage in England (Keast 1984: 16). Morrison (2000) has recently traced the medieval site's importance for women in particular, arguing that it catered extensively to illnesses associated with fertility and childbirth. The shrine claimed to possess the relic of a few drops of the Virgin's milk, and pilgrims could buy ampullae filled with water and a few drops of the milk (Morrison 2000: 5; Gillett 1946: 27). Symbols of blood and milk were connected in medieval women's lives, linking Mary's milk with the blood of Christ, so that the suckling Virgin was increasingly depicted as a backdrop of the Eucharist (Morrison 2000: 32–33).

Alongside the link with female well-being, nurture, and fertility, Walsingham's political importance was indicated by its connections with aristocracy and even royalty. In the fourteenth century, Edward II is said to have given protection to Robert Bruce of Scotland, who was suffering from leprosy, so that the latter could go on pilgrimage there in the hope of healing (Gillett 1946: 31). Another king was to prove the site's nemesis. Henry VIII, earlier a keen supporter of the shrine, made it a prime target of the Dissolution in 1538, and the Holy House and its associated statue of the Virgin and Child were destroyed. Pilgrimage to Walsingham came to a halt, seemingly forever.

Some four hundred years later, Gillett, an archeologist and Roman Catholic apologist, describes the impact of such iconoclasm on one of the buildings of the medieval pilgrimage shrine: "The Priory tumbled down. Stone by stone, successive generations, who remembered not the First Joy of the Annunciation, which had daily been recited there, carried the great church away, to build it into their houses, when formerly it might have been built into their lives" (1946: 67).

Gillett links the literal dissolution of the building with people's inability to reenact the Annunciation, or even to retain it in memory. Fragmentation of faith and of the fabric of the church appear to go hand in hand. A spiritual fall from grace is enacted as stones become mere instruments of shelter, rather than sacramentally entering and enhancing human existence. The ruined church has become an emblem not only of Henry's act of destruction, but also of the potential contained in the act of restoration.

Revival, Authenticity, and Incarnation

What is striking about the Walsingham story, perceived from a contemporary perspective, is that it contains not one "origin myth," but two. The medieval destruction of the shrine has become as paradigmatic as the Richeldis myth of construction, not least because it ultimately led to a second birth of pilgrimage to Norfolk.[6] During much of the nineteenth century, the Oxford Movement reemphasized the importance of sacramental worship within the Church of England, arguing for the "real presence" of the risen Christ in the Eucharist (Dearing 1966: 19). White (1989: 109) notes that some of the revival was jokingly termed "British Museum Religion" since so much of it was based on historical research. Romanticism and nationalism thus combined to form an attractive ideological package at a time of increasing rationalism and, of course, industrialization. Unsurprisingly, evangelicals accused Tractarians and Anglo-Catholics of a misguided medievalism in attempting to establish the "objective presence" of Christ's body and blood in isolation from the faith of believers (Cocksworth 1991: 54).

Such developments, along with the gradual establishment of Roman Catholicism in England, made their mark on Walsingham. Not much remained of the medieval site, and the location of the original Holy House had been lost. In a sense, the very lack of material "completeness" made the place more attractive to exponents of romantic revival. Charlotte Boyd (born 1837), like Richeldis a single woman of some means, had used much of her fortune restoring monastic buildings to what she perceived to be their full "Anglican" use (Jennings 1992: 7). Walsingham came to her attention, and although she was unable to persuade the owners of the priory to sell, she did manage to purchase the "Slipper Chapel," a fourteenth-century building that, in the medieval pilgrimage, had formed the last stop before pilgrims walked into Walsingham itself. What happened next is best described by Gillett (1946: 71), with his theological preferences firmly to the fore: "While yet the builders were at work, Miss Charlotte Boyd herself received the gift of Faith." From a Roman Catholic perspective, Boyd's personal spiritual revival could be interpreted as occurring at the very time when the material fabric of a genuine relic of the medieval pilgrimage was being brought back into use. Furthermore, as Gillett proclaimed, "Once again Walsingham's Slype Chapel came back into Catholic ownership and the way back to Our Lady's Land was open" (72). In this view, restoration of the building became a medium for the restoration of "true" faith on a national level.

Although Boyd died soon afterward, Roman Catholic pilgrimage to the Slipper Chapel grew from the 1930s on. In 1938, for instance, a national pilgrimage of Roman Catholic youth marked the fourth centenary of the destruction of the shrine (Gillett 1946: 75–76). What was interesting about this occasion was not only its use of pilgrimage as a means of responding to, even symbolically reversing, the Dissolution, but also its combination of liturgical elements: two High Masses at the chapel were performed alongside a blessing of sick and crippled children, and followed by a procession into Walsingham that involved placing flowers on the very spot in the priory grounds that was speculated to be the original site of the Holy House. The sacrament of Christ's living presence and incorporation into the body was therefore juxtaposed not only with a very public acknowledgement of bodily suffering (rather than a healing as such), but also with an act of physical movement from the periphery of the village to its center, restoring in liturgical memory the presence of the original shrine of the Annunciation.

By the 1930s, Roman Catholic activity at Walsingham signified more than an enactment of restoration, however; it also implied an element of competition. Anglican pilgrimage to the village was being energetically cultivated by the local priest, Alfred Hope Patten. Although he had little liking for the Roman Catholic presence in the village, Patten shared with Boyd a deeply romantic view of the medieval past (Coleman and Elsner 1999: 194–97). He had a statue of Our Lady of Walsingham carved, using as his model a medieval seal that was preserved in the British Museum. After receiving a large donation from a private benefactor, he was able to buy some land relatively near to the priory ruins. In a supreme act of theological and material restoration, he decided to rebuild the Holy House itself.

Two features of Patten's construction stand out. During the building period Patten had prayed for a sign of God's approval (Stephenson 1970: 156), and to his delight his workmen happened upon water from a disused, possibly Saxon, well—indeed the very one used by Marianne and David some sixty years later. The possible interpretation for Patten was pregnant with possibility: that he was not merely providing a copy of the medieval shrine, but was doing so at the very spot where it had originally stood. The rebirth and healing symbolized by holy water was complemented by the parallel restoration of Richeldis's building and, it was hoped, the revival of a true, pre-Reformation,

English spirituality (Colven 1990: 46–47). Furthermore, Patten placed over two hundred stones into the walls of the Holy House, mostly taken from monasteries desecrated in the Middle Ages. Thus Patten invoked the "presence" of the sacralized, pre-Reformation past in a number of dimensions: through uniting, in one building, the "real" fragments of medieval buildings; through providing a copy of Richeldis's construction; and perhaps by locating the copy on "authentic," original foundations. As the summary of a sermon at the opening of the new shrine in 1931 put it, "From henceforth Mary had come back into her own to show forth the incarnate life of her divine Son" (Colven 1990: 41).[7]

Healing Paths

The restoration of Walsingham can therefore be seen as having created a landscape of densely and powerfully charged significance. While medieval England is invoked, it reinforces a medievalism constructed in response to distinctly contemporary concerns of restoration (Coleman and Elsner 1999: 189). The Roman Catholic shrine is an explicitly national representation of the faith, yet the relatively "marginal" status of British Catholicism is curiously echoed in the peripherality of the Slipper Chapel. Anglicanism is still the established religion of England, but for most of its existence Anglo-Catholicism has been seen as a quasi-sectarian, liturgically, and even politically conservative wing of a much broader church. Both Roman and Anglo-Catholic revivalists of the earlier part of the twentieth century were seeking a definite, sacramental link with the medieval past and a biblical landscape, but only succeeded in creating a landscape that raised more theological questions than it could answer. The early revival of the village was largely characterized by the delineation of two distinct and competing (but of course partially parallel) pilgrimage traditions. Both employed the Eucharist, confession, processions, and the distribution of water (since the Slipper Chapel had a fountain) in order to relive a myth that presented Mary as pointing to the Incarnation of Jesus.

Nowadays, however, many more people visit Walsingham than ever before, and relations between the two shrines are largely ecumenical, including even the staging of joint processions. The very popularity of the place has made Walsingham even more of a multivocal religious landscape, appropriated by a much wider constituency of conservative and liberal Christians of both sides of Catholicism, as well as by tourists and amateur historians. Even a 1961 archeological excavation, which in all probability located the "true" location of the Holy House some distance from Patten's shrine, has failed to simplify the spatial dynamics of the village. The spot is on land owned by a "neutral" family that permits the two shrines occasionally to hold services at the location, but also opens the site to tourists and has marked the medieval shrine with nothing more conspicuous than a small plaque on the grass.

Of course, this lack of closure in the landscape is precisely my point. The village provides a number of powerful sites of reference for pilgrims, but it leaves open the processes of picking or even reconstructing a route that links these spiritual resources. Movement through the spaces of the village is itself a kind of therapeutic restoration, but of what, and to what extent such restoration is perceived as mimetic of a "true" past, is left to be constructed anew on each occasion. I might be regarded here as presenting pilgrimage as a contested cultural field, but in this case the metaphor of conflict is not quite accurate, or at least does not tell the whole story. Indeed, the sense of Walsingham as open to a kind of embodied poetics of pilgrimage is expressed by those at the very center of its liturgical reproduction (cf. Coleman and Elsner 1998: 46). In the foreword to a book about the village by the then Anglican administrator of the Anglo-Catholic shrine, the director of the Roman Catholic shrine writes: "This book will give an impression of Walsingham and will point us to its mystery. It still remains for pilgrim-visitors to discover the significance of Walsingham for themselves. For some the visit to the Slipper Chapel or Holy House will be of greatest significance; for others there will be a unique sacred place waiting for them in the holy land of Walsingham" (Williams 1996: x).

Given its ambiguities, in what sense can the revived Walsingham pilgrimage be said to involve healing in narrower (physical) or wider (social, psychological, theological) senses? There is no doubt that the sick in body have been incorporated within formal liturgies at both shrines throughout the revived history of the pilgrimage. And yet even the fiercest advocates of either side have not placed evidence of miraculous healing at the center of the message of the pilgrimage. In official terms, the sick are usually merely blessed and sprinkled, rather than bodily healed. Some pilgrimages explicitly focus on physically handicapped or distressed pilgrims, but most do not. The provision of accommodation designed for the physically frail is a recent innovation.

This is not to say that reports of miracles do not occur. Claude Fisher (1979), a Roman Catholic journalist and resident of Walsingham, notes that no ecclesiastical inquiries have been set up in the previous fifty years to certify that any miracle has taken place, but that he has heard of a few cases where such an inquiry might have been justified. One example deals with an elderly canon who bathed his leg in one of the two wells that are still present in the grounds of the ruined priory, and who became convinced that a two-inch gap in a bone had disappeared. The canon took the trouble to confirm with his doctor that no human explanation could be found for the cure, and returned to Walsingham to give thanks. However, one of the significant points of the story comes when Fisher states that he "made me promise not to make it known during his lifetime" (58).

Such a low-key approach to bodily cures is complemented by the location of healing in nonphysical planes. As one Anglo-Catholic bishop writes in a popular book devoted to describing the history and meaning of Walsingham: "This new edition appears at a time when the accommodation available at Walsingham is being enlarged to make special provision for the sick and handicapped. Here too is a ministry of healing which though it may not always be physical can always be spiritual" (Kemp 1990: 6).

It might be argued that these are examples of an official, sacrificial discourse prevailing over a more popular, miraculous one, but in fact, my interviews with pilgrims to both shrines indicate that hope for physical healing is present within, but is not a particularly predominant feature of, lay interpretations of the importance of the sites.[8] More common are descriptions of the place as providing a generalized "peace" and sense of reconciliation, even with death. Variations on the trope "Walsingham does things to people" are frequently expressed. Yet such apparent fetishism of place is not automatically translated into an assumption that literal physical repair will occur. Indeed, the answer to a prayer for healing may come in the form of learning to accept that one will not recover.[9] The tendency, evident at Lourdes, for well pilgrims to seek out temporarily exalted sick people is generally absent. A priest working at the Anglican shrine notes: "I think the whole business of the pilgrimage of the sick says something about the place of those who are easily marginalized from being at the center. The fact that the vast majority of people who come here on pilgrimage come from urban, underprivileged parishes . . . who need the security of what Walsingham is about and who may need almost the kind of therapy of the place."

In other words, the sense of using the pilgrimage site as a stage where the normally marginal can gain a sense of self-worth is evident, but it is not a platform that is reserved purely for those who are *physically* suffering. The sick are located within a wider interpretive framework of loss and lack of power, which can be addressed by a form of restoration that is linked to the material environment.

It would, however, be misleading to present the Walsingham pilgrimage as one where disenfranchised pilgrims become passive recipients of liturgical or psychological balm. Interactions between bodies and places can involve more dynamic, self-empowering forms of movement. Unlike, for instance, pilgrimage along the Camino to Compostela (Frey 1998: 126–36), the journey to Walsingham is not in itself normally highlighted as an essential, "authenticating" part of the spiritual experience. Pilgrims talk of the importance of getting away from their normal lives, but being *at* rather than going *to* Walsingham is the truly important thing to achieve. Once they are there, however, movement itself becomes key (Coleman 2000: 161–67). Stations of the cross, processions, and even the less formal traversing of the village in the company of others take on sacramental significance. One elderly Roman Catholic, a former nurse, noted that she found pilgrimage to Walsingham an excellent opportunity to touch her fellow Christians, much as she used very deliberately to go around touching the ailing inhabitants of an old people's home in which she had worked. In both cases, physical contact was deployed as a means of cementing social bonds rather than providing the medical healing that her nursing practices might have provided.

For some pilgrims, Walsingham is valued because it allows them to pick and choose which parts of the pilgrimage landscape to focus upon, with even the local pubs being valued as resources for the reinforcement of friendship and fellowship with others. For others, the key feature of their movement is the conviction that one is following directly in the footsteps of pre-Reformation Christians. Pilgrimage becomes the equivalent of Patten's and Boyd's forms of architectural restoration, since it plays on the sense of both symbolically and materially reestablishing a "presence" that has been lost, thus reversing the theological errors evident in iconoclasm. In addition, certain pathways through the village take on a more performative dimension, since they publicly assert the links between spiritually charged points. For instance, in the contemporary village, the normal Roman Catholic pilgrimage usually moves away from the center of the village to the Slipper Chapel. As a result, those occasions (on important feast days) when the movement is *away* from the chapel *to* the priory and original site of the original Holy House take on especially powerful significance. The latter procession can be seen as symbolizing but also enacting the reversal of a history that has resulted in the peripheralization of their faith. Other pilgrims conscientiously trace a path from one shrine to the other as an anticipation of unity and reconciliation between Christians—again, a restoration of a pre-Reformation condition. Thus, processions can imply either a competitive appropriation of pilgrimage landscape or a more ecumenical communion of souls, depending on context. They are also a means of translating explicitly sacred bodies between powerfully charged spots. Here a middle-aged Roman Catholic woman describes her experience:

> If you are in the procession there is a feeling of closeness, of unity, of doing the same thing, walking the same steps for the same reason. You are following the blessed sacrament. They may be carrying the statue of Our Lady but the blessed sacrament will be there too and this is important too, whenever there is a cure in Lourdes or anywhere else it is never because the statue of Our Lady is in front—it has always happened when they have been blessed with the blessed sacrament; through Mary to Jesus.

This statement follows the theological orthodoxy that the male figure, Jesus, rather than the female figure, Mary, is the true source of any possible healing (see Eade 1991: 63), but it also expresses the sense that the procession is a means of accompanying Our Lady and Christ through the holy landscape. Incarnation is celebrated through both Mass and the measured movement of the pilgrims, who usually sing the Ave Maria while proceeding between the village and the Slipper Chapel or vice versa. In common with many other interviewees, this woman did not claim that pilgrimage had healed her of any specific ailment, but she did note, "you come away feeling good." An important contribution to this sense of well-being was the fact that: "When I go there I feel I am near her; I am nearer to her there than I am here because she was actually there." A sense of presence is again articulated here, and despite the comment about Christ as healer, it is clear that Mary is the focus of the woman's sense of cultivating an intimate relationship with divinity. Interestingly, she talks of Mary being "actually there," and we must remember that when this pilgrim joins the major Roman Catholic processions she is not merely commemorating Mary's having visited Walsingham, she is also joining with others in transporting (an image of) Mary down the Holy Mile, and actively restoring it to the spot that Mary herself once chose.

In the case just described, pilgrimage is a means of coming close to divine figures, and reenacting a sacred narrative in the present through sacramentally charged movement. As we saw with Marianne and David, however, not all who come are quite so firm in their religious conviction. Physical engagement with the place and with fellow visitor-pilgrims can apparently have effects that extend sacramentalism and healing into more apparently secular realms. A powerful example of this phenomenon is provided by a Roman Catholic man, married to an Anglican woman, who had lost his faith in his twenties. Paul's lack of religious conviction did not prevent him from feeling close to his rather pious extended family, which contained over one hundred members. Each year, a devout relative of his who had gone to live in Walsingham arranged a family pilgrimage to the Slipper Chapel, and each year the pilgrimage caused a dilemma for Paul: should he overcome his reluctance to "rejoin" his Catholic faith, however temporarily, in order to celebrate with his family? He described one occasion when he deliberately arrived separately and late at Walsingham, avoiding the bus that had been chartered to take everybody to the village. In order to avoid participating in the family procession from the village out to the Roman Catholic shrine, he stood by the disused railway line, looking back:

> And in the distance, I saw this pilgrimage in between autumn hedgerows. And, my family doesn't dress up a lot, they're sort of a very dowdy lot, and they could have been from *any* era really. It looked absolutely wonderful, magnificent, and they were really processing, in a pilgrimage, along the lane in between the two hedgerows...and [it was] deeply moving actually, and I felt very happy...observing them, and they were my lot too, and I felt very comfortable with that, not being *totally* part of them, but being close to them.... Then I walked down across a field and joined halfway.

In my interview with him, he talked of how, before he rejected the religious beliefs of his youth, "I couldn't think of a distinction between doing things together as a family and being consciously Catholic. It was just a continuum." The Walsingham pilgrimage seemed to represent the continuing alliance between these two institutions, religion and family, a connection now made problematic because he had rejected one half of the alliance. Yet the occasion gave rise to a spontaneous and personal ritual of restoration in which he walked across the distance separating him from his family (as a group of pilgrims) and was reincorporated into the group. His language in evoking the family as simultaneously universal and personal is redolent of the myths and metaphors of undifferentiated tradition for an English Roman Catholic—rural hedgerows, the seasons, timelessness, and pilgrimage itself.[10]

So far then, I have discussed pilgrimages to Walsingham and their (narrated) effects. However, Paul's example also raises one further category of "pilgrim," and moreover one that is commonly neglected in the literature: the sometime visitor who decides to live permanently at the shrine (cf. McKevitt 1991: 93–94). Walsingham, in common with many other places of pilgrimage, has become home to many such people, who often choose to retire to a place that they have visited over a space of many decades. Those whom I have interviewed have sometimes made the connection between the place and a form of sacramentally charged lifestyle, expressing the sense that they wish to remain close to a site associated with Incarnation. A few have also linked their residence in the village with varieties of healing. In the following example, I again show how personal well-being and sacralized place become linked, although in this case it is not related to any experience of travel.

Jane is a talented musician who came to Walsingham as a lapsed Anglican, not because of any religious conviction but because of her marriage. She developed a problem with the movement of one of her arms, which did not respond to medical treatment. When Jane discussed her ailment with a friend, the latter suggested she visit a Roman Catholic priest. Jane was skeptical but, that evening, found that she could move her arm again. When she recounted the story to a priest, he recommended that she should pray, and this she did regularly while in the bath. Soon afterward, something extraordinary happened:

> I got out of the bath and I was going to the 9:30 Mass...in the village every day. I took my dog around the field and as I came back towards the house, we'd had a drought...there weren't any roses on these bushes here, and...I knew nothing about roses, Mary or anything, I'd just had this prayer with her. There was this huge orange rose, as big as my hand, at face level, and it was so stunning.... I thought no more of it. Put the dog in, went down to Mass, knelt down, next to an old chap that I know, [who] put his hand on my arm and said "I've got a message for you from the Holy Mother—you're to pick the rose, and put it by her statue, in your house."

The power of Mary's presence is not expressed here as manifesting in any of the conventional "holy" pathways of the village, but pervades the home. Although Jane did not herself refer to the fact as particularly significant, note that her prayers to Mary took place while she was immersed in water. Although this is a narrative that begins with mention of a healing—restoration of bodily function—the real point of the story is Jane's encounter with Mary and conversion to Roman Catholicism, a faith which, unlike Anglicanism, she sees as connecting her with the "actual" body and blood of Christ—and, of course, with the history of Walsingham. Furthermore, as a musician resident of the village, Jane has had the opportunity to engage repeatedly in the site's material and theological narratives, and it is striking that her story does not end with her conversion. When I interviewed her she had recently sung at a ceremony in the Slipper Chapel, commemorating a new window that had been put in to celebrate one hundred years of revived pilgrimage. Jane talked of being overpowered emotionally by the experience of taking the role of the angel Gabriel in the performance, of feeling a part of a wider whole, and moreover: "I got that feeling, oh Lord, here come the nerves, but once I got in there, I didn't notice that, because it was just so powerful, the holiness was so powerful, and other people have been moved by it too. I'm not saying they were moved by my singing, [they were] moved by the holiness, and I think are considering converting—there were some Anglicans in there—and, it has been said to me, because they felt I think the immense presence of Mary."

Many things come together in this slightly convoluted part of the narrative. Jane feels herself to be a part of the contemporary pilgrimage ceremony, but also part of a wider tradition, a revival that itself leads back to a time when Roman Catholicism was the dominant English faith. Her "part" or "voice" within the ceremony is also a central one within the wider Walsingham (and biblical) narrative, that of Gabriel. In the Slipper Chapel itself, with Mary "present," Jane is not healed as such but she is empowered to conquer her nerves (a common problem for her), and a consequence of the holiness of the experience may be that some listeners are thinking of taking the path that Jane herself once took, away from post-Reformation Christianity and toward a restored, pre-Reformation faith.

Memory and Restoration

Medieval Walsingham followed a standard, if exceptionally successful, Marian pattern for pilgrimage sites. In an age where few reliable medical cures existed, it provided hope for a wide range of ailments, including those that might have been particularly associated with Mary in her role as Holy Mother and key figure within the story of the Annunciation. Contemporary pilgrimage deals with the sick rather differently. They are located within wider narratives of restoration and revival that reflect both the complex history of the site and the place of Anglo- and Roman Catholicism in a secularizing, and skeptical, context.

There are some parallels here with other forms of modern "healing." McGuire (1988: 5) argues that it is a misconception that alternative healing techniques are only resorted to in modern America when all else fails. Most adherents are initially attracted by a larger system of beliefs, of which illness beliefs and practices form only a part. Similarly, at Walsingham practices relating to the sick form a symbolic and ideological continuum with broader notions of Incarnation, rebirth, and material restoration. Pilgrimage combines a series of sacramentally charged behaviors that invoke the physical but also the social bodies of those who come, appealing to the sociocultural concerns of Catholics—of both persuasions—who feel the need to assert their legitimacy within English Christianity. The spiritual problem faced by the majority of these Christians has less to do with confronting physical illness and more to do with the marginalization of their religious culture. Walsingham, dotted by mostly ruined buildings that recall a pre-Reformation past, incorporates architectural symbols of past suffering—even passion—alongside a permanent invitation to restore their spiritual significance in the present, not only through participation in Mass but also through sacramentally charged forms of movement that link significant parts of the village. Dubisch (1995: 170) observes that accounts associated with the Greek Orthodox shrine at Tinos imply that national identity has not been "fabricated" but rather "uncovered" by the resurrection of pilgrimage there, following the unearthing of an ancient icon. Similarly, the Walsingham pilgrimage derives much of its power—for some pilgrims—because it apparently locates contemporary practices within a tradition of English worship whose legitimacy is confirmed by the very facticity of the buildings that have been rediscovered and restored to liturgical life.

For the most part, the desecrated ruins of the village remain ruins, and the bodies of the physically sick pilgrims remain sick, but journeys made at the site provide the opportunity to engage in acts of restoration that orient the person spatially (Csordas 1994: 94), making history come alive through ritual and formal movement. When pilgrims perceive that Mary or Christ truly are present in a landscape that combines personal memory, English identity, and biblical resonances, they are also confronted with the possibility that history need not run on purely linear lines (cf. Dubisch 1995: 154), that the true miracle of the sacramental present is that it can heal the destructive mistakes of the past.

6

Of Consciousness Changes and Fortified Faith

Creativist and Catholic Pilgrimage at French Catholic Shrines

Deana L. Weibel

Scholars of pilgrimage have done much to increase our understanding of this widespread religious practice and its variations. We need, however, to become even more aware of how people with different spiritual and religious beliefs make use of the same shrines. While some pilgrimage destinations, like Jerusalem, obviously hold different meanings for people of different religions, these meanings are often complementary to a degree, with Christians, Muslims, and Jews sharing a common history and certain common understandings about the historical and religious significance of the site. It should be recognized, moreover, that even a shared belief in the healing power of pilgrimage can disguise very distinct understandings about how and why that healing takes place.

This chapter focuses primarily on the distinct experiences of pilgrims to two Roman Catholic shrines in close proximity to each other in southern France. Lourdes, arguably one of the most famous shrines in the world, is known for its allegedly miraculous healings, the devotion of its visitors, and a purported 1858 apparition of the Virgin Mary to young Bernadette Soubirous. Rocamadour is a smaller but still active shrine, well-established in its own vicinity, but with much less global renown than Lourdes. Like Lourdes, it is dedicated to the Virgin Mary, but its church buildings, including its tiny Chapelle de Notre Dame, are all built on a narrow ridge, halfway up Rocamadour's 150-meter-high cliff. Its specific origins are unknown, but it has been an active shrine since at least the eleventh century. The shrine's heyday as a pilgrimage destination was during the twelfth and thirteenth centuries, but Rocamadour is now best known, at least within France, for its beautiful, dramatic location and its proximity to the Dordogne River.

Lourdes attracts pilgrims from all over the world, most notably Roman Catholics from Europe and North America, while Rocamadour, which also draws most of its visitors from the West, receives large numbers of both secular tourists attracted to its beautiful cliff-side setting and religious pilgrims wishing to participate in a pilgrimage tradition that has existed for centuries. Unexpectedly, however, a fair proportion of pilgrims to Rocamadour, while religiously motivated, turn out not to be Catholic.

In my research at Rocamadour, I spoke with many pilgrims who had a decidedly "New Age" interpretation of the site, one often in essential conflict with the way the site is understood by its more traditional Catholic pilgrims. I came eventually to refer to these people as "religious creatives" because of their inclination to religious innovation and the development of new religious syntheses.

I examine here both Catholic and religious creativist schemas associated with pilgrimage, looking at how pilgrimage is understood as a concept, what makes certain sites suitable as pilgrimage destinations, and each group's typical motivations for pilgrimage. I discuss the way illness and healing, both physical and psychological, are conceptualized by Catholics and religious creatives, and how these notions are brought into play during the pilgrimage experience. Both kinds of pilgrims believe that healing can, and does, occur at shrines, but have different understandings about how and why healing takes place. I provide an illustrative case study of each category of pilgrim, a French Catholic and an American religious creative, and analyze what their belief systems and experiences reveal about pilgrimage in each group and about the contested nature of certain Catholic shrines.

Catholic Pilgrimage Schemas

Catholic beliefs about pilgrimage can be determined from a number of sources, including official church writings about pilgrimage, sermons, and what Catholics themselves do and say about pilgrimage. One frequently discussed understanding is that pilgrimage is a metaphor for human life, with the pilgrim making his way on foot through bad weather and worse roads to his ultimate, sacred destination, an image that is usually seen as a symbol for the good Catholic steadfastly enduring life's tribulations until finally reaching heavenly reward. This is a very common view in Christianity, with perhaps John Bunyan's Puritan classic *The Pilgrim's Progress* standing as the best-known literary example. My Catholic informants made consistent reference to this understanding, and it was an explicit part of many of the masses I attended at Catholic shrine sites.

In addition, many Catholics with whom I spoke saw pilgrimage as an inherently Christian act. A pilgrim is understood as someone conducting a holy journey, and it is a long-standing Catholic tradition to treat pilgrims with generosity and respect. In the Catholic pilgrimage schema, references in the Bible, such as Abraham being sent to wander, are held to indicate the desirability of pilgrimage as a pious activity, as are the exhortations of Marian apparitions, who are generally described as pleading with mankind to undertake acts of pilgrimage.

It should be noted that while undertaking a pilgrimage is a chance to demonstrate one's faith in an obvious way, pilgrimage is also a means of taking a break from one's daily concerns while presenting oneself as a pious person. Victor and Edith Turner assert (1978: 7) that for Catholics and other pilgrims, the "point of it all is to get out, go forth, to a far holy place approved by all."

Pilgrimage, of course, is often understood as being more than just a metaphor for Christian belief, a holy activity, and a way to break away from the fixed schedule of one's ordinary life. As we shall see, pilgrimage puts the pilgrim into sacred space, a space where it is believed transformation and healing may occur.

Religious Creatives and Creativist Pilgrimage Schemas

I use the term *religious creatives* to refer to persons whose belief systems can be described as mystical, eclectic, intentionally syncretic, highly personalized and experiential. One name often used for this movement and its participants is "New Age." However, the phrase is so vague as to mean almost anything. "New Agers," in the parlance of popular culture, are those people who believe in any or everything, a plethora of exotic and mysterious phenomena ranging from the benefits of eating organic food to reincarnation, alien abduction, and the healing powers of crystals. Recently, though, the term *New Age* has taken on a derogatory tone, and self-defined "New Agers" have practically ceased to exist. The movement itself can be characterized by its reluctance to be characterized, particularly since its adherents value flexibility and novelty. For the sake of this analysis, however, a name had to be found to refer to participants in this movement. I do not intend "religious creative" to stand as a euphemism for "New Ager," however, particularly since I believe creativism, like fundamentalism, can be understood as a style of religiosity that has been embraced by different peoples at different times. Not all religious creatives participate in the New Age, and not all New Agers can be described as religious creatives.

"Religious creatives" is my modification of a preexisting term, *Cultural Creatives*, originated by Paul Ray in a 1997 article for the marketing magazine, *American Demographics*. Ray classified Americans into several groups, which included Cultural Creatives, an "emerging" group of people that combine "a serious concern with their inner lives with a strong penchant for social activism." One defining characteristic of the Cultural Creatives is their tendency to be "experiential consumers," meaning that they tend to seek "intense, enlightening, enlivening experiences rather than things" and look for travel opportunities "that are adventuresome (but not too dangerous), educational, genuine, altruistic, and spiritual" (Ray 1997: 31, 34). It follows, therefore, that Cultural Creatives seem to hold an interest in visiting the sacred places of any religious tradition that captures the imagination and can find a place within their determinedly open-minded, syncretic, and experiential belief systems.

Religious creatives, then, are Ray's Cultural Creatives in their religious aspect. They are Westerners who see mind, body, and spirit as a single system, who see the earth as sacred, and who seek authenticity and novel experience. Religious creatives tend to believe that "all religions are true," and feel free about picking and choosing among spiritual traditions as though they were modular structures capable of being taken apart and reassembled in pleasing new forms to accommodate individual, personal values.

Among the religious creatives with whom I spoke, pilgrimage was also seen as a metaphor for life, with both pilgrimage and daily living understood as journeys toward enlightenment. As with Catholics, creatives take the view that a journey labeled a "pilgrimage," rather than just a trip or a visit, highlights the spirituality involved in this kind of travel. Creativist literature is filled with descriptions of people's pilgrimages to various locations around the globe and New Age travel agencies generally advertise many varieties of pilgrimage packages.

Religious creatives put a high priority on the freedom associated with their spirituality, and most of the creatives I interviewed felt that "dogma" was a dirty word. Because of their focus on experience, open-mindedness, and responsiveness, the notion of going on a pilgrimage is very appealing. The term *pilgrimage* is, of course, associated with the undertakings of more established religious traditions,[1] and it tends to lend some credibility to creatives' often less-than-orthodox spiritual voyages, adding an affirming air of legitimacy. Moreover, the idea of traveling to different places and expanding one's first-hand knowledge is an especially appealing notion for creatives.

Catholic and Creativist Concepts of Pilgrimage Sites

Although the sites that draw Catholics and creatives would seem to be very different, there is a certain amount of overlap that occurs, based on the tendency of creatives to "borrow" or "co-opt" sites already in use by Catholics. Catholics, however, are much less likely than creatives to make pilgrimages to non-Catholic shrines. As we shall see, even when Catholics and creatives undertake pilgrimages to the same sites, their reasons for choosing these sites are very different.

Characteristics of Catholic Pilgrimage Sites

For Catholics, there are three primary types of locations that are enticing places of pilgrimage. First are sites associated with the actual presence, whether in life or in death, of a particular religiously significant personage. Pilgrimages to Jerusalem, for example, are popular with many Christian denominations, including Catholics. Advertisements for and literature about pilgrimages to the Holy Land are filled with exhortations to walk where Jesus walked, and to experience for oneself the places one has read about in the Bible. Shrines with saintly relics, such as the chapel at Nevers where St. Bernadette's body is displayed, and locales like Fátima or Guadalupe, where apparitions of the Virgin Mary are said to have occurred, also fall into this category.

Next are sites associated with miraculous events. In many, but not all, of these places there is an overlap of sorts. A site may be valued due to the past "presence" of the Virgin Mary as well as because of continuing events that are perceived as miracles. Miracles associated with Roman Catholic pilgrimage sites include the inexplicable cures attributed to the water at Lourdes, the strange scent of roses sometimes experienced at Medjugorje, and other occurrences like weeping statues and rosaries that are said to have turned to gold. Sudden religious conversions at shrines are often also considered miraculous.

The last general type of pilgrimage site visited by Catholics is the site dedicated to a particular saint, often the Virgin Mary. These shrines can generally attract pilgrims without benefit of relics, biblical importance, or miraculous events. Pilgrimage is often taken to these churches and chapels on their saint's day, but not very often otherwise. Frequently these sites are maintained and visited by locals, and draw few from outside the immediate community. An example is the small chapel known as Notre Dame de Fèlines not far from Rocamadour, a place that is generally closed but hosts a small number of guests on Assumption.

It should be noted, however, that shrines attractive to Catholics often combine two or more characteristics of these general types of sites. For instance, many sites associated with saints, such as Marian shrines, were also strongly associated with miracles. The very presence of miracles in certain places is understood, among many Catholics I interviewed, to be the Virgin Mary's way of indicating which sites should, in fact, be visited. Miracles seem to be viewed as a kind of announcement that worship is to be rendered in a place.

Characteristics of Creativist Pilgrimage Sites

Religious creatives have a very different approach to deciding what sites are appropriate destinations for pilgrimage. For creatives, there are two major, sometimes overlapping, beliefs about shrines. One that appears frequently in interviews and creativist literature is that the best sites to visit on pilgrimage are those where the "energy" is especially strong.

While creativist ideas are determinedly idiosyncratic, one basic tenet of the New Age is that the planet Earth gives off energy that is stronger in some places than in others. One of the more frequently expressed ideas is that the earth is covered with "ley lines," a subterranean grid of energy lines analogous to the supposed energy lines in people's bodies accessed by acupuncturists. At places where two ley lines cross, a particularly strong node of energy is formed and "sensitive" people will feel this energy when they get near it. Creatives will often refer to this so-called energy as "life" energy, or "earth" energy, although some New Age authors, like Paul Devereux (1999: 4) in

Places of Power: Measuring the Sacred Energy of Ancient Sites, make an effort to define this energy in terms of magnetism, radiation, ultrasound, and other scientifically accepted phenomena.

The other major creativist belief associated with shrines is the notion that pilgrimage places are locales where a deity, very often referred to as "the Goddess," is especially present. Creativist notions of deity are often tied to notions about the energy of Earth. The planet itself is sometimes considered a goddess, and references to Gaia, as well as Mother Earth, are quite common. This mingling of Earth and the Goddess allow perceived "Earth energy" to also be considered "Goddess energy" and vice versa.

When creatives explain pilgrimage sites as places where the Goddess, in one of her many manifestations, is present, there are some parallels to the pilgrimage schemas of Roman Catholics. For instance, both types of pilgrims may pray to the "Mother" for guidance and may feel themselves to be in the presence of a sympathetic female figure. A creative at Rocamadour, for example, might pray in front of the chapel's statue of the Virgin, and be almost indistinguishable from more traditional Catholic worshippers. However, although the Catholic and the creative will be engaging in superficially similar behavior, their underlying schemas will be different.

Many religious creatives I have interviewed have emphasized their belief that all religions are different paths to the same place. This being the case, holy places associated with any religion are worthy of creativist attention. Moreover, any site dedicated to a divine female figure, whether Athena, Isis, Kali, or the Virgin Mary, is considered an appropriate place to worship the Goddess, since all female divinities throughout history have actually just been different manifestations of the Goddess.

Another common creativist belief is that the earth's energy nodes give off so much energy that spiritual people are naturally attracted to these sites, no matter what their religious persuasion. This account is used to explain why so many Christian churches are built upon the shrines of pagan peoples, be they Druids or Native Americans, and there is often a curious kind of "back-formation," where important Christian sites are assumed to have been pagan holy places without any historical evidence.

Finally, creatives tend to agree that different shrines give off different kinds of energy, and that attraction to a certain locale is an indication that one will benefit from its energy. Creativist photographer Martin Gray holds slide shows featuring images of different sacred places around the world. If an audience member is especially attracted to an image, it is an indication that he or she is meant to visit that particular shrine.

For creatives, suitable sites are any sites that produce this "mysterious attraction," and little effort is made to follow the site's interpretation and use by its more traditional pilgrims. If a creative is especially attracted to a site that does not seem to have been marked religiously by any group, it is generally assumed, once again though back-formation, to have once been a site of worship whose true significance has been forgotten over time.

The same energy that attracts a creative to a particular location or shrine is, in many cases, believed to have the ability to heal that pilgrim. Certain sites are held to possess a strong, inherent energy that may be able to "balance" the pilgrim's own "energies," much as a lodestone can be used to magnetize another piece of metal. Since illness is often attributed to an imbalance in an individual's energies, this rebalancing may in turn lead to healing. Therefore, any place that an individual feels drawn to visit is understood to be a site where healing—whether physical, mental, or emotional—may potentially take place, and thus to be inherently worthy of pilgrimage.

Communitas and Liminality: Catholic and Creativist Motivations for Pilgrimage

Victor and Edith Turner have written at length (1978) about the importance of *communitas* and liminality among the pilgrims they have studied, and when these concepts are examined with respect to the pilgrimage motivations of Catholics, their primary informants, most of their arguments seem to hold weight. Questions may be raised, however, about how well these aspects of pilgrimage fit into the experiences of religious creatives.

Catholic Motivations for Pilgrimage

Communitas is described by the Turners as a quality of full communication or communion between people that spontaneously arises in different situations, circumstances, or groups (Turner and Turner 1978: 250). For the pilgrim, they argue, it is a sense of connection to the other pilgrims that surround him or her, a feeling of solidarity that even extends to pilgrims of the past. My own Catholic informants stressed that when they and other Catholic pilgrims visited traditionally Catholic shrines, they self-consciously sought this feeling of connection to others of their faith who undertook or were undertaking the same journey.

The Turners' notion of liminality is also important in the motivations of Catholic pilgrims. They argue that pilgrimage is a "liminoid phenomenon," meaning that it has traits in common with certain liminal (literally threshold-crossing, i.e., life-crisis) rituals. For instance, both rites of passage and pilgrimage involve a temporary breaking away from mundane existence, the experience of communitas, and a "ritualized reenactment of correspondences between a religious paradigm and shared human experiences" (Turner and Turner 1978: 253–54).

The liminoid aspects of pilgrimage were often apparent in my conversations with Catholic pilgrims, many of whom characterized pilgrimage as a chance to get away from normal life. One striking example of this tendency involved Richard, an elderly French paraplegic, whose sole chance to leave his house each year was an organized pilgrimage to Lourdes. Although he told me he used to pray to be healed there, it became obvious to him that Mary was not going to grant this favor. He continued to go each year, he argued, *"pour s'embeter"* (to give her a bad time), with the hope that she would finally tire of him and send him to be with her son. I was told by Richard's friends that he enthusiastically looked forward to this pilgrimage and always cried when it was time to leave. Even though Richard had apparently given up much hope of being healed, his annual pilgrimage to Lourdes provided him with a chance to escape what he described as a rather unpleasant and frustrating day-to-day existence.

The liminoid belief that one is outside one's normal life during a pilgrimage is often emphasized through the feeling of special closeness to the divine that pilgrims typically experience at a shrine. The Turners have written that "a saint's shrine has a sort of 'hot line' to the Almighty" so that pilgrims often feel that their prayers are more likely to be answered if said there rather than in the places they pray habitually (Turner and Turner 1978: 6). This does seem to have been the case for many of the Roman Catholic pilgrims I interviewed, who felt that it was easier to communicate with Mary while at a Marian shrine.

Another of the most common reasons pilgrimages are made to Catholic shrines by Catholic pilgrims is either to request divine aid in some undertaking or to repay divine aid that is believed to have been received. Medical reasons for pilgrimage are extremely common, with pilgrims often coming to shrines to request cures for chronic illness, to pray for protection for a loved one during surgery, or to give thanks that a disease has gone into remission, often leaving ex-votos, or tokens of gratitude.

In some cases, the act of pilgrimage itself can be understood as a kind of ex-voto, an action, rather than an object, given in exchange for some miraculous favor or cure. I have interviewed pilgrims, for example, who climbed Rocamadour's Grand Escalier on their knees to request assistance for needy loved ones, and pilgrims who had completed many miles on foot to give thanks for some boon that was granted.

Finally, one of the most important motivations Roman Catholic pilgrims have for visiting a shrine is to achieve transformation of one kind or another. Pilgrims I interviewed often spoke of how their pilgrimage strengthened their faith, helping them to realize that they could endure the problems, whether physical, personal, or financial, that they were facing in their lives. Pilgrimage in these cases was a means to self-fortification.

A specific kind of transformation sometimes sought during Roman Catholic pilgrimage is physical healing. A Catholic pilgrim "is not supposed to *expect* any corporeal remedy" (Turner and Turner 1978: 14), but the hope that physical suffering will be curtailed or reduced as a result of pilgrimage is widely held. Some shrines, such as Lourdes, are believed to serve this purpose better than others. Interestingly, as science produces studies showing strong links between mental attitude, faith, and the body's ability to heal itself, the increased faith brought on by pilgrimage is being spoken of by some pilgrims as a very practical health benefit associated with their journey.

Creativist Motivations for Pilgrimage

Religious creatives' motivations for pilgrimage share some similarities with those of Catholics, but tend to follow a somewhat different pattern, one that is far less effectively described by the terms developed in the Turners' analysis of Catholic pilgrimage. For creatives, communitas appears to be a much less important motivation. Creativist groups do exist, but the typical creative has an individualized, self-oriented kind of spirituality, linked remotely or not at all to any institutional base. Thus, a religious creative is less inclined than a Catholic, for instance, to feel himself or herself part of a larger group.

In addition, there are very few, if any, purely creativist shrines, since the essence of creativism is to borrow from or appropriate the shrines of other belief systems. A creative on pilgrimage, then, is rarely in a site founded by, maintained, and controlled by members of his or her own religious inclinations. Instead, sites belonging to Hindus, Native Americans, Buddhists, Roman Catholics, and others are visited, and the creative knows that in such a site, he or she is in the spiritual minority.

Indeed, it appears that when creatives do experience communitas, it is generally with the pilgrimage site's imagined "true" founders, who are invariably described as having beliefs that seem very similar to creativist beliefs. As an example, in *A Pilgrim's Guide to Planet Earth: A Traveler's Handbook and New Age Directory*, Parmatma Singh Khalsa lists the shrine of Lourdes as "a traditional and typical spot associated with the Virgin and natural springs since the most ancient times" (1981: 95). Attraction to Lourdes, then, would link a creative with the "ancient" people who first recognized the spring, not the Catholics who say there was no spring until the 1850s.

Some creatives appear to experience some sense of communitas with a shrine's more traditional pilgrims, but this is generally mixed with a sense that these pilgrims are misguided about the site's real importance. When creatives travel in groups to pilgrimage locales, of course, there is strong mechanical solidarity within the group, sometimes mixed with an "us-against-them" recognition of the group's minority status at the shrine. In any case, a creative's experience of communitas is very different from the communitas encountered by a pilgrim to Lourdes, for example, who may recite "Hail Marys" and "Our Fathers" while surrounded by thousands of pilgrims praying the same prayer.

Liminality, however, is a condition that creatives undoubtedly experience. The creatives I interviewed often spoke of a sense of being "guided" during their pilgrimages, and although this experiential feeling of constant divine contact is commonly reported by them even outside of pilgrimage, its presence was highlighted during spiritual travel. Creatives believe themselves to be stepping outside of their normal lives during pilgrimage, and believe themselves to be transformed. These are understandings strongly linked to their schemas about the "energy" found at sacred sites.

The energy of holy places is often believed to be the reason why these sites are holy. Many creatives feel that being in the presence of this energy has a transformative effect on the pilgrim's soul, and sometimes, by extension, his or her body. While prayer and meditation hasten the process of transformation, creatives claim that merely visiting a site is enough to bring forth positive changes to one's spiritual, mental, and physical core. One creativist pilgrim I interviewed at Rocamadour, for example, complained that the site's secular tourists were weakening the shrine because they absorbed energy while visiting, but gave nothing back in return. According to this schema, proximity leads to energy absorption, whether or not the recipient is aware of what is happening.

The act of spending time at a site to absorb its positive energy, and thereby improve one's own energy, is a process I have termed *basking* due to its similarity to sitting by a fire or lying in the sunlight to absorb heat. The basker occupies a sacred site in the presence of a strong balancing force, a circumstance believed to heighten and intensify the experience and results of any meditation performed at the site. Moreover, even if a person is not aware of the beneficial energy present at a site, healing or spiritual growth may still occur. Basking is one of the most common motivations for creativist pilgrimage, often for the purely practical reason that sacred sites possess much more of this sacred energy than do more mundane locales. If one wishes to be exposed to and/or transformed by this sacred energy, one must go where it is present.

Often the desire to bask in a site's advantageous energies is accompanied by or mixed with the desire to be in the presence of a divine figure or figures, most often the aforementioned Goddess. As beneficial energy is understood to be more present at some sites than at others, the Goddess is believed to dwell more fully in particular shrines. Often these shrines are identified by the presence of feminine images, such as statues or drawings of goddesses or female saints. While some sites believed to possess strong energy are not Goddess sites, most, if not all, shrines dedicated to females are believed to be strong in Goddess energy. The two concepts are very nearly interchangeable, with basking a part of both schemas, and believed, in each case, to result in the pilgrim's healing, energy realignment, spiritual adjustment, etcetera.

Another, perhaps more practical, motivation for pilgrimage among religious creatives is that pilgrimage is, by definition, a religious activity. While Catholics undertake pilgrimage because it is understood to be something Catholics do, both a sign of piety and a way of requesting relief from illnesses and other problems, my religious creative informants sometimes seemed to participate in pilgrimage to emphasize that their spirituality was legitimate and involved the same types of activities, such as pilgrimage, conducted by members of more traditional religions. Because the New Age movement is often questioned, derided, and criticized for its lack of serious religious foundation, creatives occasionally turn to pilgrimage not only as a way to evolve spiritually and enact healing, but also as a way to validate their unorthodox spiritual beliefs by demonstrating that they do things that members of other, possibly more legitimate, religious groups do.

Finally, to echo what has already been discussed about Ray's (1997) Cultural Creatives, one of religious creatives' most driving desires—shared with others, to be sure—is to travel and to experience the exotic first-hand. Pilgrimage puts travel to foreign places into a new light, since traveling for religious purposes is often considered more legitimate than simple tourism, and because the act of visiting an exotic sacred site is thought to actually transform the visitor in some way. In addition, pilgrimage allows the religious creative to expose himself or herself to the religious traditions of diverse cultures, emphasizing the desirable personality traits of open-mindedness and adventurousness and giving the pilgrim a chance to sample from new rituals and beliefs.

Healing Schemas among Catholics and Religious Creatives

Because illness and disease have been historically outside of the direct control of human beings, religious explanations for why illness occurs and how it should be treated are common. Roman Catholic illness and healing schemas tend to follow a certain pattern, at least among those Catholics in Western societies, and these understandings tend to have dramatic differences from those held by religious creatives. What members of both groups tend to share, however, is a belief that faith can lead to healing.

The comments I make about Roman Catholic understandings about illness and healing are based on informant interviews and on information gathered from Catholic documents and rituals. Catholicism is a diverse religion, and I wish to make clear that my characterizations of Catholic beliefs are generalizations based on contact with Catholics from Western Europe and the United States.

Catholic Beliefs about Why Illness Occurs

When discussing the way illness is perceived within a religious context, one of the most basic issues to examine is why illness is believed to occur. Most

Catholic informants I interviewed shared widely held, mainstream beliefs about both physical and mental illness, including the ideas that certain diseases are genetic, that some are contagious, that some may be caused by poor diet, etcetera. This straightforward, scientific understanding of illness, however, was often shared with the belief that people become ill because it is God's will that they do so. Informants frequently used the metaphor of illness as a "cross to bear," noting that suffering was part of human existence, and that the Virgin Mary, and Jesus himself, had suffered greatly.

Some informants with whom I spoke indicated that those who suffer on earth will suffer less after death in purgatory, a view linked to the idea that illness during one's lifetime will ultimately be beneficial. Even among Catholics who disagree with this notion there tends to exist a strong respect for people who gallantly cope with a disease or illness, all the while retaining their faith, as these people are seen as good examples for everyone.

Catholics' religious beliefs also have a bearing on the way they think illness should be dealt with when it occurs. In 1995 I conducted research at Lourdes, interviewing informants about the "miraculous" water located at the shrine and how this water was believed to help the sick. When discussing the possible healing benefits of the water, many informants emphasized that when a person becomes ill, the most important thing to do is to seek conventional medical treatment. At Lourdes, of course, cures are accepted by the church as "miraculous" only after teams of doctors have examined the patient, and their thorough diagnoses and prognoses, which generally rule out divine intervention, are highly respected. Most of the informants with whom I spoke at Lourdes held positive opinions of medical doctors and science in general.

A person undergoing medical treatment, however, is generally believed by Catholics to be helped in his recovery by expressions of faith, such as prayer. A sick person may pray for improvements to his or her health, or to increase the strength of his or her faith in the face of illness. In addition, Catholic masses often have time set aside for "prayer intentions," when the congregation is asked to pray for someone experiencing illness or difficult times. Certain Catholic saints are also associated with specific types of illness, and prayers to those saints are believed to facilitate recovery. While cures the church recognizes as "miracles" are quite rare and generally require that the illness involved be categorized as incurable or untreatable by mainstream medicine, a person recovering from a normal illness who feels that he or she was assisted by prayers or by the intervention of a saint may consider the cure to be at least somewhat miraculous. Dubisch's (1995) *In a Different Place: Pilgrimage, Gender, and Politics at a Greek Island Shrine*, which focuses on Greek Orthodox rather than Roman Catholic pilgrims, very neatly describes this occurrence in a way that applies far more broadly. Dubisch writes that "any answered prayer that changes existing conditions (for example, effects a rescue or cure) could be termed a miracle insofar as it is interpreted as the working of divine power in everyday life" (71). When a person fails to recover from an illness, however, this failure is generally considered to be God's will, and not the fault of the person involved.[2]

Among the Catholics I interviewed, particularly those who participated in pilgrimages, people experiencing illness and disease were generally treated with respect. During the diocese of Cahors' 1997 pilgrimage to Lourdes, for example, about three hundred of the approximately five hundred pilgrims in the group signed on to help the sick, and only one hundred or so of the approximately five hundred were actually ill or injured, meaning that the ratio of *hospitaliers* (caretakers) to *malades* (ill) was close to three to one. The prominence of Lourdes as a pilgrimage site and its impressive accessibility for handicapped and wheelchair-bound visitors also emphasizes the respect many Catholics feel for the ill and infirm.

Catholic notions of healing and ideas about pilgrimage seem to have some significant overlap. Pilgrimage, for the sick, seems to function primarily as an activity that encourages and bolsters faith, and stronger faith is generally believed to improve a patient's ability to recover. From a very practical standpoint, going on pilgrimage can serve as a source of comfort or distraction for a sick person, taking him or her out of ordinary life and into a more exciting or pleasant environment. In addition, pilgrimage shrines are often thought of as being under the guardianship of certain saints, such as the Virgin Mary, and are therefore locales where prayers to these saints seem to believers to be especially likely to result in positive outcomes for specific maladies. Finally, certain shrines with a record of recognized cures, such as Lourdes, mark them as places where healing has taken place, and therefore most likely will again.

Creativist Beliefs about Why Illness Occurs

Creativist explanations of why disease occurs are varied, with anything from poor diet to genetics to germs to bad karma to traumatic past-life experiences being offered as possible explanations. There exists an underlying, almost universal belief among creatives in holism, the idea that the body, mind, and spirit are intricately connected. According to this belief, for instance, stress or unresolved problems can lead to illness, and symptoms such as back pain, headaches, or episodes of depression can be indications of some kind of spiritual trauma that needs to be resolved. In addition, while some creatives express suspicion about the validity of mainstream scientific explanations for illness, others take modern medical causality into account alongside alternative explanations.

When an illness has been determined to exist, creatives appear to approach its resolution with the same do-it-yourself syncretism they demonstrate when customizing their spiritual beliefs. A quick perusal of creativist literature demonstrates interest in such treatments as transcendental meditation, Brazilian trance surgery, Presbyterian sermons, Ayurvedic medicine, yoga, naturopathy, homeopathy, and energy healing.

For most creatives with whom I spoke, physical and mental healing require this kind of openness and willingness to try combinations of unusual approaches. In those cases when a sick person fails to become well, it is generally believed by creatives that this failure is due to the patient not having yet found the correct treatment or combination of therapies to meet his or her individual case. Because so many treatments from so many different societies and cultures are available to creatives, there always seems to be some degree of hope. The idea of resigning oneself to illness when the world is almost literally one's medicine cabinet seems unnecessarily pessimistic.

This attitude, however, puts responsibility for continued illness on the shoulders of the patient. Perhaps one would have already been cured if one had followed an Ayurvedic diet more closely or had managed to meditate with more concentration. The creatives interviewed rarely expressed any idea similar to the Catholic view that some illnesses are just God's will and should be borne with courage, although the belief that a disease may be serving as a means to teach the patient a life lesson is sometimes expressed.

Creativist approaches to healing tend to focus on either the beneficial qualities of herbs and special foods or on the idea of realigning one's "energies" through therapies like meditation on one's chakras or acupressure. Pilgrimage as a therapeutic practice seems to fall into the latter category, with shrines thought of as "points of energy" where the sick person's "life force" can be bolstered or corrected by that of the earth.

Case Studies

The arguments made thus far can be illustrated by two case studies, one of a French Catholic woman (whom I give the pseudonym "Jo") and one of an American creative (pseudonym "Lena"). I met both women at the shrine of Rocamadour, and conducted tape-recorded interviews with each.

Jo was in her early sixties at the time of our interview. She worked at Rocamadour as an employee for the diocese of Cahors and was nearing retirement. A recent but very reluctant divorcée, Jo turned to pilgrimage as a sort of therapy, but had actually had a long history of participation in both group and individual pilgrimages. We met while the diocese of Cahors' 1997 pilgrimage to Lourdes was being organized, and Jo was very active in the pilgrimage's implementation.

Lena, who exemplifies creativist characteristics, was an American from the Pacific Northwest in her mid-thirties. She had visited Rocamadour in 1990, and was so moved and impressed with her experience there that she decided to bring her husband with her on a second pilgrimage to the shrine. Lena was well-traveled and she and her husband were enjoying their adventures in France, but Rocamadour was, and remained, very special to her. I met Lena after one of Rocamadour's tour guides introduced us. When I later asked the guide how he had so quickly identified Lena as someone with creativist proclivities, he shrugged and answered that she was American, wasn't she?[3]

An analysis of each of these cases helps demonstrate the differences between Catholic and creativist pilgrimage and healing schemas, and highlights the way both groups tend to make sense of Catholic shrines. Although my interviews with Jo were conducted in French and my interviews with Lena were conducted in English, I present quotations from both women in paraphrased English here for the sake of consistency.

Jo, a French Catholic

Jo had a long history of pilgrimage participation, but most of it was limited to shrines in France's southwest, such as Rocamadour and Lourdes. Since Jo actually worked at Rocamadour from April through October, she had nearly continuous access to the shrine and its chapel, the Chapelle de Notre Dame de Rocamadour. Rather than taking the shrine for granted, however, Jo used her proximity to her advantage, visiting the chapel every day she worked.

She told me that she would frequently go to the chapel to meditate on her everyday concerns.

In addition to her daily prayers at Rocamadour, Jo visited Lourdes, approximately two hours away by train, at least once or twice a year. Most of her time at Lourdes, however, was not spent in contemplation, but was as a *hospitalière*, a caretaker for ill or handicapped pilgrims. The experience of being a caretaker was described by Jo as being personally thrilling and profound. Jo's need to actively help the sick, combined with a desire for quiet meditation while on pilgrimage, resulted in her generally traveling to Lourdes twice a year, once as a hospitalière during the diocese's pilgrimage and once as a member of a Catholic retreat.

Jo's understanding of what shrines are and why a person participates in pilgrimage were fairly typical for a traditional Catholic. For her, while shrines were often overrun with crowds of people and featured lots of activity, in ideal moments they were peaceful places where she could spend some time alone praying to the Virgin Mary. Both Rocamadour and Lourdes are susceptible to lots of chaos, particularly during the spring and summer months, and so Jo had to carefully choose the best times to pray in front of Lourdes' grotto or rest in Rocamadour's chapel. Another solution she found was to make small pilgrimages to a tiny shrine nearby called Notre Dame de Fèlines. She described this small church as her "*petit* Lourdes," considering it analogous to the larger pilgrimage center because both feature "a chapel, a prairie, and a castle."

This willingness to consider Fèlines a smaller version of Lourdes reflected Jo's tendency to see shrines as basically equal in their importance and power. When asked why she thought the Virgin Mary would have chosen to appear as an apparition at Lourdes rather than somewhere else, Jo replied:

> In my opinion, I think maybe God wanted Mary to appear to Bernadette because Bernadette was the poorest in the country. You saw, or maybe read, how poor Bernadette was. And the Virgin asked her to pray for the sinners. And [the apparitions took place] to renew belief and prayer. And there were miracles. There was a baby who was cured because its mother put it into the water, and so you see, there were a lot of signs. . . . To bring us closer to God, there had to be signs like that. These were all signs.

For Jo, the alleged miracles at Lourdes were intended to prove God's powers and demonstrate the verity of Catholicism.

These sorts of "signs" also seem to be present in Jo's own life. Part of the way God is believed to demonstrate his presence and authority at shrines is through the working of healings and miracles, however small, and Jo had two experiences associated with physical and emotional healing that she considered to be the evidence of divine intervention at pilgrimage sites.

Several years before our interview took place, Jo had found herself struggling with health problems associated with menopause, and surgery was called for. Unfortunately, she was supposed to have her operation right during the middle of Rocamadour's busy tourist season, at a time when neither Jo's financial situation nor her sense of responsibility would let her take any time off. Jo resorted instead to frequent prayer: "I often ask Our Lady to give me strength because I've had health problems for a few years. I had to have surgery, and during the season, I would go to Mary every day and ask her to give me enough strength to last through the season. And I didn't have to have my operation until November...I was hemorrhaging. And I went to the chapel every day, to ask Mary for enough strength to last to the end of the season. And I did." While Jo did not believe herself to have been completely healed by the power of the shrine and the grace of the Virgin Mary, she did feel that her major health problems were kept under control until a more convenient time to deal with them could be arranged.

Jo expressed satisfaction that her strong faith and Mary's intervention had helped her delay surgery, but she was prouder still of an "extraordinary" instance when she believed herself to have been emotionally cured by the Virgin Mary. After 35 or so years of marriage, Jo's husband left her very unexpectedly and she was devastated. A pilgrimage to Lourdes, however, made a dramatic impact on her ability to handle the situation:

> I went into the pools at Lourdes, and I was crying and crying and crying. And the two hospitalières who were there asked me if I was afraid. They thought I was afraid to go into the water. And I said, no, no, I'm not afraid. This isn't my first time here. It's just that I'm in the midst of a divorce. I went into the water with my husband [she means this figuratively, as men are not allowed in the women's side of the pools at Lourdes]. And then I got out, and I had my strength back. I was laughing, I was smiling, and the two hospitalières were crying. And I didn't feel the water. I couldn't tell whether the water was hot or cold, as though I'd never even gone into the water. You can't understand the courage that it gave me...I thought about it afterward, and...I thought about Bernadette, who crossed the Gave

River and didn't notice how cold the water was, and I said to myself that day, I didn't feel the cold water. I was stupefied!... It helped me very, very much. I think about it often. And it's never happened again when I've returned to the pools. I've never had that sensation again.

More dramatic and more inspiring than being able to put off necessary surgery, Jo's experience at Lourdes was the closest she felt that she had ever come to a miracle. She was able to discard much of her sorrow, and metaphorically, her husband himself, in the water at Lourdes and come back out reborn. It is interesting that her experience very closely echoed that of Saint Bernadette, whom Jo obviously saw as a role model. The idea that Saint Bernadette had a similar immunity to cold water in the same location was evidently very salient for Jo.

Analysis

Jo can be considered a traditional French Catholic, with much of her life lived in close proximity to several shrines of varying size and importance. Her schemas for shrines and pilgrimage include the idea that miracles and cures are possible, and can even impact ordinary people such as herself. For Jo, pilgrimage shrines invite pilgrimage because they have been chosen by God, often acting through his mother, Mary, to focus attention on the truth through supernatural signs. Jo's schema for illness, particularly in a religious context, is that illness is something that human beings should bear. Her willingness to delay surgery to continue working throughout the tourist season is evidence of this, as is her dedication as a hospitalière to people who are themselves struggling with illness and injury.

Lena, an American Creative

For Lena, pilgrimage was tied to her desire to travel, and could be understood as a very special subcategory of travel, one that made a strong impact on her life. At the time of our interview she was revisiting the shrine of Rocamadour, a locale she had come across only accidentally almost a decade before. She considered Rocamadour the site that instigated a life-changing spiritual transformation and was eager to show it to her husband, whom she had met since her last visit. Other religious and spiritual sites were important to her as well, such as the ancient dolmens and stone circles she had visited with friends during her initial trip to France. She describes herself as almost being led to travel to certain sites: "There were a lot of prehistoric stone circles and dolmens, so we went to all of them, and it was pretty impressive to be there. It was hard to tell whether it was impressive because people twenty thousand years ago put those stones there, or if it was impressive because of something about that particular spot, as opposed to right next door ...And a friend of mine had given me a stone for good luck. And then we went to these stone circles."

The idea that one is being pulled by or led to particular sites is typical of creatives, who tend to consider attraction to a particular site as evidence that they were "meant" to visit it. There is also nothing unusual, among creatives, about Lena's spiritual involvement with both prehistoric dolmens and a Catholic shrine site. The underlying belief is generally that all spiritual sites are really dedicated to the same energy or power, with some "resonating" more than others for particular pilgrims.

Lena's shrine schema is also typically creativist in that it combines several distinct, and sometimes contradictory, interpretations of what a shrine's true nature is. During our interview she kept restating what it was she felt at Rocamadour, and each restatement took a different point of view. For instance, she thought the site was older than even the Catholics knew: "I'm starting to realize that underneath Christianity, there's an even older religion. Like, maybe where Rocamadour is, maybe before the cathedral was built, maybe it was a site where Druids met, or maybe there was always something sacred about that spot. And so the monks felt it also and built the church there."

This view that Rocamadour had always been sacred was discussed further in her statements that there was something physically unusual about Rocamadour. She said, "I don't know because I'm not a scientist, but I feel like scientists are discovering things about atoms and atomic energy and things are not quite what they seem, so I feel like there's something about the physical structure of the area of Rocamadour that somehow creates a very positive place to be in."

Whatever this energy was, Lena felt that it was capable of having a profound effect on human beings within its range. She explained, "I was in [the chapel at] Rocamadour for a couple of hours. And I felt like I was somewhat transported into a different plane of consciousness. It was like when I'm doing yoga. At the end of an hour and a half of yoga, I'm in a different plane of consciousness."

So for Lena, prayer at Rocamadour and yoga practice led to similar states of consciousness, with her transformed state of mind at Rocamadour apparently brought about by Rocamadour's energy. However, Lena also described Rocamadour as a place inhabited by an anthropomorphic (or gynomorphic) deity of some kind. As she put it: "Basically, for me, Rocamadour boils down to that…I believe God exists, but I don't believe in Jesus suffering for our sins and I don't believe in original sin. I believe God is an entity, not a human being and I relate more to the idea of God in the feminine. And so for me, I believe God exists and I feel that one of her places of manifestation is Rocamadour."

Lena's experience of "healing" at Rocamadour can be described as primarily mental or emotional. Lena was raised as a Christian Scientist, but found her place in her family put into question when she was struck with appendicitis at age seven. Three days after her appendix had ruptured, her family, on the advice of their Christian Scientist practitioner, decided to take her to the hospital. She almost died, but the hospital's medical team was able to save her. Lena's family was very embarrassed, however, and Lena remembered her father throwing away the "get well" cards her second-grade class had sent.

Lena's perception that her family was ashamed of her for calling their religious beliefs into question led her into a very rebellious adolescence. Her family's decision to state that Lena had never gone to the hospital but had been cured by faith alone bothered her, and she eventually rejected Christian Science and her relationship with her family to some extent. By the time she was in her twenties, she was entertaining suicidal thoughts. Lena credits her trip to France, and particularly her "happenstance" visit to Rocamadour, with helping her turn her life in a more positive direction.

The healing experience Lena believes she underwent at Rocamadour seems to have occurred through "basking," with Lena sitting passively in the Chapelle de Notre Dame and receiving and being transformed by the energy that flowed into her. Part of this experience seemed to be a sense of being in some kind of mothering presence. Lena stated, "I think life is really, really hard and how do we make it through? It's amazing. How do we make it through each day? And [in the chapel] I felt…it felt very much like a lullaby almost, to sit and be soothed and be very calm, like [in a comforting voice], "It's okay."

As she was being "soothed" in this manner, Lena also felt that something was happening to her mentally that proved the effect the site and its energy were having on her. She told me, "A lot of times when I'm doing yoga I'll have visions! And I had visions, I can't remember what they were, but I had visions in the chapel. So for me, I knew this was a *very* powerful spot, and a *very* safe spot."

In a letter sent to me after Lena had returned to the United States, she further described her understanding of her experience at Rocamadour: "I just sat in front of the statue and learned about compassion, love, joy, and moving forward in life, even though, inevitably, pain lies ahead as well."

While Lena's second trip to Rocamadour involved her husband and a French friend of theirs, and it was therefore not possible for Lena to replicate her earlier consciousness-changing experiences at the shrine, she was looking forward to another trip to Rocamadour where she could spend some time in solitude. She wrote, "It is so powerful there as to leave me speechless, wanting to be alone in the chapel, sitting in prayer and contemplation until I am satiated. My next visit I shall rent a motorcycle so that I can make my own way to Rocamadour, on my own time."

Analysis

Lena can be understood as a fairly typical creative, combining an interest and belief in a variety of spiritual phenomena (deities, energy, Druids, yoga, etcetera) into a personal and constantly flexible religious system. Contradictions are built into the creativist style, so it is not surprising that Lena's certainty about whether she was praying before a feminine entity or in the presence of a physical structure charged with some mysterious atomic energy tended to waver. In any case, Lena's pilgrimage schema seemed to lead her to understand that, at Rocamadour, she was in the company of some overwhelming yet safe, powerful yet soothing, being or energy, and that this being or energy was able to change her consciousness, emotions, and mind while she sat passively, meditating and praying in its presence.

The healing Lena experienced can best be described as emotional or psychological, and something that was definitely needed for her to be able to move on with her life. Although she expressed recognition that life would always have both pleasant and painful moments, she did not feel that there was anything honorable about suffering, and strongly disliked the emphasis that Christianity places on the suffering of Jesus on the cross. For Lena, illness and suffering will occur in life, but rather than tolerating them or denying them (like her Christian Scientist family), Lena's approach was to recognize them and combat them with prayer, yoga, pilgrimage, and anything else that would expose her to positive energy.

Closing Thoughts

Scholars of religious pilgrimage must better account for all visitors to the shrines they study, even when these pilgrims seem like odd outliers in an otherwise consistent group. In their Introduction to *Image and Pilgrimage in Christian Culture*, Victor and Edith Turner (1978: 21–22) acknowledge the existence of "countercultural pilgrimages" to Glastonbury that tie prehistoric sites to stories of Atlanteans or "Saucerians" from outer space. Although these beliefs would seem to fit into the "New Age" category, little attempt is made to understand them or fit them into any overlying religious movement like creativism. As a result, more subtle components of these "countercultural" beliefs, such as the view that basking in a sacred site's energy can initiate healing, have been neglected.

In addition, the intentional syncretism of creativist pilgrims has been underexamined in pilgrimage research. The creativist approach to pilgrimage and healing taken by many "New Agers"—who feel that spiritual, mental, and physical transformations can take place anywhere strong energy is present, from the vortexes of Sedona to the Ganges River and Roman Catholic shrines—deserves another look since it has also been seen in other societies and other time periods, such as in ancient Rome, which took up worshipping the deities of many of the peoples it conquered, or in some contemporary Hindu sects.

Religious creativism, like religious fundamentalism, is a style of religious belief. Creatives' syncretic notions about healing and the way the universe works appear to be spreading and becoming more mainstream as time passes. It should not be surprising, therefore, that the practice of pilgrimage has also responded to the impact of creativism, and that pilgrimage sites around the world have begun to be increasingly used as places for prayer and healing by people with creativist proclivities.

7

Healing "the Wounds That Are Not Visible"

A Vietnam Veterans' Motorcycle Pilgrimage

Jill Dubisch

In May, 1996, I and my partner made a motorcycle journey across the United States in memory of a man we never knew.[1] The man's name was Vincent Trujillo, and he had been active in the motorcycle pilgrimage called the Run for the Wall, an annual journey of Vietnam veterans from California to the Vietnam Veterans Memorial in Washington, D.C. Trujillo had died the previous August from AIDS, contracted through a blood transfusion he had received while being treated for cancer caused by exposure to Agent Orange in Vietnam. Thus, while his name was not on the Wall, Trujillo died of the "invisible wounds" he had received during the Vietnam War. The Run for the Wall that year was dedicated to his memory.

"Not all wounds are visible" reads a patch that one rider on this journey wore on his motorcycle jacket. This refers not only to wounds such as those suffered by Vincent Trujillo—the hidden but nonetheless often deadly damage inflicted upon those who were exposed to Agent Orange in the course of the Vietnam War—but also to those no less debilitating injuries to the soul and psyche suffered by many of the veterans who returned from Vietnam. Such injuries have persisted for decades, some of them evident immediately upon the veteran's return, others only surfacing years later. Often grouped under the heading of Post Traumatic Stress Disorder (PTSD), these symptoms of unhealed wounds take many forms: drug and alcohol addiction, flashbacks and nightmares, insomnia, mental problems, and overwhelming feelings of survivor guilt.[2]

135

It is to address these problems, and to address the still unresolved issues that have been the consequence of "America's longest war," that veterans took to their motorcycles for that long cross-country journey in May 1996. This was not an isolated or one-time journey, however; rather it was a pilgrimage that had taken place annually since 1989, and that has continued to the present. In this journey, Vietnam veterans and their supporters—spouses, family, friends, and others interested in the cause—ride from California to Washington, D.C. This journey, the Run for the Wall (or simply "the Run"), leaves the West Coast in mid-May, crossing the country in ten days and arriving in Washington, D.C., the Friday of Memorial Day weekend. On Sunday of that weekend, the group joins a large motorcycle rally called "Rolling Thunder," which parades from the Pentagon parking lot through downtown D.C., ending up at the Wall.[3]

But the objective of the journey does not lie only in the destination. All along the course of this cross-country pilgrimage the Run is joined by riders who will make all or part of the journey. Participants are greeted in small towns across the "heartland of America" with ceremonies, meals, and entertainment. For many of the veterans who take part in the Run, it is the welcome they receive in such communities that constitutes much of the healing power of this pilgrimage.

While healing of individual wounds of war is a major purpose of the Run, it has an explicit political purpose as well, for it seeks to call attention to, and to rally support for, the prisoner of war/missing in action (POW/MIA) issue.[4] In calling attention to the plight of those still unaccounted for from the Vietnam War, and of those who, some believe, are still alive as prisoners of war, the Run protests what the participants see as the U.S. government's abandonment of those who fought in that war. By extension, it also addresses that government's perceived neglect of veterans' issues in general, including treatment of PTSD and the damage caused by exposure to Agent Orange.[5] While commitment to the POW/MIA issue varies among participants, the fact that one is riding for others, and not simply for oneself, is an important dimension of the healing process. The Run also seeks to reconstruct the memory of Vietnam, both for participants and for those encountered along the way, and in so doing, to create a positive image and identity for veterans.

The Run for the Wall began as a spontaneous event. In 1989, a group of biker veterans decided to ride to the Vietnam Veterans Memorial, both in support of bringing home all those Americans still unaccounted for in Vietnam and, as one of the organizers put it, "to say good-by" to their comrades whose names were on the Wall. This ride was originally planned as a one-time event. But the reception that greeted the riders in the communities where they stopped along the way was so overwhelming and unexpected, that, as the same individual put it, "We knew we would have to do it again." And so the Run for the Wall has become an annual pilgrimage, increasing in numbers over the years and moving from a small group of friends to an organization with a board of directors and a Web site. Though the pilgrimage alters its route somewhat from one year to the next, it still always makes the cross-country journey in time to arrive for the Memorial Day weekend every year. And the Run has now added rituals of memorialization for those killed in Afghanistan and Iraq, as well as support for soldiers fighting there and for those who have returned, many of whom are already experiencing some of the post-conflict traumas with which Vietnam veterans are all too familiar.

The Run for the Wall is not the only pilgrimage to the Vietnam Veterans Memorial; both individual and collective pilgrimages have occurred from the time of the memorial's dedication. However, several important features of the Run make it unique among such journeys, not the least of which is the fact that it is made on motorcycles. Before examining some of these features, I first discuss some of the background of the Vietnam war and the reasons it has left so many "invisible wounds," wounds that still, thirty years after the war's end, can cause those who fought grief and pain that are sometimes startling in their freshness and intensity. To watch these veterans break down in uncontrollable grief as they confront the names of dead comrades at the Wall, or to hear the stories of those who are unable even to contemplate visiting this moving national shrine, makes it clear that for these veterans, the war is far from over.

Remembering and Forgetting the Vietnam War

The controversy over the Vietnam War has lasted longer than the war itself. Although direct military involvement took place over a fifteen-year period, the battle over the meaning of the Vietnam War has now gone on for more than forty years (coloring even the 2004 presidential election). Unresolved conflicts over the meaning of the Vietnam War have created what Kristen Hass (1998:1) characterizes as "a restless memory that continues to haunt the

American imagination." For those on the Run for the Wall, it is not only the historical meaning of the Vietnam War that is contested, but also what it means to have fought in that war. For many of these biker veterans, their goal is to build an identity and a sense of themselves that is free of the negative assessment that both they and others have had of them for having participated in the Vietnam War.

From the beginning of its entanglements in Vietnam in the 1950s, the U.S. government was unable to establish a solid public consensus that the war in Southeast Asia was necessary for U.S. national security. Moreover, many American soldiers and American civilians had difficulty making strategic sense out of U.S. military policy there. A recurring theme in first-hand accounts by Americans who served in Vietnam, regardless of what they felt about the overall purpose of the war, is the incomprehensibility, and sometimes seeming lunacy, of U.S. military strategy there. And because the Vietnam War ended badly, it provided no good foundation for a unifying narrative about the war. Instead, disagreements that began in the 1950s over America's role in Vietnam continue today. The failure of U.S. military efforts in Vietnam threatened a core American belief—the conviction that the United States was invincible—and in doing so, it created a crisis of meaning for many Americans, and particularly for many of those who had fought in that war. Was the Vietnam War fought for "just" purposes, to protect freedom both at home and abroad? Or was it simply a vast military blunder with no defensible moral or strategic purpose?

For the men and women who fought it, these conflicts over the Vietnam War are more than academic debates. They are struggles over the meaning of a significant, and often defining, period of their lives. Conflicts over the meaning of the Vietnam War have become struggles over their understandings of themselves. As one veteran on the Run put it, "When I went over, I was John Wayne. When I returned I was a piece of shit." How can such veterans create a sense of pride and self-respect for having served their country when the country preferred to forget the war in which they fought? How can they find meaning in the death and destruction they witnessed when to this day the country has been unable to create a meaningful national narrative about that war? And for many combat veterans, perhaps the worst question of all: Why did I survive when many of my comrades were killed? Questions such as these link the larger political conflicts over the meaning of the Vietnam War with the private needs of Vietnam veterans, particularly those who are still struggling to create a sense of themselves that allows them to come to terms with having once fought in an unpopular war.

The search for a new narrative about the Vietnam War is part of the motivation that leads veterans and others to join the Run for the Wall. Through political action and healing rituals, the Run provides an opportunity for its participants to find answers and to fashion new meanings about the Vietnam War, about the Americans who never returned from Southeast Asia, and about those who returned but never heard someone outside their own families say, "Welcome Home."

On the Run for the Wall, one way to create an acceptable collective memory of the Vietnam War is, in the words of a T-shirt we saw several times on the Run, to "forget the war" but "remember the warrior." Thus, nearly all of the rituals and much of the conversation on the Run focus on those, living and dead, who fought the war, rather than on the reasons for which the war itself was fought. Public ceremonies on the Run remind us of the dead and the missing, the need to heal the wounds of war, or the honor due to Vietnam veterans because they served their country when asked. The favored memory is that of soldiers doing their duty, not of a nation torn by conflict. "Forget the war, remember the warrior" messages demand that the nation accept the full human consequences of sending men and women to fight wars, including those wars that were lost.

Yet, for most of these Vietnam veterans, remembering the warrior also means revisiting the horrors of war. This includes facing the damage done to youthful optimism and idealism in a conflict where friends were killed in battles that seemed to make no sense, and remembering again their return to a divided society that could not welcome them home. Making sense of one's own role in the Vietnam War also requires making sense of the deaths of comrades, and honoring them as fallen warriors. The Run for the Wall provides a space for such memorialization and for the expression of grief, a grief that is often closely tied to survivor guilt. "My name should be up there," is a comment we have heard from a number of veterans as they have faced the long line of names engraved upon the black granite surface of the Wall.

Because the particular conditions of the Vietnam War provided little context for grieving, this added to the difficulty of coping with the sudden deaths of close friends. Most of the dead were whisked away from the combat zone as quickly as possible and the bodies flown back to the United States. Bodies left in the field might be used as booby traps by the enemy, or as bait for ambushes, or be mutilated or degraded, adding to the horror of the death of comrades. In addition, little space was provided in the combat zone for mourning, and the expression of grief was not encouraged. As psychologist Jonathan Shay notes (1994:63): "American military culture in Vietnam regarded tears as dangerous but above all as demeaning, the sign of a weakling, a loser. To weep was to lose one's dignity among American soldiers in Vietnam."

For many veterans we have met, it is the Wall, and not the individual graves, that is the focus of this mourning. It is at the Wall that they confront the reality of the deaths of comrades. It is there that they leave offerings. It is there that the dead speak to them and there that, as "Wall folklore" has it, one brings back the soul of a dead person by touching his name. And it is there that finally they can shed the tears that many have not been able to shed before. It is for these reasons that the Vietnam Veterans Memorial is such a powerful magnet for pilgrimage. And it is its capacity to define a space and place for the expression of unhealed grief that makes it such an important therapeutic focus for the Run for the Wall's healing mission.

In addition to the need for healing and for mourning, the issue of whether POWs might still be held captive in Southeast Asia and the goal of identifying and repatriating the remains of every American MIA have provided a motivation for joining the Run and a concrete way for some Vietnam veterans to begin constructing new, more acceptable memories about the Vietnam War and their role in it. By devoting energy to a movement on behalf of POWs and MIAs, veterans can find what Robert Jay Lifton terms a "survivor mission" (Lifton 1992), a task that gives purpose to having escaped death while friends and comrades died. Focusing attention on POWs and MIAs as *victims* of the Vietnam War also helps construct an image of all those who fought as heroes rather than as villains or failed warriors. If the war can remain a current issue through a focus on POWs and MIAs, there is still time to redeem the experience. Hence the POW/MIA issue plays an important role in the individual and collective redemption that is part of the Run for the Wall's healing process.

At the same time, not all those who participate in the Run for the Wall are motivated by the need for healing, by a commitment to the POW/MIA issue, or even necessarily by a desire to visit the Wall. We have met a number of participants in the Run who joined simply because it was an exciting motorcycle event, a chance to take part in a cross-country ride with a large group of fellow bikers. For many of these individuals, their transformation from riders to pilgrims came in the course of the journey itself. For Vietnam veterans, such a transformation often comes as a result of the memories— and the pain—that participation in the Run evokes. Often these individuals were unaware that they even had any need for healing; they thought Vietnam was behind them, that they had "got on with their lives." The rituals of commemoration performed during the course of the journey, the conversations with other veterans, and the visits to the various Vietnam memorials along the route all serve to reveal the unhealed wounds from the veteran's past and to commit him to the Run as a pilgrimage. For the nonveteran participating in the Run, the events can create a similar sense of commitment, whether to the POW/MIA cause, or to the support of veterans, or both. ("I wasn't there, but I care," reads one T-shirt from the Run.) In the process, bikers who had simply joined the Run as a lark become dedicated pilgrims who may return to the Run year after year.

Whether they join with an explicit mission in mind or not, many participants nonetheless have come because, like pilgrims to other special places, they have felt a "call" (cf. Weibel, this volume). "I saw a flyer in my local Harley shop and I just felt I had to come," is a typical response we received when we asked people why they joined the Run. Or "as soon as I heard about it, I knew I had to go." In addition, a number of veterans have been urged to go by wives, friends, and other Run participants who felt that the event could provide some sense of healing for the still unhealed wounds of the Vietnam War. Thus, not all pilgrims on the Run begin their journey as such. It is through their experience of the journey itself that their transformation takes place.

A Typical Day on the Run for the Wall, 1998

It is hard to oversleep on the Run. The group departs from its overnight stop at 8:00 every morning, but many of the riders arise well before that, at 5:00 or 6:00.[6] The roar of Harleys warming up at the motels and campgrounds where the Run participants have spent the night is more effective than any alarm clock in getting everyone up and ready for the road.

It is day three of the Run and we wake up in Gallup, New Mexico, to a chilly but sunny morning. In an efficient routine that is the result of several years' participation in the Run, we dress, pack and load our Honda Gold Wing, then head for the KOA campground where the Run is to gather for departure. Turning into the entrance to the Gallup KOA, we wheel our bike into the row of bikes lined up for departure. Today we are riding near the front of the pack, next to our friend R.C., one of the Run's several chaplains, and directly behind the Missing Man formation, which honors those who never returned from war. Then we head for the picnic tables where the other riders are gathered. As on most mornings of the Run, a free breakfast is provided for the riders by local individuals and groups, in this case by the management of the KOA. This morning it is coffee and breakfast burritos. We eat, chat with our fellow riders, and greet friends who have just arrived to join the group.

At 7:30 that year's Run leader calls us all together for a riders' meeting. As he does every morning, he reviews the rules of the road. There will be 150 or more of us riding together for several hundred miles that day, for the most part two abreast and in tight formation, and safety is of the utmost importance. The leader reviews the day's itinerary, thanks those who have hosted us in Gallup, and makes various other announcements. We have the day's raffle drawing, with half the money paid for tickets going to the Run. Then R.C. gives a blessing, after which the leader shouts, "Five minutes!" and the riders scramble to mount their bikes. With a loud blast of horns, the group is off, through the town of Gallup with a police escort and out onto the interstate, headed for Albuquerque.

As we speed down the highway, gripped once again by the rhythm of the road, the roar of the bikes, and the wind in our faces, the day begins to warm up. At our gas stop in Grants, New Mexico, riders shed jacket liners and other warm gear in preparation for the increasing heat that we know lies ahead of us. Just outside Albuquerque we stop again, briefly, waiting for our escort of Albuquerque motorcycle police to arrive to escort us through the city. They are an impressive sight when they arrive, over twenty uniformed police mounted on white Kawasakis. We admire their precision and skill as they lead our over one hundred motorcycles safely and expertly through the intricacies of the I-40 and I-25 interchange and across several lanes of heavy traffic to our exit just north of the city. We have arrived safely for our lunch stop at Chick's Harley-Davidson of Albuquerque, where a free lunch awaits us—as well as the chance to shop and attend to the various mechanical needs of our bikes.

From Chick's, we head north, climbing into the mountains of the Sangre de Christo Range and toward Santa Fe. At the Santa Fe exit we leave the highway to thread our way through urban traffic, a harrowing journey with several close calls, despite our Santa Fe police escort. Another police escort takes us through the small but sprawling town of Espanola, and then we are free of traffic and beginning our climb toward Taos. We ride staggered now, as we wind our way along the beautiful Rio Grande gorge, and for a space of time rare on this intense journey, we can enjoy the scenery around us and the graceful swaying of the ride as the road curves between high rock walls.

Just south of Taos we turn and here the road becomes more difficult as it first climbs and then descends in a series of heart-stopping hairpin turns made all the more intimidating by the fact that we must negotiate each of them in such close proximity to other motorcycles. At last we emerge onto a straight flat road that stretches across a high, wide green mountain valley toward the aptly named tiny town of Eagle's Nest. Here, in this beautiful remote place surrounded by snow-capped peaks, stands one of the Run's most moving stops—the Vietnam Veterans' Memorial at Angel Fire. Its chapel is visible from the road, a white wing of a building perched on a hill part way up the valley. As we turn up the road to the memorial, other bikers waiting at the top wave and greet us, exchanging heart-felt hugs with the incoming riders as they park and dismount in the memorial's parking lot.

The Angel Fire memorial was built by physician Victor Westphall, who lost his son, David, in Vietnam in 1968. Until his death in 2003, Dr. Westphall would wait each year in his wheelchair to greet the riders as we trooped inside the memorial to partake of the refreshments that awaited us and to visit the museum filled with pictures and other artifacts of the Vietnam War. (Dr. Westphall's grave now stands on the hilltop next to the memorial.) But it is the chapel, furnished only with simple descending rows of seats and a large cross, that draws our attention on this and every other ride we have made to Angel Fire. For many of the veterans we have encountered on the Run, it was this stop at Angel Fire that first awakened memories of Vietnam and began their healing journey. And for my partner and me also, though we were not veterans, Angel Fire was the place that first impressed upon us the power of this highly emotional pilgrimage. During our first Run for the Wall in 1996, this little chapel was filled with the voices of biker veterans singing "Amazing Grace" at a memorial service for Vincent Trujillo, the biker veteran who had died the previous year from Agent Orange. Although services have not been held in the chapel during succeeding Run visits, we always pay a visit to the chapel, along with a few other riders who come to leave an offering at the foot of the cross, to shed tears of memory, or simply to sit in quiet contemplation in the chapel's peaceful interior.

The afternoon has turned cloudy and cold here high in the New Mexico mountains, and the darkened skies and damp air threaten rain. The group of now quite weary bikers mounts up for the last leg of the day's journey, out of the valley and further down the mountains into the little town of Cimarron. With warnings to be careful of gravel on the road and to watch out for deer that will be starting to graze along the roadsides at dusk, we set off.

Our reception in Cimarron is typical of the welcome extended to the Run in the small towns that make up what is often referred to as "the heartland of America": dinner at the local parish hall, greetings from local officials; coffee, juice and doughnuts at our send-off in the morning; a group picture that is taken every year by a local photographer. Although a local bar has brought in a band for the occasion, there is little partying that evening by the weary (and mostly middle-aged) bikers. One after-dinner drink and we ourselves are ready to stumble off to our motel room and to bed for a little sleep to prepare us for the next day's ride.

Although each day has its own characteristics, its own events, its own landscape, its own sensations and emotions, this day has been typical of the rhythm and routines that make up this cross-country pilgrimage. But although they play a role, these rhythm and routines do not by themselves make this journey a pilgrimage.

The Run for the Wall as Pilgrimage

We are sometimes asked why we refer to the Run for the Wall as a "pilgrimage." The simplest answer is that this is the term the participants themselves use. At a deeper level, however, the term pilgrimage is justified by the inclusion in the Run for the Wall of many, if not all, of the elements characteristic of any "classic" pilgrimage. At the heart of a pilgrimage, after all, is the idea of a journey, and at the heart of the journey is the idea that traveling to a different or special place will bring about a change in one's life, in one's viewpoint, in one's state of being.

The only thing that differentiates the Run for the Wall from classic forms of pilgrimage is that it is not based in a particular religious tradition. But pilgrimage need not be religious. The Run for the Wall might be termed a *secular pilgrimage*, that is, one that takes place outside a specific religious tradition, and that does not have as its goal a religiously defined destination such as a famous shrine or miracle site.[7] This does not mean, however, that such pilgrimage cannot have a spiritual dimension. The Run for the Wall, in addition to incorporating Christian rituals (such as morning prayers before each day's journey), also includes Native American and even some New Age spirituality, as well as a more general sense of spiritual mission.

Several features mark the Run for the Wall as a pilgrimage: the separation from ordinary life, the journey made under conditions of danger and hardship, the rituals performed along the way that recall the dead and the missing, the sense of liminality created by the roar of a hundred or more motorcycles as they journey across the country, and the power of a sacred destination. Pilgrimages are often transformative, and this is characteristic of the Run as well, for it seeks to transform public consciousness of veterans and of the POW/MIA issue, as well as to effect healing in the individuals who participate.

While the POW/MIA issue is the ostensible public focus of the Run, it is the Run's nature as a healing pilgrimage that draws many to participate in it. Moreover, this healing has in recent years come to encompass more than healing of the wounds of the Vietnam War. One veteran wrote the following to the Run for the Wall Web site:

> We are on a mission to ensure that our POW/MIAs are not forgotten. We are on a mission to help the victims of all wars to recover from their injuries. The wounds that we help to heal are the ones that no one can see. They are the emotional wounds from the losses that have occurred as a result of military service. Many times participants are not even aware of the impact of those wounds, until they participate in RFTW [the Run for the Wall]. Not every one who participates can go all the way to the WALL. Regardless of their level of participation, they experience the healing that occurs on this mission.

Before turning to a discussion of how the Run serves to heal, however, I want to examine an important element of the Run for the Wall as pilgrimage: the fact that it is made on motorcycles.

Among the groups that offer support and hospitality to the Run in the course of its journey are various motorcycle groups and veterans' organizations. In addition, there are biker clubs whose membership is composed solely of Vietnam veterans, or, in some cases, in-country combat veterans only, which also participate in and/or support the Run. And while certainly not all, or even a majority of, Vietnam veterans have taken to motorcycle riding, and only a minority of bikers are veterans, still the proportion of Vietnam veterans who are bikers is disproportionate within the general population.[8] An examination of why this is so gives some clues to the ways in which the Run for the Wall functions as a healing pilgrimage.

Among the combat veterans who returned home from Vietnam in the 1960s and 1970s were some who shared certain important characteristics with the "hardcore" bikers of that era. Both groups were small and socially isolated. Both were patriotic and pro-military, although not necessarily progovernment. Both were strongly focused on the notion of freedom, an important concept among bikers. Both believed deeply in the idea of "brotherhood," which creates bikers' sense of community and solidarity.[9] For these reasons, many Vietnam veterans who had been motorcycle riders before the war, or who were drawn to motorcycle riding after it, found a comfortable social world within the world of biker clubs, a world that reflected some of their own experiences and world view. And it is from the blending of the values and rituals of these veterans with the values and rituals of this biker subculture that the Run for the Wall was created.

The concept of brotherhood is undoubtedly one of the attractions of biker culture for Vietnam veterans. It is a world where they can relive, in some form, at least, the bonds of brotherhood and shared risk that they experienced when they were young warriors. Among Run for the Wall riders, the ideals of brotherhood include giving other riders any assistance they might need in dealing with a disabled bike, giving money to those having financial problems getting to D.C. or back home, and most importantly, providing emotional and moral support for riders troubled by wartime memories, the pain of wartime losses, or fear of seeing the Wall.

In addition to a common devotion to freedom and brotherhood, biker and military subcultures also share certain symbols and rituals. For both bikers and soldiers the *parade* is the primary vehicle for displaying their unity, coordination, and power. For bikers, their parade is the *run*. While there may be fun involved, runs typically are organized to serve a serious organizational or political purpose. In the case of the Run for the Wall, the political purpose is the POW/MIA issue, which gives many of the riders a "survivor mission," a way of focusing their energies on the behalf of others and relieving, to some extent at least, the survivor guilt that afflicts so many veterans we have encountered.

But there is more to the attraction of motorcycling than a sense of camaraderie and commitment to a purpose. Many of those who ride the Run for the Wall see motorcycling as an inner journey that can deepen their understanding of themselves and, at the same time, put them in touch with the world around them. For at least some of the Vietnam combat veterans who ride the Run for the Wall, this inner journey is not about self-development; it is about psychological survival. For them the road is where they find temporary peace as the roar of the wind and the thunder of the bike overwhelm the voices from their past that make peace of mind rare and precious. These moments are not a luxury; they are essential. One Run regular, whose post-Vietnam life has been a long struggle against the physical and emotional wounds left by the war, put it this way, "I ride my bike to stay sane. The last time they let me out of the loony bin, I got this bike. It's just about the only thing that makes sense to me. Without it, and the stuff I take for pain, I'd be locked up somewhere again." Another Run for the Wall rider whose high-stress career collapsed with the onset of PTSD nearly a quarter century after he left Vietnam put it this way: "When I wasn't working I was out riding my bike at one hundred miles an hour in the dead of night. It was all that kept me together. It was the only place I could escape the pressure. When I couldn't take the stress, I'd go out and ride." In such cases, the motorcycle is both escape and therapy for those still struggling with the aftermath of their Vietnam experience.

It is important to note that motorcycle riding is an intensely physical and absorbing experience, a feature that ties the Run for the Wall to many other pilgrimages (including a number discussed in this volume) in which the pilgrim's body becomes the means and locus of both pilgrimage and healing, and may be subject to hardship and sacrifice in the process. In addition, the bodies of Run participants may also become representations of their goals, beliefs, and identities through T-shirts, patches, pins, and other emblems that, in common with biker culture more generally, are used to decorate the outfits worn by participants in the Run. Such items express political opinions, display slogans of biker culture, demonstrate support for veterans and their causes, commemorate one's military service, and (through display of annual patches or wearing of T-shirts) bear witness to the duration and frequency of one's participation in the Run itself.

Healing the Veteran

Participants in the Run speak of their pilgrimage as a journey of "healing." However, the wounds of Vietnam that afflict the participants in the Run are, for the most part, not the obvious ones. Rather they are less visible ailments such as PTSD, the effects of exposure to Agent Orange, addictions, guilt, anger, and loss.

It is useful here to make a distinction between "curing" and "healing," with "curing" referring to the effects of the biomedical system, which eliminates or corrects the source of the biomedically caused "disease."[10] "Healing," on the other hand, is a broader concept that involves dealing with the psychic, social, and cognitive consequences of disease or trauma and restoring the patient to emotional, psychological, and/or social wholeness. A number of the veterans on the Run for the Wall have had extensive contact with the dominant medical system, especially through VA hospitals, as they sought help for physical and psychological problems that are the consequences of their war experiences. Few of them can be said to have found a "cure" for their most troubling problems. The Run for the Wall provides a support group that offers its participants healing for "the wounds that are not visible," including grief and loss, guilt, alienation, PTSD, and other effects of participation in the Vietnam War. Such healing may thus take place in the absence of what the medical system might term a "cure." This support group differs from the therapy groups in which some veterans have participated in VA hospitals in several respects, the most important of which is probably the ritual nature of the Run as a pilgrimage journey.

While the therapeutic effectiveness of rituals has long been acknowledged by anthropologists and others, the exact means by which rituals heal is often unclear. One view sees rituals as healing through a process of catharsis, which is "the key to successful ritual" (Walter 1993: 82). The release of emotion, it is argued, brings both psychological relief and physical healing. As part of this process, healing rituals may first heighten the anxiety of the person being healed, increasing the power of the emotional release. Thus, the veteran on the Run for the Wall feels increasing anxiety and pain as the Wall draws closer, climaxing in the painful confrontation with the Wall itself and with the dead whose names are inscribed there. With tears streaming down their faces, veterans locate the names of dead comrades on the Wall, and lay their offerings beneath the names, or wander the Wall's length, seeking to absorb the tragedy of over fifty-five thousand names engraved in the polished black granite. Others, unable to bear the pain, collapse on nearby benches, accompanied by supportive friends. The pain is highly personal and individual, yet collective as well, as participants from the Run support and comfort each other during this difficult confrontation.

However, while catharsis may be one element of ritual healing, it does not completely explain the process. Nor is the journey to the Wall, even in the company of other veterans, all that is involved in the healing. In one case study, for example, a group of Vietnam veterans suffering from PTSD was taken from a VA medical center by bus to the Wall. While according to the various psychological tests administered to these vets before and after the visit, there was some improvement in their condition, this improvement was apparently not lasting (Watson et al. 1995). To judge by the accounts of Run for the Wall participants, the Run for the Wall is a more effective healing process than the more straightforward visit to the Vietnam Veterans Memorial recounted in this study. There are several reasons for this.

First, the Run is a ritual, and rituals have a particular power often not found in other forms of therapeutic activities. Second, the Run is built around a set of American cultural symbols with powerful, positive meaning for many of the vets: the "welcome home" offered to veterans by communities along the way, the riding together with other veterans and supporters, the commitment to the POW/MIA issue, and the ceremonies performed in the course of the journey that commemorate the veterans, the dead, and the missing. As Thomas Csordas states, "The key to the therapeutic effectiveness of systems of religious healing is precisely this ability to reorganize or restructure the conceptual worlds of people who are ill" (1983: 346). On the Run, such "restructuring" involves, in part, the replacing of the veteran's hostile homecoming reception with the positive "welcome home," and of shame at having fought in an unpopular war with a sense of pride. Third, because it is more than a one-time event, the Run is able to sustain a sense of brotherhood and community among many of its participants beyond the actual duration of the pilgrimage.

In various ways then, the Run for the Wall is similar to other support groups, such as Alcoholics Anonymous. Such groups often address physical and psychological problems that cannot be addressed by the society's conventional systems of healing (including the western biomedical system). Individuals involved in such groups are often socially marginal in one respect or another, or are in difficult situations in which they feel they have little control over their lives. An extreme example of the marginalized veteran is the one who "comes out of the woods" to join the Run, an image often evoked by participants. Although a few of the vets on the Run fit this image literally, others have reported being almost as socially isolated before they joined the Run. (They are, in the words of one Run organizer, "MIAs—Missing in America.") On the Run, such individuals find themselves with others who have had similar experiences and who can provide the suffering individual with understanding and support. In addition, through association with the group, a person is offered a framework of meaning within which suffering can be understood. And finally, when the support group includes participating in some extraordinary experience, whether it is entering a trance state, walking over hot coals, or riding a motorcycle across the country, sufferers can achieve a sense of self-worth and empowerment, thus "moving...from a negative state of illness to a positive state of health through a persuasive rhetoric of empowerment and transformation" (Danforth 1989: 7). Like individuals in other societies who become lifelong members of their ritual therapy groups, many of those who participate in the Run for the Wall feel the therapeutic need to return for the Run year after year. However, the Run differs from most other such therapy groups in that, while it is concerned with individual healing, it is focused on a collective experience (the Vietnam War), rather than on purely individual experience (such as childhood trauma), as the source of the individual's problems.

Vietnam, Healing, and the Construction of Meaning

Central to the healing process is the construction of meaning. Many of the young men who fought in Vietnam had their faith in themselves—and the values of their culture—shaken by the experience. As one veteran traveling to the Wall put it, "You're taught to believe in God, you don't harass anyone, you don't kill...You have some values, and all of a sudden it just don't mean nothing" (Battiata 1984). As psychologist Jonathan Shay points out in *Achilles in Vietnam* (1994: 31), "The most ancient traditions of Western culture instruct us to base our self-respect on firmness of character," and we want to believe that our own moral courage will hold firm even under the most difficult circumstances. Such a belief in their own good character was challenged by the actions many soldiers found themselves committing while in combat situations, creating the fear that such actions might in fact represent their *real* character.[11]

Once the veterans returned home, their belief that those who fought in defense of their country would be warmly welcomed was challenged by the indifference or sometimes hostility with which many of them felt they were received. Many veterans report that civilians they encountered didn't really want to hear about the war, even when they themselves asked the vet what it had been like "over there." In addition, behaviors that had been appropriate, necessary, and even commendable in the combat conditions of Vietnam were regarded with disgust and horror by many civilians back home.

A number of Vietnam veterans suffered a variety of obvious physical and mental problems following their return from the war: drug and alcohol problems, broken relationships, PTSD, the effects of Agent Orange, and so on. On the other hand, a number of the veterans on the Run have told us that they had "got on with their lives" after returning home, and that for many years they felt there was nothing to confront or deal with from their Vietnam experience. Often it was some particular event that awakened memories and emotions of that experience and thus brought them to participate in the Run for the Wall. This event might be a physical or mental breakdown, a life-altering event such as a death or divorce, "mid-life crisis," or an encounter with a place or situation connected with the war that broke down the barriers that had been built against such memories over the years. Seeing the news of the dedication of the Vietnam Veterans Memorial, for example, had such an effect on many veterans.

To these difficulties is added the lingering—and often surprisingly fresh—grief that many of these veterans still feel for their dead comrades years after the war's end. Moreover, many Vietnam veterans harbor strong feelings of guilt, not only guilt over acts that they might have committed while in the heat of combat, but also guilt that they "failed" to save dead comrades. In some cases there is guilt that, while they served in Vietnam, it was in noncombat roles, such as clerks and support personnel, which did not expose them to the dangers experienced by those in combat. And many suffer simply from "survivor guilt," that they have lived to go on with their lives when so many of their comrades did not.

How does the Run for the Wall address these issues and how does it seek to heal these "invisible wounds"? It does so, in part, by constructing a new narrative of the Vietnam War and of those who fought in it, a narrative that seeks to make meaningful the confusing and traumatic experiences that often defied such meaning. An early writer on what was at the time called "traumatic memory" points out that memory is an action: *"it is the action of telling a story.*... The teller must not only know how to do it, but must also know how to associate the happening with the other events of his life, how to put it in its place in that life history which for each of us is an essential element of his personality" (Janet 1925: 662). Such stories can be part of a shared cultural identity, such as the identity veterans can develop *as* veterans. John Braithwaite, in his analysis of cultural communication among Vietnam veterans (1990: 164–65), refers to these stories as "myth," not in the sense of myth as falsehood, but as a speech form that "provides speakers with a way to apply and express significant aspects of their cultural identity." These stories deal with a variety of phenomena common to many, if not all, veterans (not just experiences of the war, but veterans' homecoming, dealing with the VA, marital problems, etc.), and place such experiences in a common cultural milieu. The self is thus fit into a larger narrative.

Recent discussions of the role of narrative in experience have suggested that there cannot even *be* "experience" in any meaningful way unless we can construct a narrative. This narrative, however, is constructed in a cultural context. If there are past experiences that are difficult or impossible to talk about, it may be not so much that language is inadequate, or even simply that memory is too painful, but rather that "sometimes there are situations or events...that are the occasions of 'experiences' that cannot be expressed in the terms that language (or, more broadly, the symbolic order) offers *at that moment*" (van Alphen 1999: 26). Such a situation has been reported for Holocaust survivors, as well as survivors of individual rather than collective trauma, and has also been a problem for Vietnam veterans, many of whom felt unable to talk about their war experiences. Part of the reason for this is that the Vietnam War itself "had no conventional narrative structure—a war without a clear beginning or end, without well-articulated goals, fought sometimes with scant regard for geographic boundaries, and indeed, remaining undeclared, technically not a war at all" (Allen 1995: 94). Because the Vietnam War lacked a recognizable narrative structure, that is, a way to talk about it that fit with stories of other wars, many veterans found it hard to tell others about what they had experienced.

The Run for the Wall thus offers veterans a "symbolic order" in which a narrative can be created, and in which experience can be articulated and reclaimed. Through participation in the Run, veterans and their supporters create meaning out of psychological and emotional pain, and a new narrative is articulated that seeks to integrate the Vietnam experience into individual and collective biography. But this new narrative does not begin at an intellectual or cognitive level. It begins with the highly sensory act of motorcycle riding. The long motorcycle ride across the country and the successful arrival at the Wall take physical and psychological suffering and translate them into physical (and psychological) accomplishment. Painful emotions and memories may be aroused in the course of the journey, but they occur in the course of a pilgrimage that demands attention and skill, and in the company of others who can provide understanding and support.

But there is more involved in ritual healing than physical accomplishment and somatic mastery. As things come together in bodily motion, so they come together in a cognitive way as new structures of meaning are created. For the veteran on the Run, suffering is due to the experiences of Vietnam and the resulting trauma. Part of the trauma, at least for some, was the controversy over, and opposition to, the war on the home front and the lack of a positive reception upon the veterans' return. Part of the therapy of the Run for the Wall, then, lies in the ritual "welcome home" that is received on the Run, both from fellow veterans and from noncombatants and communities along the way. Individual suffering becomes transformed into meaningful shared experience, and is made even more effective by the rallying of communal support. The veteran is not just a wounded suffering individual who feels inadequate because he has not been able to adapt or cope after his experience (or because after leading a "normal" life he finds himself in midlife reliving his trauma), and not just someone experiencing a personal problem or defeat. Rather, he is a returned warrior who, with self-sacrificing patriotism, fought for freedom, and who, betrayed by the government that sent him to fight and the citizens he fought to protect, is finally receiving some of the recognition he deserves. The slogan mentioned earlier sums up an important part of this construction of a new narrative of the war: "Forget the War, Remember the Warrior." This slogan declares that we should put the controversial politics of the Vietnam War behind us and instead focus on those who sacrificed to fight in that war and are still suffering its consequences.

A final word needs to be said about the ultimate goal of this pilgrimage—the Vietnam Veterans Memorial in Washington, D.C. "The Wall" plays an important role not only in constructing the pilgrimage itself—it is, after all, the *Run for the Wall*—but also in the process of healing for many veterans. It is clear from the conversations of Run participants that they view confrontation with the Wall, however emotionally difficult it may be, as an essential part of the healing process. And the Wall plays its own part in the construction of the Vietnam narrative, for part of the power of the Vietnam Veterans Memorial lies in its ability to absorb, reflect, and inspire multiple meanings. As Sellers and Walter (1993: 189) suggest, it "is one of the few war memorials … that allows, yet does not force, repentance for our part in the war as well as honour for those who died." The memorial is both a place that evokes pain and one that helps to heal. Here the dead can be mourned, and pain and grief given expression and form, regardless of one's view of the rightness or wrongness of the Vietnam conflict, or of war in general.[12] And it is here that the Vietnam veterans end their long, cross-country pilgrimage and confront their past, a painful encounter that is both the culmination of their journey and, for many, the beginning of the process of reconstruction and recovery.

Embers, Dust, and Ashes

Pilgrimage and Healing
at the Burning Man Festival

Lee Gilmore

*B*urning Man is one of the most fascinating and intensely creative cultural phenomena to emerge at the end of the twentieth century. An annual festival of art, ritual, performance, community, and fire, Burning Man has taken place in northwestern Nevada's Black Rock Desert since 1991, and is now attended by over thirty-five thousand individuals from around the globe. During the week preceding Labor Day (late August/early September) an extraordinary temporary metropolis springs to life on the barren desert floor. Laid out on a semicircular grid of streets that stretches more than a mile from end to end, "Black Rock City" features distinct neighborhoods of "theme camps" and "villages," as well as a phenomenal array of art installations.[1] In addition, Black Rock City proudly offers basic civic amenities, including an internal peacekeeping force of "rangers," medical services, several "alternative" daily newspapers, dozens of "pirate" radio stations, and a central cafe. At the heart of it all is the infamous "Burning Man" itself—a forty-foot effigy of wood, neon, and pyrotechnics that serves as the central locus of the city's design, and which is ceremonially and spectacularly burned, marking the traditional climax of the event.

The realities of survival in the desert are also very much a part of the Burning Man experience. The Black Rock Desert is an extremely harsh and arid environment, with temperatures that range from a sweltering one-hundred-plus degrees during the day to a bitter forty degrees overnight. Rainstorms, dust storms, and winds up to seventy miles per hour are not uncommon. To

155

this ancient lakebed—a four-hundred-square-mile expanse of flat hardpan alkali called the "playa"—participants are required to bring everything they need to survive, including food, shelter, and at least two gallons of water per person per day. This desolate landscape invites the imagination to populate its open terrain, as participants create a mind-boggling array of expressive projects, producing a visual contrast between emptiness and abundance. The desert evokes a potent imagery of mystery, abstraction, and limitlessness as well as of hardship, sacrifice, and solitude that creates a context for an esoteric experience in a quasi-mythical setting.

Among the most consistently reported experiences shared by participants in Burning Man is that of transformation—thousands of individuals have journeyed to this desert festival and returned with the feeling that their lives have irrevocably changed in ways that foster personal and cultural healing. People come to Burning Man seeking experiences beyond the commonplace and the commodified, and most are not disappointed. Many participants return to the desert year after year, seeking to reach beyond ordinary consumer lifestyles and corporate cultures, and to connect with alternate expressions of self within community. In this annual voyage, participants enact a kind of pilgrimage, typically defined as, "a round trip journey undertaken by a person or persons who consider their destination sacred" (Smith 1995: 841). Yet Burning Man participants do not typically view Black Rock City as sacred in the same way that, for example, a pilgrim to Lourdes or Mecca would. Nevertheless, the journey to Burning Man is experienced and described as a pilgrimage by many participants, and also bears many of the standard characteristics of rites of passage. Therefore, I prefer to think of pilgrimage as a (1) ritualized journey to a (2) specific, culturally imbued geographic location intended to (3) connect individuals to a collective experience of (4) something beyond their ordinary existence, something perhaps sacred, transcendent, healing, or transformative, however the individuals and communities involved choose to conceive those ideas, and that (5) can emerge in either religious or secular contexts.

My analysis shows that in many of its features Burning Man invites comparison to Victor Turner's theories of ritual process in general and pilgrimage in particular. Building upon the foundation laid by French anthropologist Arnold van Gennep (1960), Turner (1967; 1969; 1974) is well-known for his conceptualization of three distinct phases through which participants in rites of passage are said to progress. The first phase is *separation* from the mundane world into the *liminal realm,* described as a special space and time betwixt and between the sacred and the profane. Liminality is also characterized by an experience Turner called *communitas,* which is marked by feelings of communal unity and egalitarianism that disrupts the *structure* of conventional hierarchical relationships. The final stage, according to Turner, is *aggregation,* whereby one returns to the mundane or secular world, yet with the new status or experiential knowledge gained through the rite.

Noting that the traditional liturgy and sacraments of his own Catholic faith offer little in the way of the sort of liminal experiences identified in field work with the Ndembu, Turner and his wife looked to the phenomenon of pilgrimage in the Christian world where they perceived the processes of liminality, anti-structure, and communitas as more readily identifiable (Turner and Turner 1978). They argued that the traditional journey and hardships encountered in a pilgrimage to a sacred site served to create the necessary conditions in which to encounter the *liminoid* through separation from one's daily life and community, to an encounter with a miraculous and divine sacred center in the context of a shared common experience with other pilgrims, and finally, through the reentry into society with renewed or enhanced status. Within pilgrimage, the Turners identified the following attributes of liminality in passage rites:

> Release from mundane structure; homogenization of status; simplicity of dress and behavior; communitas; ordeal; reflection on the meaning of basic religious and cultural values; ritualized enactment of correspondences between religious paradigms and shared human experiences; emergence of the integral person from multiple personae; movement from a mundane center to a sacred periphery which suddenly, transiently, becomes central for the individual, an *axis mundi* of his faith; movement itself, a symbol of communitas, which changes with time, as against stasis which represents structure; individuality posed against the institutionalized milieu; and so forth. (Turner and Turner 1978: 34)

Here, I examine the ways in which those who attend the Burning Man festival enact a pilgrimage that shares many of these attributes, mirroring Turner's theories. By performing a collective journey to a space between the worlds of the ordinary and the extraordinary, participants are frequently marked by transformations that reach deeply and unexpectedly into their lives in an enduring fashion. Although most Burning Man participants I spoke with did not typically gloss their experiences in terms of "healing," they did frequently refer to experiences of profound life transformations, the effects of which ripple out into their lives beyond the festival. In this sense, many participants can be said to experience various manifestations of personal, spiritual, or psychological change and healing. Participation in Burning Man does not generally entail a quest for physical healing, but rather engages with a more holistic desire to heal or transform the total self, as well as to heal and transform society. As Meredith McGuire found in her study, *Ritual Healing in Suburban America*, many of the increasingly popular alternative healing practices engaged in by middle-class Americans, "provide very important functions for their adherents: meaning, order, and a sense of personal empowerment" (1988: 14). It is this sense of meaning, order, and personal empowerment as a way to heal the total self—mind, body, and spirit within diverse and particular cultural and community contexts—that Burning Man may provide for participants. This includes a perception on the part of many individuals that some degree of cultural transformation and healing is possible through the agency of Burning Man, as participants take the experiences and ideologies encountered at the event out into wider social spheres.

This analysis examines the heterogeneous nature of Burning Man by investigating participants' narratives and through exploring some of the ritualistic facets of the event that contribute to personal and cultural healing. At the same time, this analysis recognizes that not all participants experience this festival in ways that neatly replicate Turner's theories. My research draws on nine years of participation in the festival itself, as well as within San Francisco Bay Area–based communities that have emerged among those who have attended, and also in Internet communities related to Burning Man that span the globe. This includes numerous conversations and interviews with several participants and key organizers, as well as an online survey of Burning Man participants conducted in the summer of 2004. I will return in greater depth to the themes of ritual, pilgrimage, and healing but must first further contextualize the background and outlook of the festival.

History and Ideology

The humble beginnings of this event as an informal gathering of friends on a San Francisco beach in 1986 fail to suggest its subsequent phenomenal growth and success. A man named Larry Harvey, working at the time as a landscape carpenter, arranged an informal get together with some friends on summer solstice eve to build and burn an eight-foot-high wooden humanoid figure.[2] Harvey insists that he had no consciously preconceived ideas about the "meaning" of this act, despite the legends that have since accumulated around these origins.[3] The impromptu gathering immediately attracted a number of onlookers who spontaneously found ways to participate in the moment with music and dance, and as an enjoyable time was a had by all, they decided to do it again the following year. By 1988, approximately 150–200 people joined in and the effigy became "officially" named the Burning Man. By 1990, the event's popularity had outstripped the resources available to a free beach party. The local park police stepped in to prohibit burning the Man, now a towering forty-foot figure, and the approximately 800 people in attendance grew restless and unruly. At this point, organizers teamed up with the San Francisco Cacophony Society, a group of pranksters and artists notorious for organizing "situationist happenings," many of whom had already been attending the event in recent years. The event was reorganized as "a Zone Trip" to the Black Rock Desert.[4] The original invitation read:

> An established Cacophony tradition, the Zone Trip is an extended event that takes place outside of our local area of time and place. On this particular expedition, we shall travel to a vast, desolate white expanse stretching onward to the horizon in all directions... A place where you could gain nothing or lose everything and no one would ever know. A place well beyond that which you think you understand. We will be accompanied by the Burning Man, a 40-foot tall wooden icon that will travel with us into the Zone and there meet with destiny. This excursion is an opportunity to leave your old self and be reborn through the cleansing fires of the trackless, pure desert. (Cacophony Society 1990)

As one of these original travelers described it, "The Zone was some other dimensional place, it could be the past, the future, something weird, it didn't matter. We were going there, and we would challenge it and be better for it" (Brill 1998). Thus, the suggestion that transformation was possible through this collective journey was built into the earliest concepts and evocations of Burning Man.

Fewer than one hundred individuals made the trek to the desert that first time, but the event proceeded to grow exponentially over the next several years. In 2004, nearly thirty-five thousand individuals attended Burning

Man. After successfully contending with numerous external and internal challenges stemming from the event's remarkable growth, the organizers of the event formed the Burning Man LLC in order to provide a measure of financial and social stability. This organization now employs several full-time salaried staff, including a communications manager, a community services manager, a site manager, an administrative manager, and a curator, among others. There are also numerous part-time and contracting staff, in addition to the several thousand volunteers that help make the event happen.

There are doubtless as many ways to frame the experience of Burning Man as there are participants and individuals to experience it, and this inherent heterogeneity is built into stated goals. Although the continuously evolving annual festival has several ritualistic features, there is very little in the way of an "officially" prescribed or "correct" way to engage in and experience the festival. Individuals are explicitly encouraged to create their own categories and frames of interpretation and to find their own meanings. As one long-time participant (and former organizer) wrote, "Burning Man employs ritual, but it is ritual removed from the context of theology. Unhindered by dogma, ritual becomes a vessel that can be filled with direct experience. Burning Man is about having that experience, not about explaining it. In fact, if you can explain it, you're probably not paying attention" (Mangrum 1998).

Despite this refusal of prescribed meaning, there is nevertheless a cultural ethos and distinct ideology connected with the event that encompasses principals of personal, social, and environmental responsibility. For example, festival attendees and organizers have adopted certain slogans that encourage responsible and engaged participation, such as the Bureau of Land Management's motto "Leave No Trace," intended to educate attendees about the importance of meticulously cleaning up their camps as well as the entire event site at the festival's conclusion.

Burning Man also enforces a strict policy against vending and commodification that sets it apart from other festivals on this scale, such as the Rainbow Gathering, the new Woodstock concerts, or Neo-pagan festivals such as the Pagan Spirit Gathering (See Niman 1997; Pike 2001). With the exception of ice and coffee, the proceeds of which benefit the local communities of Gerlach and Empire, Nevada, no products are offered for sale during the event. Although many corporate entities have approached the organizers, they consistently refuse all offers of corporate sponsorship, and most participants would react very negatively to such commercialization. Participants are even encouraged to cover or creatively alter the logos and brand names on the items that they bring with them to Black Rock City. Burning Man does charge an entrance fee (in 2004, between 175 and 350 dollars, depending on date of purchase) to help cover the enormous costs of organizing an event of this nature in the middle of nowhere.

Consumer researcher Rob Kozinets (2002) has examined the ways in which Burning Man simultaneously resists and participates in traditional market economies. Noting that participants must necessarily engage in commerce with corporate interests in order to obtain supplies to bring to the event, he also observes that once they have arrived at the festival site itself they distance themselves from corporate consumption and refuse market logics in favor of gift giving and obscuring products' brand-name origins. He concludes that "rather than providing a resolution to the many extant social tensions in contemporary life—such as the one surrounding markets logics, their beneficial and oppressive elements—it offers a conceptual space set apart within which to temporarily consider, to play with and within those contradictions. It falls short of some ideal and uncontaminated state, but it may be all the consumer emancipation most consumers want or need" (36).

In opposing corporate consumption and commodification, Burning Man organizers prefer to describe the event as a "gift economy" in which participants are inspired to share of themselves as a way of participating in the larger community. In this way, Burning Man participants engage in what Lewis Hyde (1979) has described as an "erotic" commerce, that is, a gift-giving economy based on relationship, attraction, and union, that binds communities together by creating ties between individuals.

The most often stated value at Burning Man is "No Spectators," reflecting a community ethos that strongly encourages attendees to be actively engaged as "participants" in the event, rather than to remain distant as passive spectators. This injunction is also reflected in most of the event's other core values, including the expressed ideals of both "radical self-expression" and "radical self-reliance." As Larry Harvey explains,

> Self-expression might be anything. We don't dictate that. What we do ask, however, is that participants commune with themselves, that they regard their own reality, that essential inner portion of experience that makes them feel real, as if it were a vision. I like to say that visions aren't defined by light which falls upon them, but that they shine forth with their own light—they radiate outward, they

illumine the world, they redefine reality. No one can say what that vision might be. We just ask people to invent some way of sharing it with others. (Van Rhey 2000)

By expressing this inner vision through art and performance, Burning Man participants engage in a process of self-reflexivity that mirrors some core inner aspect of themselves and that engages dialectically with the dominant culture. This can be seen in the incredible range of costuming that is displayed at Burning Man, as individuals "perform" a host of cultural symbols—horned "demons," winged "angels," and blue-skinned "faeries" are not uncommon sights. Others perform their inner vision through creating and/or participating with interactive art installations, while others demonstrate their commitment to community by volunteering for the event.

Participation in Burning Man is also encouraged through the stated value of "radical self-reliance." On one level, this emphasis means simply that participants must bring all of their own supplies to the festival. Yet this is also seen as having additional significance for both the Burning Man community as well as for society at large. Harvey has proposed that, "the celebrated doctrine of 'radical self-reliance,' by which participants are vested with complete responsibility for creating their personal visions within a severe natural environment, promotes a high degree of collaboration" (Van Rhey 1999). Elsewhere, he has theorized that, "if you're going to survive in the coming world, you're going to have to learn radical self-reliance in an environment like this and then take that self-reliance and turn it into connection with other people, and then turn it into connection with the whole universe out there" (Harvey 1998). Thus, "radical self-reliance" is not intended to breed isolation, solipsism, or greed, but rather to encourage individuals to turn that self-reliance outward by sharing of themselves in the context of the greater community, and thereby supporting the goals of Burning Man's key ideological tenet—participation.

Performing Ritual, Enacting Pilgrimage

One prominent and endlessly creative form of participation at Burning Man is through ritual. Although ideally stripped of dogmatic content, ritual is an explicitly encouraged aspect of the festival. Some ritual aspects of Burning Man are silly and irreverent while others are quite serious; most encompass a mixture of motivations. The most conspicuous ritual feature in which nearly all festival attendees participate is "the Burn"—the conflagration of the Burning Man effigy itself—which marks the traditional climax of the event. The wooden figure is elevated on a platform (itself an increasingly elaborate work of art in recent years), lit with multicolored shafts of neon, and filled with pyrotechnics designed to explode in a carefully orchestrated sequence.

During the days and weeks preceding the annual burn, the community's collective levels of excitement and anticipation rise, fostering heightened expectations and charging perceptions of the moment with elevated significance. One participant told me of the Burn's importance in his own experience, saying: "In the beginning, the Burn was complete catharsis. The first time, I had no idea what to expect.... For one, it was so different from the rituals that I knew—my Bar Mitzvah was nothing like this! The drums, the night, the flames, the spectacle, combined into an intoxicating whole. When the Man burned, you knew that something was happening. Shit was coming down. The old, the heavy, the burdensome, was going up in flames." Many participants will toss an object into the central fire of the Burning Man itself, as a form of personal sacrifice, or as a way to symbolically release a burden or pain that they no longer wish to endure. The same participant quoted above also told me of the unexpected potency he had discovered in this simple ritual act:

> When we begin, as dusk falls on the night of the Burn, we begin to concentrate on what is to come and enter what some might call a sacred space. Energy is focused on a ritual that has more meaning for me than any other during the year, with the possible exception of Passover. It started by writing things that we wish to get rid of in our lives on pieces of paper, pouring in gunpowder and wrapping them around with—what else—duct tape. After the Man burned, he fell into a long, heaping bonfire.... We threw in the packets, and with them went whatever we had written. In the weeks and months to come, I would think of the things that I had written and watch for them. The ritual made me more aware.

Fire rituals have also been performed with many other artworks. A series of especially moving examples were the Temples created by artist David Best—the Temple of Tears (2001), the Temple of Joy (2002), the Temple of Honor (2003), and the Temple of Stars (2004). Constructed of intricately cut plywood (remnants of three dimensional skeletal dinosaur puzzles) in 2001, 2002, and 2004, and by elaborate papier-mâché in 2003, each manifestation of the Temple was intended to be a chapel-like structure in which participants were invited to congregate to honor loss and remember the dead. As the artist conceived the piece, the first incarnation of the Temple was intended as "a place where participants can commemorate, remember, venerate, bid farewell, excoriate, exorcise, celebrate, and above all, honor those whose loss has moved them. Parents, friends, loved ones, ancestors, the unborn, those who chose to exit this plane by their hand . . . in short anyone who has had a loss and that means everyone, is welcome to pause and meditate on the meaning of pain and loss" (Best and Haye 2001). Although the theme shifted somewhat with each passing year, as reflected in the pieces' changing titles, the ritual intentions and utilizations remained more or less the same. Nearly every available space on the Temples' walls had been inscribed with memorials to the beloved dead, such as "ancestors, guide me in the river of life until I join you," and "Mom, you need no novenas to be in my heart" (Pike 2005). For several days during the event, participants who visited the structure discovered a deeply reverent and introspective space devoted to remembering and honoring the dead. People sat in corners and stood along walls, weeping and quietly contemplating their most personal and painful sorrows. Finally, on the night following the burning of the Man, the Temples have been set aflame. The Temples provided poignant reminders of loss that served to transport participants back to the gravity of the "real" world, while also creating powerful and accessible healing rituals.

Most of the other rites enacted at the festival tend to be smaller in scale, involving individual, personally significant acts, or rites shared by groups of friends and campmates. For example, a simple communal rite took place amongst a group that I camped with during the event in 2000. Several campmates felt that the infrastructure required to host a large "theme camp" at Burning Man had grown unwieldy and unenjoyable, and that the group itself had become uncomfortably large. It was determined that it was time to "kill" the camp and in response, a flag emblazoned with the camp name and logo— a corruption of a well-known corporate brand, Motel 666—was draped atop an empty coffin. The group marched in a funeral procession—complete with a trumpet sounding "Taps"—to the site where the Man had burned on the previous night. A communion of sorts, consisting of a bottle of Jamison's Irish Whiskey and a bag of peanuts (said to have been the only food and alcohol that the original camp founders had brought with them their first year), was passed around the gathered assembly. Individuals stood one by one to say a few words about the history of the group, what "the Motel" had meant to them, and to recognize some of the group's original founders who were not present. Finally, the coffin was ignited with bottle rockets. In this way campmates both reinforced their shared identity as "Moteliers" while also recognizing, releasing, and healing some of the tensions that had emerged within the group.

Beyond these intentionally devised rituals and performances, the very act of making the trip to Burning Man has ritualistic elements, as attested to by one participant:

> Going to Burning Man is rife with ritual, if only because it is hard to avoid the feeling in significant motions repeated at predictable intervals. Even packing, you go through what you took in previous years, patch what needs to be patched, or buy something to make this year easier. There is the simple layer of significance: what you forget to pack, you do not have, and the playa is large, hot, and dry. Moreover, there are the memories that the act evokes from years past. The item you thought lost that was then found, the shirt that you wore when you met so-and-so.

The necessary preparations, often repeated year after year, combined with the journey to a distant and unforgiving environment, combine to give participants a sense that they are performing ritualized behaviors and enacting a pilgrimage.

As noted earlier, Burning Man pilgrims can be readily identified as passing through the stages in a rite of passage—separation, liminality, and aggregation—as identified by Turner and van Gennep. They separate from their mundane daily and usually urban contexts, cross a threshold into the para-urban festival setting of Black Rock City, and return home often with a changed perspective or renewed understanding of themselves in the world. Another commonly described feature of pilgrimages that is readily identifiable within Burning Man is that of hardship and sacrifice. As the Turners noted, "for many pilgrims the journey itself is something of a penance.... But these fresh and unpredictable troubles represent, at the same time, a release from the ingrown ills of home" (1978: 7). Pilgrimages, they argued, tend to be "voluntary obligations" that provide a radical reorientation away from ordinary time, space, and social norms, and thus, "this freedom of choice itself negates the obligatoriness of a life embedded in social structure" (Turner and Turner 1978: 8; see also Turner 1974: 175). By making this journey to the desert, participants undertake varying degrees of personal sacrifice and hardship. In addition to enduring the harsh physical environment of the desert playa, participants often make enormous commitments of time, energy, and money, well above the cost of tickets and supplies, in order to create elaborate art projects and theme camps. It is also worth mentioning that many Christian pilgrimages were historically associated with simultaneously occurring festivals that were often among the real draws for hundreds and thousands of pilgrims (Turner and Turner 1978: 36). With its strong emphasis on playfulness and a healthy dose of decadent display, the carnivalesque aspects of Burning Man can certainly be seen to function within that legacy.

The spatial metaphors inherent in theories of liminality are also entirely applicable here, as seen in participants' actual movement from home to desert and back again. In the early days when Burning Man was a Cacophony Society "Zone Trip," participants actively and literally invoked liminoid threshold metaphors. Upon the group's arrival in the desert, a line was drawn on the ground, across which all participants simultaneously stepped, thus symbolizing their collective entrance into "the zone." As one writer described it, "We all got out of our cars as one member drew a long line on the desert floor creating what we accepted as a 'Zone gateway.' This was one of our Cacophony rituals, for the zone as we defined it took on many forms; it could be a weird house, a particularly strange neighborhood (like Covina, CA), or a desolate, deserted warehouse. Today it was the base of a mountain range in Northern Nevada. We crossed the line and knew we were definitely not in Kansas anymore" (Brill 1998).

Once pilgrims arrive on the playa, they enter into an otherworldly zone marked by a strong feeling of what Turner surely would have identified as communitas. There is a very real sense in which many of the standard hierarchical roles we live with in the dominant culture fall away at Burning Man by means of the shared experiences all must undergo by their presence in the desert and their participation in the festival's rites. In this way, Turner's vision of the egalitarian aura of communitas arising in an encounter with liminality is manifest, as all participants become equal before "the Man" and within nature. Indeed, many individuals cite "community" as one of the key reasons why they go to this festival, and it is also often one of the most pragmatic ways in which individuals take the event home with them. The connections with others that are forged or deepened during the festival often have real and lasting impacts that transform participants' daily lives well beyond the event itself.

Transformation, Healing, and Community

Transformation and healing may or may not be consciously or intentionally pursued by participants who make the pilgrimage to Burning Man, but many do experience profound and real change in their lives as a result of their participation in the festival, transformations that frequently facilitate healing around issues of personal and social identity. One woman I spoke with, who had attended the event for eight consecutive years when I spoke with her in 2000, attested to the ways in which the altered sense of reality and culture she experienced at Burning Man had profoundly transformed her consciousness:

> I realized part of the trouble with the life I have outside of Burning Man has to do with being regulated by a lot of things that are really socially constructed and that aren't true [and] don't matter.... Because so many things can spring up spontaneously [here] you can have all kinds of realizations and insights that you wouldn't have ordinarily in the world. You get to stop and think and move in a different way because it's a different culture out here. I realized I wanted to live my life outside of Burning Man as though I were still at Burning Man, and made a vow like that.... My life has taken miraculous amazing turns that I would never have predicted and never have thought would be likely because of that decision and it came from this environment, it sprang organically from being here.... I went from [working with] computers into teaching tantra and meditation. I decided that I wasn't going to be bound by a lot of social conventions. I decided to experiment and be much more risk taking emotionally in the way that I ordered my relationships, which I don't think I could have done if I hadn't been out here and felt like it's a giant petri dish that I can experiment in. [It's] also [helped me] to remain open to magic and synchronicity and that weird impulse that says "Hey, go do this thing" even though it makes no rational sense to do that.

This sense of being freed of "artificial" limitations was echoed by another participant who told me that Burning Man had changed his life by helping to free him of his own perceived constraints and to transgress some of the social controls imposed by the dominant culture without risking his status as a "normal" and functional person within that society, significantly changing his approach. He said Burning Man gave him,

> The ability to change my life by really feeling in control of it—by facing the stark nature of the site, then challenging myself to not just exist but excel there. The community surrounding me there is self-selected...people interested in what is beyond a mundane, normal existence. [Burning Man helps us see] that *more* can we all be in both taking care of ourselves and then giving beyond the necessary to improve and enrich the lives of those around us.... It is a sacred space that allows a spiritual safety for this kind of personal challenging and experimentation. It is different than your normal surroundings and allows you to be abnormal without sacrificing your safe, normal existence back home.

He went on to say that the power of Burning Man includes, "living on the blank canvas. Being part of the ephemeral art that is painted there has taught me to see beneath some of my layers, my fears and [to] grow brighter as a life force."

Another individual, who lived and worked in Ecuador as a tour guide, told me that before he had gone to Burning Man he had experienced "duality" within himself, and felt that his "urban persona" and "jungle persona" were uncomfortably split. Burning Man, however, gave him the experience he needed to balance these two parts of himself into one, saying "I'm the same person in the jungle that I am in the city now." He attributed this healing to the people and the sense of community that he experienced in Black Rock City, saying that the event provides, "what you really need in life. You get a much clearer vision of yourself, and give in to your inner-childhood and eliminate distractions."

A man who volunteered with the Department of Public Works (DPW), the volunteer group that goes out to the desert a month or more in advance of the event to build the needed infrastructure, relayed a similar story. He told me that Burning Man had given him, "a way to completely shift my world, to force myself to pay attention to myself and really be honest with myself." For him, Black Rock City is

A space where I can practice being a better human, and try to make this world a little better. This place gives me a good testing ground for that. Everything here is accelerated, so much stimuli and so many people that you have to keep moving. It helps me shed layers of insecurity.... In a sense I was drawn spiritually [to Burning Man] because it's a celebration of life.... If a community is an organism, then this is a more healthy organism—all the cells are functioning.

Another and perhaps more surprising instance of an individual whose perspective on life and spirituality was transformed by the event was a young evangelical Christian pastor from the Midwest. His intent in his pilgrimage to Burning Man in 2000 was to distribute five thousand bottles of water and packets of seeds as a "gesture of prophetic witness" (Bohlender 2000).[5] After conversing with several other participants during the event, he discovered that many of his own preconceptions about what lay at the heart of Burning Man had been challenged, as he was profoundly struck by the ways in which the event fulfilled people's need to connect with one another in a community. He returned to find that Burning Man had changed his "personal definition of weird" and had deepened his own relationship to God. He wrote about this in an essay that he initially posted to his church's Web site:

I no longer find it weird when people express themselves in ways I never thought of.... I think God likes our rough, creative ideas better than professional presentation. I have a gut feeling he delights in our most creative attempt to get his attention, because it shows our heart. With this in mind, I find it weird that the church world appears to have been made from a cookie cutter. While worshipping a God that values creativity, the church has managed to squash it at every turn.... Particularly in America, we have homogenized worship to the point where our distinctive, given to us to by God to be celebrated, [gifts] have dissolved into an evangelical unitarianism.... I do find it weird that the church strives to convenience people when people really thrive on challenge. Getting to Burning Man is a challenge, but it's a challenge people rise to. The church in America has done everything they can to remove all challenge from attending, in hopes that if it's convenient, people will stumble into a walk with God.... Let me make it simple for you. Following God, pursuing him, is not as easy as getting to Burning Man. (Bohlender 2000)

In this instance, it can be seen that the transformative power of Burning Man does not necessarily preclude other, even mainstream or evangelical spiritual traditions, and can in some cases even enhance them. This was also the case with the individual quoted earlier who noted that Burning Man provided a far more exhilarating rite of passage than his Bar Mitzvah had, but was of less annual spiritual significance to him than Passover. Yet another individual, a lifelong Quaker, described how Burning Man had changed his life by quoting: "'I will entice you into the desert and there I will speak to you in the depths of your heart,' Hosea 2:14. It happened to me. I won't presume to speak for the meaning for anyone else." He added, "I'm reasonably sure my life would have changed anyway, but Burning Man provided a well-defined vehicle for it."

The Power of Community

Perhaps the most enduring power of Burning Man is manifested in the firm bonds of community that have been formed through the event and that for many continue year round. In asking various individuals how, specifically, Burning Man had changed their lives, I found that one of the most common responses was by way of community. Numerous and overlapping communities have sprung up across the country through networks and friendships formed at Black Rock City, as well as over the Internet and in regional gatherings. Indeed, a number of individuals have gotten married and formed other long-lasting relationships through connections seeded at Burning Man. Some individuals reported that this sense of community had been largely absent in their lives before going to Burning Man, and in creating and sustaining these communities, many experienced a kind of healing.

One participant told me, "It has changed my life by introducing me to a group of creative people. I have a community of friends who I am in contact with all year through the Internet and gatherings." Another woman said, "I found my community, a larger group of kindred spirits than I'd ever expected to find, which makes me generally more open to people." Yet another individual affirmed the positive changes that Burning Man had brought into his life by means of the community he had found there, noting,

> While I did not experience anything like the epiphanies that many
> other friends have—I've seen this happen, but must admit that I did
> not experience that level of change—I was reminded that there are

others out there who don't fit well into the constraints that mainstream society dictates. It *did* restore a community to my life, which had been absent for a decade and a half. This has been a huge plus, in my experience.... I was both reminded and reassured to again be a part of a community where people were close, and trusting of one another, and openly emotional in situations that did *not* involve death or disaster, which is, all too frequently, the only times you tend to see open and honest emotion in most of our society. I'd say that I may be happier about my life and choices in part because of my Burning Man experiences, because a lot of those choices have gone contrary to what I was "supposed" to do, or expected to do.

Through Burning Man, many people who sometimes feel like outcasts in the dominant culture have found a place where they can express themselves, and where their eccentricities can be shared and celebrated. As one participant asserted, "I felt like I had come home. I found fellow freaks to help me fly my freak flag." And yet another participant, telling me about his first experience at Burning Man, said, "It's given me a psychological release unlike anything else. I can be strange and crazy and nobody cares! And if they do, it's *so* fucking positive!"

In some ways, individuals who discover powerful new communities through Burning Man may never completely reassimilate back into mainstream society after the festival is over. Instead, they seek to aggregate their new experiences—which they find to be more satisfying, connected, and holistic, as well as more inter- and intrapersonally healing—with their old realities. They do this by taking the new identities and communities discovered at Burning Man back into the dominant culture with them, and attempting to pass these values through to other parts of our culture.

Cultural Transformation

An underlying theme of the transformational experiences attested to by many Burning Man participants is a sense that the event is culturally transformative as well. Because of the myriad ways in which individuals bring these experiences back home with them, from personal epiphanies to newly forged or strengthened community ties, many participants carry the hope that Burning Man can help to create and sustain possibilities for broader cultural transformations. One such participant says,

Over the last three years Burning Man has proved to me that there is a vital, viable, below-the-radar movement in this culture to recreate society in accordance with human values (as opposed to oppressive corporate values). I look at Burning Man as a training ground for those who wish to survive through, and thrive after, the coming chaos engendered by the downward economic spiral and militarization that has accelerated these last few years. I'm glad, and proud, to be part of that movement; it's a group of people who think for themselves at the same time they're thinking about each other.

Another woman told me that through Burning Man she had

Learned to question society's value system. For example, at Burning Man everyone is a participant and therefore we are allowed to interact with them on a personal level. Why is it that if you say 'hi' to a stranger at Safeway you are looked at like a freak but at Burning Man it is a great way to meet people you may never have had the chance to meet? Also, at Burning Man you are encouraged to be generous and helpful, whereas in society people are too busy for one another and use each other as rungs to climb upon to get higher up their ladders. I also appreciate the Leave No Trace aspect of Burning Man where people are encouraged to take responsibility for their messes. In normal society, we have been programmed to believe that our mess is someone else's responsibility.

Harvey has his own ideas about the possibilities for cultural transformation manifested by Burning Man, and has sought to embed these values into the event by means of shaping its infrastructure and parameters, as well as through publicly articulating his ideas. In one essay, he suggested that

Burning Man is certainly a kind of party, but it is also a carefully crafted social experiment. Talk of community at Burning Man is not merely shorthand for a loosely shared life-style. The physical and social infrastructures of Black Rock City are devised with certain goals in mind. We have tried to create an environment that functions as an incubator of the social process that give rise to human culture and this, by extension, functions as a critique of society at large. This utopian agenda may appear grandiose, but in our actual efforts, sustained over fifteen years, we have employed very pragmatic methods. Every year we literally wipe the blank face of the Black Rock Desert clean, and, unencumbered by historic dispositions of property, power or established social status, originate our world anew. Black Rock City does not exist to illustrate some exalted theory of human nature. Instead, we have worked with human nature, year after year, with the sole purpose of producing a model of society that connects people in a dynamic way. (Harvey 2000)

Harvey concludes this essay with an acknowledgment of Burning Man's personally and culturally transformative potential by proposing that

> The significance of Burning Man extends beyond the event. Burning Man is not confined to the artificial limits of Black Rock City. It is more than an event. It has become a social movement. Very typically, participants found significant new relationships or resolve to undertake ambitious projects as a result of their experience. Just as often, they end old relationships, deciding to get divorced or quit their jobs. The typical statement one hears sounds like a conversion experience: "Burning Man has changed my life," and this is manifestly true. Few remain indifferent or return sated, as from a consumption-oriented experience. These changes also have a larger social consequence. The prospect of thousands of people sharing resources and engaging in highly cooperative, collaborative, and creative endeavors, has inspired many to begin new enterprises or originate their own events. These efforts are extremely diverse, but are based on certain principles participants absorbed at Burning Man. Burning Man, the organization, exists throughout the year and, increasingly, via the Internet, it has become a crossroads for much of this activity. (Harvey 2000)

One of the ways in which the Burning Man phenomenon is successfully reaching out to a broader sphere of influence is through a number of homegrown "spin-off" events. These events are not coordinated by the main Burning Man organization, but rather have sprung to life by various regional communities' desires to continue to live in the spirit of Burning Man throughout the year and in other parts of the country. Among the more established of these spin-off events is an event called Burning Flipside, hosted since 1998 by a group from Austin, Texas, at a private campground outside of Austin over the Memorial Day weekend. Attended by over thirteen hundred people in 2004, Burning Flipside mirrors Burning Man in some of its key features by including theme camps, rangers, and a large effigy at the center of camp that is, of course, burned at the event's conclusion. Other regional gatherings include "SynOrgy" in the western Utah desert, "Toast" in Arizona, and "Playa del Fuego" in Delaware. Some individuals and groups even journey to the Black Rock Desert at other times of the year.

During the summer of 2001, a long-time leader in the Burning Man organization known as Danger Ranger undertook an extensive cross-country road trip in order to engage with various local communities that participate in Burning Man, and to encourage them to start organizing their own regional "Burning Man–like" events. A chronicle of his travels-in-progress was posted to Burning Man's Web site so that people back home in San Francisco and around the world could participate in his journey as it unfolded (see http://roadtrip.burningman.com). As the Burning Man festival continues to evolve over the years, the concept of seeding smaller, derivative events in different areas is seen by the organizers as the festival's next stage. These are just a few of the more tangible ways that Burning Man is manifesting small but measurable effects on society. As individuals continue to be inspired by the event in endlessly surprising and creative ways, the parts have ever more potential to affect the whole.

"Burning Out" and "Burning On"

Despite the significant extent to which narratives of personal transformation and cultural healing are readily discernible in Burning Man, it is also important to remember Burning Man's inherent heterogeneity. Indeed, the event leaves itself intentionally open to divergent interpretations and ways of being experienced. While for many it is a profoundly life-changing and even spiritual experience, others specifically noted the absence of radical life changes or shifts of consciousness as a result of their experiences with Burning Man, and did not generally frame or experience their lives in any "spiritual" terms. For some, Burning Man is only a grand party, an excuse for debauchery and a license for transgressive behavior that is disconnected from any overt sense of "the sacred." This too is just as much part of the overall experience as is spiritual transformation or psychological healing. Individuals are typically disposed to construct their experiences in life within the parameters of their own unique contexts and worldviews.

Even those who have experienced profound life adjustments and transformations of consciousness through Burning Man often outgrow what was once a deeply radical experience. After attending for several years in a row, the festival begins to lose some of its initial magic for those who now know what to expect and for whom the experience has become almost routine. Some formerly avid participants have stopped attending as they have "burned out," and chosen to move on to new interests and life experiences. One woman described her decision to stop attending Burning Man, saying that it had become, "too big, the event interferes with my appreciation for the desert environment, it's losing its impact on my psyche, and it's time to seek new perspective adjustment tools." Another individual told me that he feels there are now "too many people [and] too much spectacle for the sake of spectacle. [I'm] moving on in my own life. I've been involved with Burning Man year-round for the last three years and I want a break." Still another woman, who had been a very active participant and an integral organizer since the event first began trekking to the desert, saw this process as only natural. Individuals, she said, get what they need out of the event and then often reach a certain point where they need to move forward and take that experience out into other parts of the world and their own lives.

It has been argued that pilgrimage is better contextualized as an arena of competing secular and religious discourses that can serve to both break down societal structures (as Turner theorized) and to support dominant ideologies. More often, pilgrimage can be shown to serve multiple functions simultaneously. As Eade and Sallnow wrote (1991: 5), "It is necessary to develop a view of pilgrimage not merely as a field of social relations but also as *a realm of competing discourses*. Indeed, much of what Turner has to say could be seen as representative of a particular discourse *about* pilgrimage rather than as an empirical description *of* it, one which might well co-exist or compete with alternative discourses." Although Turner tended to essentialize ritual in general, and pilgrimage in particular, as fitting into a universal mode, he also acknowledged that the communitas of pilgrimage was only an ideal, and that often its "anti-structure" only served to reinforce structure: "Communitas, however, is not structure with its signs reversed, minuses instead of pluses, but rather the *fons et origo* of all structures and, at the same time, their critique.... Some might say that pure communitas knows only harmonies and no disharmonies or conflict; I am suggesting that the social mode appropriate to all pilgrimages represents a mutually energizing compromise between structure and communitas" (1974: 202, 206). While these statements do contain broad generalizations about the nature of pilgrimages, they also contain an awareness of the complex and occasionally conflicting social operations taking place within them.

Such cautions are particularly applicable to secular pilgrimages such as Burning Man, for despite the relative ease with which rites of passage theory is applicable to this festival, it also refuses the mantle of pilgrimage by subverting traditional and popular perceptions of ritual and spiritual practice. Numerous other discourses could no doubt be shown to, and do, operate within Burning Man. Yet despite the genuinely complex and multifarious nature of Burning Man, it also seems apparent that one of its manifestations is as a contemporary pilgrimage, and one that clearly demonstrates most of the qualities that Turner associated with rites of passage. This is demonstrated in the numerous examples given above, as well as within thousands of other stories that cannot be told here.

Moreover, Turner's theories about rites of passage and liminality have manifestly infiltrated the North American and Western consciousness such that many now take his ideas about rites of passage to be paradigmatic. In part, perhaps one of the reasons why Burning Man can be shown to fit so neatly into a Turnerian framework is the fact that Harvey and other key contributors to the event are familiar with the work of Turner and other scholars of religion and anthropology, including Mircea Eliade, whose ideas influenced Turner.[6] Indeed the Man itself, with the spokes of the city's streets radiating around it in concentric circles, can readily be perceived as an exemplar of Eliade's axis mundi—a manifestation of the sacred center of the cosmos. Eliade (1954: 5) maintained that, "reality is conferred through participation in the 'symbolism of the Center,'" and that creation was seen by the archaic or premodern mind to have emerged from a central point where heaven and earth meet. For Eliade, the axis mundi is the location of *heirophany,* the eruption of the sacred into the profane world. Indeed, in Black Rock City, the Man forms the axis around which time and space are fixed—time because the Burn is generally perceived as the festival's climactic zenith, and space because the Man forms the city's locus around which streets are laid in concentric circles and in relation to which much of the other art is perceived or placed. This is but one instance of the ways in which Burning Man is perhaps one of the more candid and enigmatic contemporary phenomena in which it can clearly be seen that theories of religion, ritual, and culture not only reflect, but also shape their subjects.

Many people make the pilgrimage to Burning Man in order to experience something beyond themselves, to touch, for a moment and in their own individual ways, a sense of something sacred and meaningful in their own lives.

Through this journey, many individuals experience radical self-transformations in ways that invite comparison to Turner's theories of rites of passage, liminality, and communitas. Yet the festival is very much a set of competing discourses, and in the end pilgrimage narratives are but one template by which to contextualize the diverse experiences of Burning Man. Yet because the event is by design a creature of contradictions, it facilitates profound reorientations in time and space that often do lead to marked changes in consciousness, personal transformations, and new cultural possibilities. In an age when many have refused the dogma of their hereditary, traditional religions, Burning Man provides a new setting in which to fulfill desires for spiritual healing through connection, release, and renewal.

9 —— ⑤

Plants and Healing on the Wixárika (Huichol) Peyote Pilgrimage

Stacy B. Schaefer

eep in the northern Mexican desert in the state of San Luis Potosí is Wirikuta, the holy land of the Wixárika (Huichol) people. Wixáritari make annual pilgrimages to Wirikuta, the place where the peyote lives and where their gods dwell. Located at the eastern cardinal direction in Wixárika cosmology, Wirikuta lies at the heart of Wixárika culture, and is ever-present in the thoughts of individuals through their myths, songs, and rituals, especially the pilgrimage. Beginning at a young age, many Wixárika children learn about Wirikuta and its wonders, anticipating the day they may go on the pilgrimage with their families to know this sacred desert. One young girl attending the elementary school in the Wixárika community of San Andrés Cohamiata described her pilgrimage experience this way:

> Wirikuta [the sacred peyote desert] is one of the most beautiful places I know. There all of our gods are reunited and they protect us. Many times my father has spoken to me about this place and when I listened I got the urge to go there.... We journeyed to Wirikuta in the same way that the gods traveled. We walked numerous days to the same places that they had passed. We try to see what our gods saw and learn their lessons; that's why we go to Wirikuta. Wirikuta is the place we want to go to. I feel happy to know that I will be able to return there on another occasion [pilgrimage]. When I go to Wirikuta I don't want to leave...My name is Santiaga, and I am 9 years old. (Instituto Nacional Indigenista 1992)

While presently the peyote pilgrimage is carried out primarily by Wixárika people, in the past it was a more widely spread practice in the indigenous Mexican world. Essential to the pilgrimage are the peyote cactus, *Lophophora williamsii*, and tobacco, *Nicotiana rustica*. Both are revered and play integral roles in the pilgrimage as sacraments with healing powers that enable pilgrims to communicate with the spirit world. The external surroundings of the vast peyote desert, coupled with the internal neurochemical interactions that occur from ingesting these psychoactive plants, create an "other worldly" cognitive space conducive for contemplating one's life, healing ailments and psychological wounds, and seeking greater purpose and meaning in life. These plants, and the dynamic interplay they have on the body and mind, can be interpreted within the concept of "psychointegrator plants" developed by Winkelman (1996). According to Winkelman, psychoactive plants used as ritual sacraments can serve as catalysts that evoke "systemic conditions" that can predispose individuals to experience mystical and transpersonal events.

The first sections of this chapter present a short introduction to the history of the religious use of peyote in Mexico, a general description of the peyote pilgrimage, and a review of previous ethnographic studies of the Wixárika pilgrimage. The concept of psychointegrator plants and their role in pilgrimage are explored next in the sections on botanical, pharmacological, ritual, and symbolic aspects of peyote and tobacco. The role of the shaman in the pilgrimage as specialist in esoteric knowledge, spiritual guide, teacher, and healer is discussed in the subsequent section. This is followed by a description of individual Wixárika pilgrims, several of whom are shaman apprentices, their reasons for going on the pilgrimage, and a discussion of the kinds of healings that take place on the journey.

History and Ethnography of the Pilgrimage

The peyote pilgrimage Wixárika people take to Wirikuta in the San Luis Potosí desert of northern Mexico is an ancient religious practice that has endured through the centuries.[1] The origins of this pilgrimage are unclear. Spanish chroniclers writing in the sixteenth and seventeenth centuries describe the use of peyote, a psychoactive cactus, in rituals they observed among the Mexica or Aztecs (Sahagun 1950–1969; Ruiz de Alarcón 1984).

According to these reports, northern desert-dwelling hunter-gatherers called Teochichimec were credited with having introduced this vision-producing plant to the Mexica and other indigenous groups in central Mexico centuries before Europeans arrived to the New World. Missionary documents from the area surrounding Wixárika territory in the Sierra Madre Occidental, in the states of Jalisco and Zacatecas, reveal that despite zealous attempts by the clergy to put an end to indigenous beliefs and practices, Wixáritari held firmly to their peyote traditions. Neither religious indoctrination or enslavement by Spanish military to work the silver mines in Zacatecas and San Luis Potosí deterred Wixáritari efforts to make pilgrimages, albeit clandestinely, to Wirikuta, their revered peyote desert.[2]

Presently, groups of Wixáritari leave their sierra homelands annually to travel to the sacred desert of Wirikuta. Some older Wixáritari remember making this pilgrimage on foot, completing it in a month's time. Nowadays pilgrims rely on trucks and buses for their transportation. They usually complete the journey in approximately a week, sometimes less. Most pilgrimages occur between the months of December to April.

The number of times a person makes the pilgrimage in his or her lifetime varies greatly. Some Wixáritari may make this trip only once or twice in their lifetimes, others go twenty times or more to the peyote desert, still others may never visit Wirikuta. The pilgrims usually are members of a traditional temple group or an extended family ranch group.[3] Both temple and ranch groups are charged with caring for specific gods and carrying out ceremonial responsibilities over five consecutive years. For temple members this undoubtedly includes at least one to five pilgrimages to the peyote desert.[4]

Wirikuta and all of the shrines, caves, rocks, hills, and water sources visited on the pilgrimage, from the mountains to the desert, are fundamental places in Wixárika sacred landscapes. These places are so deeply etched into their rituals, ceremonies, myths, songs, and cosmology that most Wixáritari are familiar with them even if they have never participated in the pilgrimage. Wirikuta is the eastern cardinal point in Wixárika cosmology and is also the sacred center of their world; herein lies the entrance to the upper world of the gods and spirits. Pilgrims, as caretakers for specific gods, ritually act out their creation myths in order to renew the world, providing their deities with offerings as prayers for plentiful rains, fertile crops, and abundant deer. On a more personal level, some Wixáritari go on the pilgrimage in hopes of gaining esoteric knowledge in their quest to become cultural specialists as shamans, master musicians, or master artists. Other pilgrims are motivated to make this trip in order to heal themselves or loved ones, to reconcile personal problems, or to strengthen family bonds.

Over the last five centuries Wixáritari have successfully maintained many of their cultural beliefs and practices, including their peyote pilgrimage. This is rapidly changing. Today, in the twenty-first century, increasingly more Wixáritari leave their homelands to find work in *el norte* (the United States), leaving fewer people to carry out the pilgrimage. Mestizos and foreigners are encroaching on Wixárika land in the Sierra Madre Occidental, as well as on the peyote desert. The future health of peyote populations and their native habitat is endangered. In addition, very real legal entanglements exist for pilgrims who encounter military authorities unfamiliar with Wixárika traditions. Soldiers posted at highway checkpoints in the Mexican states that Wixáritari travel on their pilgrimage do not know or understand conflicting national laws and international treaties on the religious use of peyote (Schaefer 1998).

Considering the physical, economic and legal hardships pilgrims may encounter on the path, why do Wixáritari continue to make this journey? In the mid-1960s the shaman apprentice, Ramon Medina Silva, now deceased, explained to anthropologists Peter T. Furst (1969b) and the late Barbara G. Myerhoff (1974) that Wixáritari go on the peyote pilgrimage "to find our life." Ramon Medina's words about the powerful life-renewing purpose of the peyote pilgrimage provide as compelling a reason for Wixárika pilgrims to carry out this challenging journey today, at the beginning of the new millennium, as they did almost half a century ago.

Studies of the Peyote Pilgrimage

Since the 1960s various accounts have been written of the Wixárika peyote pilgrimage. Especially important are the pioneering works of Mexican journalist Fernando Benitez (1968) and American anthropologists Peter T. Furst (1969a, 1969b, 1972) and Barbara Myerhoff (1974, 1975, 1978a, 1978b) who brought this remarkable journey to the attention of a Western audience. All three authors describe some of the sacred places Wixáritari visit and the rituals performed on the pilgrimage to Wirikuta. Furst (Furst and Anguiano 1976) relates how these places are described in song by the leading shaman of the harvest ceremony (Tatei Neixa), in which he magically transforms young children into hummingbirds and metaphysically makes the pilgrimage with them to the sacred land of peyote.

In her study of the peyote pilgrimage, Myerhoff referred to the work of Victor Turner (1969). She analyzed the pilgrimage in terms of societal values, morals, and norms. Turner's concept of *communitas*, in which the pilgrimage experience is an opportunity for the participants to express their objection to rigid roles and statuses that exist within society, influenced Myerhoff and her interpretation of the Wixárika pilgrimage. Myerhoff stressed the importance of the shaman and his leading role as religious guide and skilled navigator into sacred time and space on the path to the "Sacred Land" of Wirikuta. The transformation of the pilgrims from the mundane world to the sacred, from separate, individual identities to one unified group, Myerhoff states (1975: 44–45), enable the pilgrims to experience life in "paradise," however briefly that may be. Myerhoff distinguishes the shaman as the only member who has regular access to this other world, and it is his role as caretaker of the pilgrims to protect them from "their own yearnings and frailty" and help them integrate these experiences into their everyday lives.

The role of reversals in the pilgrimage was also highlighted in Myerhoff's analyses (1974, 1978a, 1978b). Names, directions, and social status are metaphorically inverted, and mortal pilgrims symbolically become their immortal deities at the time of the world's creation. Drawing on Turner's approach to ritual as performance, in which the participants use and articulate symbols to create meaning, Myerhoff analyzed three key symbols that figure prominently in the beliefs and rituals of the pilgrimage: deer, maize, and peyote. Deer, according to Myerhoff, represent a romantic notion of time past when Wixáritari relied on hunting for subsistence. Maize reflects the mundane world Wixáritari live in today. Peyote symbolizes "the spiritual, the private, and free part of life" (Myerhoff 1974: 262). The unification of all three elements brings these different times and realities together, making the spiritual realm tangible to the pilgrims.

The literature published by Furst, Myerhoff, and Benitez brought the Wixáritari and their sacred journey to the peyote into public view. Their portrayals of the pilgrimage captured the interests of social scientists and the imagination of many college students and an avid reading public. This was at a time when the fabulous tales of Carlos Castañeda and his adventures with Don Juan fueled the imagination of disenchanted youth.[5] Documentary films made about this peyote pilgrimage have also sparked the interest of many people. Videos by Furst (1969b), Muller (1977), and Maybury-Lewis (1992) have circulated in the United States, and an untold number of others have been made by Mexican, European, and Japanese documentary filmmakers as well. Consequently, over the last four decades popular literature and media on the Wixárika peyote pilgrimage have catered to Westerners in search of spiritual guidance and their interests in psychedelic experiences. *Huichol Sacred Pilgrimage to Wirikuta* (Boyll 1991), *Toltecs of the New Millennium* (Sánchez 1996), *Flowers of Wirikuta* (Pinkson 1995), and *El Venado Azul* (Blanco 1991) are four examples of such works.

Elsewhere I have written on the importance and meaning of peyote in Wixárika culture and how peyote and the pilgrimage to Wirikuta can be viewed on a multiplicity of levels (Schaefer 1996a, 1996b). My focus in this chapter is to highlight the interrelationship between the pilgrims and their sacred plants—peyote and tobacco—to discuss the healing aspects of these plants and the journey, and to explore the reasons some Wixáritari participate in the pilgrimage.

The Role of Psychointegrator Plants

Peyote and tobacco are important plants treated as sacraments throughout the pilgrimage. Botanical, pharmacological, ritual, and symbolic aspects of both these plants are examined in this section. Insights into the creative means in which Wixáritari have integrated peyote and tobacco into the cultural dimensions of their pilgrimage and worldview are presented, and a discussion of the healing properties of these two plants follows.

Peyote

Peyote is a visionary cactus that inhabits the Chihuahuan Desert. Its range spans the distance from the Mexican state of San Luis Potosí to parts of south and west Texas. Strands of dried peyote in archaeological sites, funerary sculpture, and Spanish chronicles attest to the importance of peyote and its ritual use from around 5,000 B.C. among rock-shelter dwelling hunters and gatherers (Furst 1989; Boyd and Dering 1996) to the postclassic period (1200 to Spanish Conquest) in the Aztec and Chichimec cultures (Sahagun 1950–1969). Over sixty alkaloids have been identified in peyote. Mescaline (3,4,5-trimethoxyphenethylamine is the alkaloid most responsible for peyote's vision-producing effects. Mescaline alkaloid analysis of dried plant material has been reported to vary between 1 and 6 percent of the whole dried plant (Crosby and McLaughlin 1973: 416). The mescaline content most likely varies from plant to plant. Wixáritari classify peyote according to one of five colors: blue, white, yellow, red, and speckled. Several shaman consultants have pointed out the different colored peyote in Wirikuta to Bauml and me. It appears they recognize these distinguishing characteristics based on the coloration of the plant epidermis or the color of the internal tissue of the root. To an untrained eye these differences are extremely subtle. Not nearly as subtle are the differences in strength between the different colored plants. Blue and yellow peyote are praised as the strongest, followed by white and speckled; red is the weakest in potency. Wixáritari harvest the spineless cactus slightly below the soil level (leaving the tap root in place). Then they carefully remove the white tufts of fuzz. They place the entire cactus button in their mouths, making sure to slowly chew it well before swallowing it. While in Wirikuta, Wixáritari dry some of the peyote they harvest to use at a later time, grinding the dried tops into a powder and mixing it with water to drink. The strength does not diminish if the plant is dried.

Mescaline, the major mind-altering alkaloid in peyote, interacts with the brain's naturally occurring neurotransmitters: norepinephrine, serotonin, and dopamine. Chemically it most closely resembles norepinephrine. Abundantly concentrated in the limbic system of the brain, norepinephrine affects emotions, engendering love, hate, joy, and sadness. Greater clarity of thought is also evoked by the release of this neurotransmitter, and it plays an important role in regulating general behavioral response to sensory stimulation. Norepinephrine neurons descend to the spinal cord and influence the regulation of muscles in the arms and legs (Snyder 1996: 146, 205). The serotonin system, with particularly dense projections of axons in the limbic system, involves sleep, mood, appetite, and depression. Serotonin neurotransmitters also affect the secretion of growth hormones, influence sensory-motor processes in behavior, and act as a vasoconstrictor stimulating the smooth muscles (Winkelman 1996: 30). Finally, dopamine neurons, known to be linked to motor abilities and Parkinson's disease, are also designed to maintain thoughts and perceptions in accord with the reality of one's mundane environment (Snyder 1996: 209). Mescaline appears to suppress the release of dopamine and consequently shuts down the brain from habitual routines related to social behavioral displays (Winkelman 1996: 43)

Peyote inebriation alters sensory perception. Visual, auditory, olfactory, tactile, and gustatory senses are enhanced. Some Wixáritari hear music and compose new songs from the peyote experience. Others describe unusual feelings as if snakes were slithering in and around their bodies. Bitter tastes, such as the juice from peyote, taste sweet, and brilliant colored visions burst across one's field of vision (see Schaefer 1996a). Emotional responses to external and internal stimuli evoke deep-seated feelings, such as sorrow, ecstasy, and love, and are often expressed through tears and laughter. Cognitively, the overall peyote experience reinforces general cultural principles of Wixárika worldview, and provides the pilgrim with a more profound understanding of oneself and one's place in the cosmos. Behavioral effects are determined by the number of peyote tops eaten and the quantity of mescaline and other alkaloids present in them. Small amounts of peyote provoke excitatory effects, provide greater endurance and alertness, and assuage hunger and thirst. The visions seen under low doses of this plant consist primarily of brightly colored pulsating geometric designs in constant movement as they transform from one shape to the next. Sufficiently large amounts of consumed peyote can on occasion produce the visual effect of being repelled through a dark tunnel, ending in a sea of bright light, followed by visionary images of anthropomorphic forms.

A Wixárika man described to me one such visionary experience he had after eating numerous peyote and staring into the fire:

> I felt I saw the fire turn into tissue paper...the form of the fire disappeared and I saw only tissue paper in the glowing form of flowers like the ones we make when we are going to sacrifice a calf. There were many colors of this flowerlike tissue paper.... then in the very center of the fire I saw in the distance a person; afterwards the mara'akame [shaman] told me it was Tatewari, Grandfather Fire. I saw the entrance to the temple, even though we were in Wirikuta, and I entered the temple. (Schaefer 1996a: 156, 158)

Under these conditions of peyote inebriation the individual draws inward, eyes closed, body still, and journeys through an altered state of consciousness very much akin to lucid dreaming.

Often, shamans are consulted on the amount of peyote for pilgrims to consume since they are knowledgeable about doses and are well-experienced travelers to these other realms of consciousness. Peyote is ingested numerous times throughout the pilgrimage. After the first cluster of peyote is found and metaphorically hunted like deer, prayers uttered by the pilgrims and offerings left in thanks prepare the setting for the initial ingestion of peyote. Pilgrims may enjoy eating small quantities of peyote while they continue harvesting peyote in the desert landscape. Ceremonies in Wirikuta require the leading shaman to sing the entire night to call upon the presence of the gods. Pilgrims with religious responsibilities, such as temple members, will consume peyote five times during the night; at dawn some may continue eating peyote until they tune out external stimuli and travel within themselves. This also occurs when individuals make the pilgrimage as a vision quest and specifically consume large quantities of peyote in order to communicate with the gods and learn from them.

Tobacco

Another important psychointegrator plant, often overlooked but crucial to the success of the peyote pilgrimage, is tobacco, specifically *Nicotiana rustica*, or *makutse* as Wixárika call it. Makutse leaves are placed in a specially woven miniature bag that is attached to a dried deer face mask made from the first hunted deer of the season. The deer face and the tobacco bag must be carried in front of the pilgrims. Together they guide and protect the participants on the journey. Pilgrims smoke makutse in conjunction with peyote consumption. The particular species of tobacco is most likely the oldest of the nicotine-producing tobaccos cultivated by indigenous peoples in the Americas in pre-Contact times. Perhaps one reason for this is because of its potency in nicotine alkaloids (Wilbert 1987: 6). *Nicotiana rustica* cultivated by Wixáritari may contain nicotine alkaloids in its leaves as high as 18.76 percent (±2.6 percent). *Nicotiana tabacum*, used for commercial cigarettes, has a much lower nicotine content ranging from 0.6 to 9.0 percent (Siegel, Collings, and Diaz 1977: 22; Wilbert 1987: 134).

Nicotine, when smoked as a cigarette, vaporizes into the smoke and particles of ashes that dissolve in the mucous membrane of the inside surface of the lungs. Upon reaching the lungs, the nicotine particles are rapidly absorbed and are carried directly to the heart. From there much of the blood containing nicotine goes straight to the brain in seven seconds (Wilbert 1987: 146). High concentrations of nicotine are retained in the brain for about thirty minutes before the nicotine travels away from the brain and concentrates in the liver, kidneys, salivary glands, and stomach (McKim 1991: 171). Nicotine occupies and stimulates nicotinic cholinergic receptor sites in the central nervous system, prompting the release of the neurotransmitters acetylcholine, norepinephrine, dopamine, serotonin, epinephrine, vasopressin, growth hormone, and ACTH (Benowitz 1988: 1318). Nicotine also excites the nicotinic receptors in the spinal cord and the autonomic ganglia, which are collections of nerves or nerve cell bodies outside of the central nervous system.

Wixáritari smoke tobacco, and then ingest peyote. Both mescaline and tobacco stimulate the release of serotonin, norepinephrine, dopamine, and in the case of nicotine, epinephrine. The effects of nicotine and mescaline are widespread, creeping their way throughout the body from the peripheral nervous system to the central nervous system to act at many places simultaneously and thus potentiating or compounding the effects of these visionary plants. Nicotine and mescaline most likely enhance each other's visionary effects.[6]

The Integration of Peyote and Tobacco in the Pilgrimage

The cognitive constructs that Wixáritari have created around the ritual use of these two psychointegrator plants, especially in relation to the pilgrimage, point to the deep structures, the beliefs and practices, this culture has built around their visionary plant-informed experiences. Music, songs, woven or embroidered designs, even certain kinds of knowledge are said by Wixáritari to come to them while inebriated. They acknowledge these messages as special gifts that only their gods can provide. Partaking of these two plants enables individuals to become actively involved in their own personal evolution. Seeking to become a shaman or master artisan, healing oneself or a loved one, even setting out on a new path, such as returning to Wixárika cultural lifeways after having spent years in the larger mestizo world, are all very much in keeping with their cultural values and activities in daily and ritual life.

Recognizing the strength and power of this tobacco, only shamans cultivate makutse near their ranches. The first leaves of the makutse plants are trimmed and taken to the temple where they are anointed with blood from the first deer hunted before the peyote pilgrimage. Then a special ceremony is held to make the miniature sacred tobacco bag, the *wainuri*. This bag is the single most important ritual object of the temple and its members, and its origin is explained in the creation myth of the peyote pilgrimage, when the earth goddess, 'Utüanaka, wove this bag in order to find the path to Wirikuta.

Usually a prominent male shaman of the temple will weave the wainuri.

Sometimes a woman will be selected to perform this major ritual task. One of the most important requirements for this role as weaver of the tobacco bag is that the person must have the ability to sing. Whoever weaves the wainuri carries a tremendous responsibility, because the special makutse cuttings to be placed inside of it contain the heart memory of the gods. Making the wain-uri for the pilgrimage can be a healing event in and of itself. One woman I know was selected to weave the wainuri. According to the leading shaman of the temple, the act of her making the tobacco bag would be part of her own healing ritual. This woman's daughter described to me some of the details of this undertaking:

> My mother has made the little bag for four or five years now ... before she became too sick. She was sick a lot, and then one hun-dred of her cattle died. Because she was sick so much the shaman told her she had to weave the bag. She did not want to, saying, "I am a woman, why do I have to sing?" ... and she had to sing before weav-ing it. She had to sing and she went to Werikuata [a sacred place in the Sierra] like those who go to ask for help. There she passed the night along, singing to all the sacred places. She sang with Kauyu-marie [the deer god who serves as messenger]. He is the one who selected her and he had to help her. (Schaefer 2002: 245–46)

The miniature tobacco bag is attached to the front of the head of the hunted deer, which has been cleaned and dried so that it appears as a deer mask. The deer mask with the wainuri, the tobacco bag, must always be in the very front of the line of pilgrims, as it guides them on the road to Wirikuta. It is placed in front of the shaman while he sings and leads the pilgrims to find the peyote.

Tobacco cigarettes are smoked during the pilgrimage before and after peyote consumption. On a pharmacological level it is quite plausible that nicotine increases attention span, concentration, and the ability to perform tasks while inebriated with peyote. One Wixárika shaman with whom Bauml and I spoke explained that smoking tobacco does change the effect one feels from eating peyote. Relating the ritual process, he said that first one has to make an arrow and leave it where the first peyotes were hunted and con-sumed;

> And then you pray ... that you will get something from it [the pey-ote] that you will gain knowledge, see things, not get nauseous or

vomit...and then when you smoke the makutse you will not feel so *empeyotado*. Even if you eat lots of peyote you will not feel it that much...it makes one feel it very gently, that's how the people do it ...Because if you eat peyote you feel differently, sometimes [the peyote] is gentle, sometimes it is very heavy...and then you hear things from far away, people talking from far over there. But with makutse, no, it lessens the feeling of being drunk with the peyote...so that you come down, that's why they smoke...you get the urge to smoke when you eat peyote.

Healing Aspects of the Plants

Peyote and tobacco are revered by Wixáritari for their healing and visionary powers. The combination of the two is reputed to make the peyote experience gentler and to help smooth out the journey. Both plants are used as healing agents, as medicine. Laboratory studies indicate that some of the peyote alkaloids (hordenine) have antibiotic qualities, inhibiting the growth of penicillin-resistant strains of the bacteria *Staphylococcus aureus* (McCleary, Sypherd and Walkington 1960: 247–49). Peyote is used to cure intestinal problems, to relieve pain and fevers, and to treat scorpion stings and snake bites. It is made into a poultice and applied externally to arthritic joints, cuts, and bruises. Juice from peyote is used by some as drops to lubricate eyes dry from cataracts. Some pregnant women consume peyote to bring on labor, as well as to ease pain caused by uterine contractions. Peyote is also known to increase lactation in nursing mothers (Schaefer 1996b). Tobacco and its smoke are used in purification rituals, as well as in prayer. Nicotine in tobacco can enhance concentration, and it may also have an antidepressant effect (McKim 1991: 174).

The therapeutic effect of psychointegrative plants on brain systems and consciousness proposed by Michael Winkelman (1996) is an intriguing idea that merits review here in relation to peyote and tobacco and the influences they have on Wixárika pilgrims. To paraphrase Winkelman and his reference to the work of MacLean (1990), there are three kinds of brain systems functioning in human beings: the R-complex or reptilian brain, the paleomammalian brain, and the neomammalian brain associated with the neocortex. The R-complex typically manages the cognition required for the body's behavioral actions, including habitual routines, and is characterized as regulating large amounts of dopamine. The paleomammalian brain is comprised of the limbic system and serves as an integrating agent for emotion and memory and for processing sensory and motor functions. It plays a crucial role in engendering feelings of attachment, emotional security, and identity, and functions as a link between the R-complex and the frontal cortex. The neocortex, which surrounds the brain, houses the vast majority of neurons in the human central nervous system (Hooper and Teresi 1986). Psychointegrative plants function to integrate all three brain system processes. They interfere with habitual behavior associated with the R-complex, and in fact, mescaline and nicotine inhibit the release of dopamine neurotransmitters that are so prevalent in this brain system.

Peyote and tobacco, plants deemed sacred by Wixáritari, can serve to evoke the processing of important memories and emotions, as seen by the means in which mescaline and nicotine interact with norepinephrine and serotonin systems. Peyote and tobacco are instrumental in helping people systematically integrate those parts of their unconscious into a more holistic understanding of themselves. These experiences enable individuals to discover a greater sense of certainty and meaning in life, framed within the cosmological constructs of Wixárika culture. In essence, peyote and tobacco, as psychointegrator plants, facilitate the healing and union of the body, the mind, the soul, and the psyche.

Healing and Training of Shamans during the Pilgrimage

A successful pilgrimage and effective healings on the journey are only possible under the guidance of a shaman. Shamans are specialists in the esoteric knowledge of the Wixárika world, and act as healers and counselors, purifying individuals with their feathered power wands, and interpreting the dreams and peyote-induced visions that pilgrims discuss with them. On the pilgrimage, a shaman is also a botanist and pharmacologist. His knowledge of the plants in this desert environment is extensive, and he advises pilgrims on the different kinds of peyote and quantities of them to consume. One shaman is the designated leader of the pilgrimage. However, more often then not, there are also other shamans making the journey who attend to the specific needs of those who ask them for help.

One particularly important ritual that takes place early in the pilgrimage is the purification rite that prepares the pilgrims for the experiences that may unfold on the journey. All the pilgrims must confess to the shaman leader in front of the entire group any transgressions or wrongdoings they may have committed. The most serious missteps are theft, murder, and adultery. In the latter case a rope is used to tie knots for all the people with whom an individual identifies as a sexual partner. After the confessions are told, the shaman purifies everyone by "sweeping" his plumed wand of power over and around the bodies of all the pilgrims. This concept of purification, and the ritual of confession that enacts it, is a profound part of the healings that take place on the pilgrimage. One shaman named Rafael, with whom Bauml and I have been working, has participated in close to twenty pilgrimages. He related to us his first one to Wirikuta and the cleansing experience he had after having eaten peyote. He was a boy at the time, a preadolescent, and had run away from home to join the peyote pilgrims because he wanted to see Wirikuta. He also wanted to learn to play the violin. Now he is a master violin player renowned in the region for his musical abilities. This is Rafael's description, recorded in January 2001:

> The first time I ate peyote I ate a small amount to see if it would bring me luck. I wanted to play the violin.... Then I felt this way... some animals appeared, they were like dinosaurs, and a big snake [appeared]; they were all huge, really big! I was surprised to see them ...they asked me what I was thinking, what I was feeling.
>
> Well, at that time I lost myself [traveling with the peyote]. I thought my companions no longer lived, not even my brother. Only the offerings we had left were there and these animals were alive. No, they told me, your companions have sinned, but over there where the offerings are, are the things you have been thinking about. Look, over there is a violin. It's yours but first you have to confess your wrongdoings they told me. Look at the others who confessed, they are dirty, as if they had mucous all over them. We don't like the way they are. God doesn't want them to be dirty.
>
> So, we will clean [purify] you. And they cleaned me with their tongues. Their tongues were enormous! They cleaned me all over. Then a light like a star appeared, it came from over there where the sun rises. First they cleaned me, then the light fell all around me and cleaned me all over. Then I appeared like a bright light, a really beautiful light...then they took me...up to the sky.

A significant number of Wixárika go on the pilgrimage as part of their apprenticeship in learning to become a shaman.[7] This apprenticeship demands that the initiate be married; otherwise he must remain single and chaste throughout the duration of this undertaking, which can last five years or more. Because of the esoteric nature of this training, which entails acquiring an understanding of, and navigating within, various altered states of consciousness, shaman apprentices are especially sensitive to their own personal problems and must learn to heal their own wounds before they are able to heal others. Hardships endured on the pilgrimage, such as fasting, drinking little water, exposure to extreme hot and cold temperatures in the desert, and physical and mental fatigue predispose pilgrims both mentally and pharmacologically to the powerful experiences brought on by peyote and tobacco consumption. This is particularly true for shamans and shaman initiates. As discussed earlier, the interaction of these plant alkaloids within the brain stimulates the expression of emotions, bringing the pilgrim face to face with a host of feelings he or she carries deep within. The heightened degree of awareness and concentration that accompanies this brain activity enables the individual to examine challenges, difficulties, and problems in a different light.

Individuals' Stories and Their Reasons for Making this Life-Transforming Pilgrimage

In the pilgrimages I participated in, there were several men learning to become shamans. Each individual's personal, social, and family dynamics were brought into the pilgrimage along with the rituals and lessons to be learned from the journey.

Marital infidelity is one such challenge that must be addressed and reconciled on this journey. Pancho, a young man whom I have known since he was a young boy, has accompanied us on two pilgrimages as part of his shaman apprenticeship. His grandmother, Nicolasa, arranged his marriage to his wife Rosa, so that his spouse could assist him in completing this training. Ideally the shaman initiate's wife works together with her husband, helping him achieve this specialist training. And ideally, married couples should remain faithful to each other throughout the entire apprenticeship. Pancho's marital problems had troubled him for some time and were often on his mind. He talked freely about them to me. Rosa refused to carry out her wifely duties.

She would not cook for him, nor would she sew his clothes. In fact, she did very little work at all around the rancho. When their first child was born, she shrugged off her motherly responsibilities, leaving Pancho to care for their baby. He raised the little girl on powdered milk formula. Several times Rosa ran away from the rancho only to return weeks, sometimes several months, later. The last time she left him, Pancho told me, she found another Wixárika man and lived with him. This partner treated her abusively, and she returned home to Pancho, hoping he would take her back, pregnant with the other man's child. Months later she gave birth to a little boy.

Pancho and Rosa's family worked with the couple to help them overcome their marital problems. Now on the pilgrimage, even greater reconciliation had to be made between the two. In addition to the confession ritual, they had to work together, making and leaving votive offerings in sacred places on the way. In their prayers, Pancho and Rosa prayed as a family, and Nicolosa, his grandmother and the leading shaman on this pilgrimage, purified and blessed the two along with their daughter and Rosa's baby boy. When it came time for everyone to ritually partake of the peyote in Wirikuta, the real unification took place. Nicolasa gave Pancho and Rosa blessed peyote to eat, and then gave their two-year-old daughter a small peyote button and put a small piece of the peyote in the mouth of the baby. Rosa quickly gave the baby her breast to suckle to help the peyote go down its throat. Later, Pancho's daughter demonstrated her liking for the peyote, taking more from their bags to eat. She became the center of attention when all eyes watched and laughed in good humor at her drunkenlike behavior from the peyote. It was also a for-tuitous sign to Pancho and his wife that their daughter's affinity for the pey-ote might indicate a proclivity toward becoming a shaman when she grew older.

Healing social wrongs is another motivation for pilgrimage. Isidro, another shaman apprentice who is in his mid- to late thirties, and is Pancho's uncle, also accompanied us on two pilgrimages. He was trying to come to terms with a terrible period in his life that needed healing. Early in his life Isidro's fam-ily recognized his calling to become a shaman from his affinity for peyote. Isidro's older sister Angélica, recounted to me the following event when he was young:

> My father was planting [in the milpa]. We were working also, I think
> [my father] brought peyote with him so that he would have more

energy to do the work. He left it [peyote] where we had left our things. Later he did not know that [my brother] was eating some of this because it was dry like the meat of deer, that's how the peyote was that he left there [where] my brother sat waiting by our things. When we got closer to my brother it seemed that he was eating peyote and I told [my father]. Oh really [my father said], and he took it away from him so that he would not get dizzy [inebriated from eating it]. He [my brother] was crying.... Then [my father] carried the peyote far away and put it where my brother would not see it, so that he would not become empeyotado [inebriated]. Afterwards we went back to work. Upon returning we saw that the peyote was there. I think [my brother] looked for and found the peyote because he felt bad and heard where it was [the peyote called out to him]. He went over to where the peyote was hidden, far away, and was eating all of it, lots of it. Then two hours later he was just sitting there, doing nothing, for about two or three hours he just sat there. Then he stood up, and yes he was empeyotado.

When Isidro reached his early teenage years, his father died. Shortly afterward he moved with his mother, Nicolasa, and his younger brothers and sister to the Mexican city of Zacatecas. Isidro was united with a young woman in a marriage arranged by his mother, and began his shaman apprenticeship. His life changed abruptly when he was unjustly accused of murdering a mestizo man and sent away to a prison on Isla Maria, an island off the Pacific Coast. Isidro was the only Wixárika in this island penal colony; the rest were mestizos. His prison term lasted for years. During that time, word spread of his healing powers and some of the inmates called upon him to cure them. Isidro's innocence of the crime he was accused of was finally recognized and he was released from prison. He returned to his family who was living back in the sierra, to find that his wife had deserted him during his time in prison. There were many difficult adjustments he had to make in all areas of his life. Nicolasa arranged another marriage for him with a Wixárika woman from a different sierra community, one who had been her patient. Starting again with his new wife improved Isidro's outlook on life. Another important element that was guiding him through these hard times was his renewed commitment to completing his shamanic training. This meant he would have to make more pilgrimages to Wirikuta. In the two pilgrimages in which Bauml and I participated with him, he was very pious in his prayers and actions. Nicolasa served as his guide along the journey. He looked upon these journeys as a way to right the wrongs that had happened to him, and through our travels to the various sacred places on the pilgrimage and his ingestion of peyote, he sought to obtain visions, songs, knowledge, and power from Kauyumarie, the divine deer who is the shaman's messenger, and from the other gods. Isidro also had to make a special stop on the pilgrimage in Zacatecas, to report his activities and whereabouts to the correctional authorities as part of the terms of his release from prison.

Wixárika women who desire to have children may also look upon the pilgrimage as an opportunity to heal any infertility problems they and their husbands may have. One woman I know had tried for years to have a second child. After she and her husband's return from their pilgrimage to Wirikuta as part of a temple group, she became pregnant and marveled to me about the healing she received there (Schaefer 1996a: 164–65). During two of the pilgrimages in which Bauml and I participated, we had a chance to observe the healing that Nicolasa, the leading shaman, carried out with Isidro's wife, Lili. Lili had never been able to conceive, and she was reaching the end of her reproductive years without a child. She yearned for a child, so much so that Nicolasa arranged for Lili and Isidro to adopt Joaquin's (Isidro's brother's) young son. After endless turmoil between Joaquin and his wife over this exchange, Lili and Isidro were resigned to returning the little boy to his biological parents. Now, Lili and Isidro had great hopes that going on this pilgrimage would enable them to have a child. At all of the sacred places we visited on the journey, Nicolasa instructed Lili to lie on the ground and lift her blouse so her abdomen was exposed. Nicolasa touched Lili's bare stomach with her feathered power wands and sprayed onto it, from her mouth, holy water collected at the sacred places. Nicolasa did the same for Isidro.

In the early part of the pilgrimage, when we passed through Zacatecas, we traveled a little further to the Catholic shrine of the Santo Niño de Atocha, before heading to the desert. This shrine is a kind of mecca for thousands of mestizo pilgrims who come to ask the child saint for miracles, especially ones that will heal physical ailments. With the help of Nicolasa, Lili and Isidro left offerings to the Santo Niño to help Lili bear a child. The couple bought miniature images of this young saint to leave in Wirikuta, where they hunted and consumed peyote with the hopes that the gods would look favorably upon them and give them this gift of life, as well as visions to help Isidro on his shaman's path.

Women and fertility are prominent themes in the origin myth of the peyote pilgrimage. Lili and Isidro's prayers and special ceremonies on their pilgrimage to Wirikuta are a most fitting way to work within Wixárika cultural beliefs to heal their problem. According to the origin myth, the earth goddess 'Utüanaka wove the first tobacco pouch, and, in so doing, found the path to Wirikuta. 'Utüanaka was accompanied by two other goddesses on the pilgrimage. Upon reaching a lake near the present-day city of Zacatecas, 'Utüanaka and the two other goddesses began to menstruate. Kauyumarie, the deer god, looked to see if they had vaginas and fertile wombs. 'Utüanaka and one of her companions, the goddess Wiri 'uwi, were fertile and were permitted to enter into the peyote desert. The third goddess was barren. She was denied the opportunity to accompany the other goddesses, and she turned into a mountain nearby. 'Utüanaka and Wiri 'uwi arrived at Wirikuta, and discovered peyote and the brilliant splendor it could show them, as well as the miraculous powers it held. The goddesses also became pregnant. 'Utüanaka took peyote and her knowledge of it to share with her community. Wiri 'uwi remained in the desert to become the mother of peyote.

Interestingly, on the second pilgrimage we took with Nicolasa and her family, Lili began to menstruate when we entered Wirikuta. Nicolasa cut some strands of hair around the crown of her head, to neutralize the "heat" she exuded. This event was viewed by Nicolasa as a "good" sign that Lili would be able to conceive and give birth to a child.

In regards to the physiological and pharmacological interactions taking place in pilgrims during the journey, it is all but impossible to clinically study this aspect of the experience, just as it is extremely difficult to acquire a personal understanding of the visions another encounters under the influence of peyote and tobacco. It is possible however, to follow the life trajectories of these pilgrims and the direction their paths take after the pilgrimage. A year and a half after taking the second pilgrimage with the Wixárika families, Pancho, the shaman initiate, and his wife Rosa have a much more harmonious marriage. Rosa is a dedicated mother and wife, and Pancho has accepted Rosa's son, born from a different father, as his own. Although Lili, the wife of Isidro, has yet to become pregnant, Isidro revealed to me that after the second trip to Wirikuta he had a dream in which the messenger god, Kauyumarie, appeared to him. This is the first crucial step in becoming a shaman.

Healing in a Broader Context

Every pilgrimage is unique, and none of the participants can fully anticipate the people or events they may encounter along the way. During two different pilgrimages, I witnessed the manner in which shamans attempted to heal outsiders on the sacred journey; in both situations the outsiders were mestizos. The first incident took place with a mestizo man from Mexico City who, with another mestizo friend, had come along on the pilgrimage carried out by a temple group. Throughout the journey, pilgrims not only fast, but also abstain from drinking alcohol. It turned out that the mestizo was an alcoholic and had brought his own supply of alcohol along. The night before we entered Wirikuta, we were camped and everyone was asleep except for this mestizo. In the wee hours of the night, he began to cry and shout in Spanish that we should all wake up, he had not confessed well. He wanted everyone to hear his real confession, that he wanted to kill his parents. He wailed on like this until his mestizo companion and one of the shamans took him aside, and calmed him down, and he fell asleep. The following day, when we were in Wirikuta and everyone was partaking of the peyote, this shaman noticed that the man was not eating any. The shaman confronted the man and instructed him to eat twenty peyote. The shaman said he would eat the same amount, then together they could get to the root of his problems and he could be healed. The mestizo, not willing to comply, was later dropped off by his companion on the side of the highway to find his own way home. The pilgrims, puzzled by the troubled mestizo's behavior, did not understand why he did not want to eat peyote and be healed by the shaman.

On another pilgrimage I observed a most remarkable healing. The pilgrims on this journey were Nicolasa and her extended family, along with Bauml and myself. We had reached the sacred springs, known to the travelers as Tatei Matiniere. Here, at the fresh water springs on the edge of the desert, we left prayer offerings and received blessings with the sacred water from the springs and a cleansing from Nicolasa with her power wands. Next to the springs is a mestizo pueblo. Wixáritari passing through the pueblo on the pilgrimage have grown wary of some of the residents, especially the youths who steal the offerings they leave at the springs shortly after the pilgrims have departed. This time, as we were leaving the springs and passing back through the pueblo, a mestizo woman with a baby in her arms stopped us, asking if any of the pilgrims was a shaman. The woman explained that she had a daughter at her house in town that was seriously ill with *empacho*, (stomach problems), and none of the doctors to whom she had taken the girl had been able to cure her. Nicolasa agreed to see the woman's daughter.

We followed the distressed woman to her house and found her daughter, around three years of age, asleep on the bed. The little girl awoke; she looked sickly and weak. Her face was pale and she was thin, with a distended stomach. Upon realizing that there were strangers in her house and all eyes were on her, she began to cry. Her mother comforted her and gently laid her down so that Nicolasa could examine her. Nicolasa palpated her stomach with her hands and then used her power wands to "sweep" the little girl, concentrating her attention on the girl's stomach. Throughout all of this, the young patient cried continuously. Then Nicolasa sucked some object from the girl's belly, spat the object into her hand, examined it and threw it through the door to the outside. This caused the girl to cry even more. Requesting a glass of water, Nicolasa took a large sip of the water and sprayed it onto the girl's belly. She repeated this several times and then gave the glass with the remaining water to the little girl to drink. The girl's mother was asked to provide a candle, which she did, and Nicolasa instructed her to leave the candle for her daughter in the waters of Tatei Matiniere. The reason that her daughter and so many other people in this pueblo are sick, Nicolasa explained to the woman, is because the local kids steal the offerings. The people in the pueblo live right next to the springs, yet they themselves do not leave offerings. For these reasons the gods are angry and they take their wrath upon the people by bringing illnesses. Nicolasa told the woman that she must have faith in Wixárika healers. The woman responded by recounting that ever since she was a child she remembered the Wixáritari coming through to leave offerings at the springs. She knows Wixáritari have special healing powers because on various occasions some of them cured local people in the pueblo. As we took our leave, the young patient sat up, got up from the bed, and walked around us with a smile on her face. She was like a new person, looking healthy and happy. It certainly did seem as if she had miraculously recovered. On our way out of town, the young girl waved goodbye to us from the doorway of her house, at which time Nicolasa said to the rest of us that the girl would continue to get sick until her mother realized that her daughter was meant to be a healer and helped her achieve this goal.

In sum, Wixárika do not exclude outsiders from their experiences while on the pilgrimage. Rather, they may incorporate these people into their rituals, situating them within Wixárika cultural beliefs and worldview. Healing non-Wixárika on the pilgrimage, as discussed above, is an example of ways pilgrims integrate others into their sacred journey. Wixáritari pilgrims do not proselytize outsiders with their religious convictions, nor do shamans advertise themselves as special healers. However, these pilgrims do feel a responsibility to communicate with the gods with their prayers and offerings, and ask for their intervention to balance the forces of nature and to provide good health, luck, and productivity for all.

Health and Renewal from the Land of Peyote, the Place of Origins

The pilgrimage that Wixáritari make to the peyote desert of San Luis Potosí is a sacred journey that enables the participants to work toward finding solutions in a creative and supportive social environment to problems in their lives. A number of participants go to Wirikuta as part of their training in becoming shamans. An important part of this spiritual quest is the hope of many of the participants that they will be healed and gain greater understanding of the world around them. On the pilgrimage, shamans may extend their healing powers to outsiders so that they too may benefit from good luck and health in their lives.

Essential to the pilgrimage are the sacred peyote and tobacco, and the visions pilgrims experience from having consumed them. The pharmacological activity that occurs from ingestion of these plants helps enable participants to integrate their thoughts, feelings, and sensations into a more holistic sense of self. With the guidance of the shamans as pharmacologists, therapists, and spiritual counselors, the pilgrims are able to understand these experiences within the cognitive framework of Wixárika culture and worldview. They have gone to Wirikuta, the furthest eastern cardinal direction in their cosmological map, the place of their origins where the gods reside. With the assistance of their sacred plants, peyote and tobacco, and of their prayers and rituals, they have renewed the world again. The leading shaman has safely guided their journey to the world of the gods and helped interpret the meaning of these divine communications.

Completing the pilgrimage to Wirikuta also fulfills family and community ritual responsibilities. The gods have been called upon to provide plentiful rain, fertile crops, and abundant deer and cattle for their families and

temple group, and the pilgrims have left offerings in thanks for their involvement in human affairs. In sum, the pilgrimage is a ritual undertaking that
unifies families and communities, reinforces cultural beliefs, practices and values, and serves as a means by which pilgrims can work toward their own
individual development. On this personal level, the pilgrimage helps the individual seekers find greater health, awareness, understanding, and meaning; in
essence it enables the seekers to "find their lives."

The Janai Purnima Pilgrimage of the Tamang Shamans of Nepal

An Experiential Study

Larry G. Peters

The Sociocultural Context of Janai Purnima

*T*he Tamang are of Tibetan ethnicity and constitute one of the largest tribal groups in Nepal. Nepal is at the geographic crossroads of the great Hindu and Buddhist civilizations of India and Tibet, and the Tamang shamans of the Kathmandu Valley with whom I've apprenticed have developed a unique blend of both these spiritualities, assimilated with a much more ancient, Tibetan, oral, pre-Buddhist, animistic tradition called "Bön" or "Bönpo." Furthermore, the resulting shamanic belief system functions alongside a Tamang hereditary Lamaistic Buddhist tradition. My field research site is Boudhanath, currently a busy urban town of perhaps one hundred thousand people, primarily Tamang and recent Tibetan immigrants, located about six miles northeast of Kathmandu. The Tamang shamans there are primarily spiritual healers, while the Tamang lamas have distinct social responsibilities that include conducting the death rites (Peters 1998).

Pilgrimage is a crucial practice for Tamang shamans (*jhankri*, Ta: *bombo*).[1] It provides community healing and is also a means of initiating candidates. Shamanic pilgrimages occur on certain full moon days. Probably the most important of these, for shamans of all ethnicities residing in Nepal, is Janai Purnima, which falls on the full moon ending the lunar month of Saun (July/August). *Purnima* means "day of the full moon." This full moon day has a number of religious/ritual events. It is when higher-caste adult Hindu males change their sacred yellow threads *(janai)*, thus "Janai Purnima." In Nepal, Buddhists and Hindus of the other castes, tribes, and genders follow a similar rite this day, having red strings tied around their wrists (right for males, left for females) that restrict *(bandhan)* evil and provide protection *(raksha)*, called "Raksha Bandhan." Hindu Brahmins, ascetic mendicants *(sadhu, followers of Shiva)*, and shamans who have pilgrimaged to the sacred shrines on this day, bestow Raksha Bandhan on the throngs of laypersons who gather at the holy places. Janai Purnima is also the time of year that offerings are made to honor the ancient holy men. Janai Purnima is associated with the ending of the monsoon period. Thus there are agricultural ceremonies. It is the day shamans go on pilgrimage to acquire power and perform soul-calling healings for community members in need. Thus Janai Purnima is a pan-Nepali religious holiday and festive occasion for all faiths, castes, genders, and ages, and it has numerous individual purposes. As Miller (1997) puts it, "It holds something for everybody."

There are many important pilgrimage sites for shamans in Nepal. On Janai Purnima, small groups consisting of a master shaman (guru) and his/her disciples *(chela)* journey along with hosts of other Nepalis to various sacred shrines. The most popular of these sacred power places at the time of Janai Purnima is the Shiva shrine of Gosainkunda Lake, more than fifteen thousand feet high in the Langtang Himalayas, forty miles north of Kathmandu, or at the magnificent temple at Kumbeswar in nearby Patan. The sacred bathing pools *(kunda)* and the sacred healing waters at various other Shiva shrines in Nepal, including Kumbeswar, are thought to have their source in Gosainkunda Lake and, like Gosainkunda, to have been miraculously created by Shiva (see Dowman and Bubriski 1995).[2]

Janai Purnima marks the end of the deities' month-long world retreat and a resumption of shamanic ritual *(puja)* when deities can again be invoked in shamanic healing ceremonies. For one month the gods and goddesses have been on retreat in the lower world, rejuvenating their power *(shakti)*. For this month, the shamans' drums *(dhyangro)* have also been silent. "Major" healing puja that require the use of drums to invoke the deities are not performed during the month of Saun. Drums are not used in healing and purification rites again until Janai Purnima, when the deities resume their aid to humankind. As Miller (1997: 13) describes it, "Saun means a month of sickness and trouble. Hill people dread its coming each year. For during Saun the gods have gone down to the underworld leaving men defenseless against the attacks of other invisible forces that bring sickness, disaster, and death. Saun is a time to be endured until the gods begin to return from their underworld sojourn. With the full moon, the reentry begins."

I have gone on pilgrimage many times with my Tamang shaman-gurus, Gajendra Bombo (now deceased) and Aama Bombo (Mother Shaman), both of whom are from Boudhanath (Peters 1997a, 1998). This chapter describes the four Janai Purnima pilgrimages in which I have participated as an initiate shaman, and the rites of healing we performed on this day that the deities return.

When there are large crowds, as is typical during Janai Purnima, we spend only fifteen or twenty minutes in ceremony and dance at the sacred bathing pools. The sacred shrines themselves, which are always nearby, are usually little more than unhewn rocks with ceremonial offerings of flowers, ochre, and rice strewn about them. When our group begins the trek home after the short stay, we proudly adorn the sides of our drums with leaves from *titi paati* shrubs growing near the shrines. Titi paati is sacred to Shiva, and is evidence to all that we have been amidst divinity and have thereby acquired power. When we arrive back in Boudhanath, people in need of healing leave ritual food and drink offerings *(sagun)* in front of their houses, and we stop to perform the sacred pilgrimage dance *(tirtha nach)* taught to us by our guru, which may include performing soul-callings. The dance and healings now performed for those leaving offerings are the same as the shamans and initiates had done earlier at the shrine. Since our guru is well known and highly regarded, there are always about a half-dozen offerings left for us in Boudhanath, where we had begun our pilgrimage thirty-six hours earlier. But now we embody the healing power of Shiva. We have brought the healing powers back to the community.

The Pilgrimage Costume

Shamans in Boudhanath rarely wear full ritual attire except on pilgrimage. The shaman's ritual costume is a white shirt and skirt, long red and white scarves that tie around the forehead and hang down in back nearly to the ground, and a peacock-feather and porcupine-quill headdress or "crown" bound in a gold and/or red cloth band. One or two straps of bells and two or three rosaries *(mala)* are crisscrossed over the shaman's torso, and most shamans carry a carved wooden-handled two-sided drum. This drum is made of stretched hide, usually goatskin, less frequently deer, over a frame of hazel wood, and played with a curved snakelike cane drumstick. For pilgrimage, Aama paints both sides with a trident (symbol of Shiva), and with images of sun, moon, and a spirit serpent *(nag)*. Gajendra's drum had a male and female side, male with a trident and female with a lotus, the symbol of the Mother Goddess. White dots painted on the edge of the drumheads represent the planets and stars.

The costume symbolizes the Tamang shamanic cosmos. Because it's a totally oral tradition, details might vary from shaman to shaman, yet there is general consensus. Most of the major elements of the costume are explained in the sacred legends and histories (Ta: *she-rab*; meaning "wisdom") sung by the shamans during ritual. The peacock-feather headdress, for example, was a gift from the goddess Ghang Selmo Lhamo, daughter of Ghesar, the Heavenly God. One version of this goddess' she-rab states that the Truth Era or Golden Age ended due to an act of deception when the light or rainbow bridge connecting heaven and earth was severed. The result of this break has been a decline in morality and a corresponding increase in suffering. In the Truth Era, there was no need for shamans because humans were immortal like the gods. But when it ended, death, suffering, and illness beset the world. At that point, Ghang Selmo Lhamo felt compassion for humankind and initiated shamanism. As gifts of healing, she gave the peacock-feather and porcupine-quill headdress and water vessel (Ta: *bumba*), important cultural symbols and sacred shamanic "power objects," to the first human shaman, Selhi Häzer Bön. He in turn transmitted the Truth Era tradition to the lineage of ancestral shamans that continues into the present era (the dark Kali Yuga). It is from this link to the Golden Age that current Tamang shamans derive their spiritual authority (Peters 1990).

The names of these legendary founders of shamanism reflect the guiding principles of the Tamang shamanic vocation. *Lhamo* means "female goddess" and *Ghang* refers to her "great" status. *Mo* is a feminine suffix. *Sel* in both the name of the goddess and the first shaman is translated "to remove grievances," "remedy evil," "dispel darkness," and "cure disease" (see Jaschke 1972). Thus Ghang Selmo Lhamo is the Great Goddess who dispels darkness, remedies evil, etcetera. In Tamang, *Häzer* means a beam of light or a sunbeam. Thus Selhi Häzer Bon is the shaman *(Bön)* of the healing light.

The peacock feathers given by Ghang Selmo Lhamo, the golden band in which they are set, and the long red and white scarves, are symbols of the shaman's ability to trance-journey. They are the "rainbow bridge" that rein-states the severed connection with heaven that existed in the Golden Age. They are thus paths of "magical flight," the axis by which shamans soul jour-ney, that is, ascend and descend from the earth to the upper and lower worlds (Peters 1990). Further, the deities descend to take their place upon the porcu-pine quills set in the headdress when we drum and call them to accompany, assist, and protect us on our pilgrimage.

Gajendra, my first teacher, taught me that the shaman's drum is a horse upon which shamans fly into the sky. There are important founding myths of ancestral shamans flying on drums (Peters 1998). As a cultural symbol, the shaman's drum reflects the syncretic nature of Tamang shamanism. The painted tridents are symbols of the Great God, Shiva, while the dagger-type handle is associated with Tibetan Buddhism. However the drum itself is specifically Nepalese and shamanic and different from either the much larger two-sided lama ritual drums or the smaller hand drum *(damaru)* associated with Shiva or Lamaist ritual used by some Tibetan shamans (Peters 1997b).[3]

According to Aama, Shiva gave shamans the white frock in the Truth Era as the appropriate apparel to wear on pilgrimage because it is white and thus ritually "pure." The shamans wear two types of rosaries (mala). Aama typically wears two rosaries of brown *rudraksya* seeds, crisscrossed over each shoulder and under her arms, and one of black *ridha* seeds around her neck. These seeds are both from sacred trees, but rudraksya is ordinarily worn by Hindus because it is associated with Shiva in the form of Rudra, one of his wrathful aspects and one of his many names that emphasize the way sorcer-ers and evil spirits perceive his powers. In fact, Shiva is said to reside in rudraksya seeds. On the other hand, the black ridha rosary is worn only by shamans, primarily during ceremony, and is often used for divination. They are symbols of the vocation and of the lineage of ancestral shamans and, like the rudraksya, protect the shaman and frighten the evil spirits and sorcerers. Both types of rosary contain 108 beads. One shaman told me this reflects the twelve months of the year and seven planets, sun, and moon of the Tamang cosmos (multiplied, these numbers equal 108).[4]

One of each type of seed, and a copper coin, is put inside most shamans' drums.[5] Herein they are said to be "witnesses" that ensure by their power that the bad spirits the shaman exorcises from patients with help from the drum will keep their "promise" to return to their "proper places" and no longer cause human misfortune. The dagger handle of the drum and the dagger *(phurba)* the shamans carry in the waistbands of their pilgrimage skirts are used to subdue the wicked spirits *(laagu)* and compel them to obey the shaman's commands. When we don our costumes and carry the sacred paraphernalia, we understand that we are reconnecting with the sacred heritage of the Truth Era, when Shiva initiated the first pilgrimage. The thousands of pilgrims who visit the sacred Shiva sites on Janai Purnima are likewise following the model of his primordial Golden Age journey.

It is said that Shiva formed Gosainkunda Lake during the Truth Era in order to heal himself after he ingested a world-threatening poison that he extracted from the ocean at the request of the other deities. It was they who had created the poison, but Shiva alone among the gods was able to remove it. Afterward, he created Gosainkunda with his trident, and lay in its healing water. Gosainkunda Lake, like the other waters sacred to Shiva, is frequented by pilgrims seeking to heal their physical and spiritual poisons. In other words, the Janai Purnima pilgrimage reenacts myth and deed of the Truth Era. For the layperson, bathing or applying the holy water, in order to be healed in the model of Shiva, is one primary purpose for the pilgrimage.

Thus, the Janai Purnima pilgrimage celebrates the deities' return to this world, Shiva's own healing, his world-saving cleansing of the ocean and, at the same time, the return of the deities' healing powers to the community.

The Pilgrimage as Initiation: Separation

Scholars generally agree that pilgrimages can be rites of passage or initiation; that is, a ritual process by which a person's social status, role, and psychological condition are transformed. A complete rite of passage has three phases: separation, transition, and worldly return (Campbell 1968; van Gennep 1960; Turner 1967). In the context of this pilgrimage, the separation is from the familiar cultural world (ordinary reality) to access the sacred and "pure" nonordinary reality of the Golden Age, which has separate schemata giving sense and order to everyday life. In other words, "separation" represents a return to the very beginning of things, the pristine Truth Era, which, as Gajendra told, was when deities and humans lived together and the traditional ways were first established (see Eliade 1964; Harner 1990). The ensuing transition phase of the ritual journey includes tests, obstacles, and battles that the candidate, in the image of the deities' mythic deeds, needs to endure, followed by a successful "return" to the world with a gift or power acquired from Shiva that empowers the shaman's work and benefits the community.

The pilgrimage begins the night before the full moon day at our guru's home, where we play our drums for the first time in a month. First candles are lit; flowers, rice, and other food offerings made to the divinities; and various types of incense are burned to cleanse and purify the puja room before we call on the deities to empower our costumes and ritual gear. My guru and fellow shaman disciples say that the smell of burning titi paati leaves is offensive to sorcerers so that they, and the bad spirits they "play," are driven away and cannot stay or enter the room. Thus, a clean ritual space is created into which we can call, by song and drum, the deities and spirits of the village, surrounding areas, and those on the road to the shrine. Aama explains that, while she plays the drum, she "sees" the spirits and invites them to our gathering, to bless and to accompany us on the pilgrimage. As the shamans begin singing and drumming to invoke them, the spirits enter the room and cause the shamans to shake. The belts of bells crisscrossed over their shaking torsos chime to announce that the arriving spirits are embodying them.[6]

The shamans then sing the she-rab, telling the legends of Ghang Selmo Lhamo and Selhi Häzer Bön, as well as the sacred histories that empower our costumes, drums, and other sacred objects. Sometimes the singing and invocations take a whole night. Then, early at dawn on the full moon day, we help each other into our costumes and begin our pilgrimage to the shrine.

When we leave our guru's house, we perform the sacred shamans' pilgrimage dance for the first time in her courtyard. Aama's family leaves an offering for us, typical of those we will receive later on our return from the pilgrimage: a metal plate of uncooked husked rice *(chamal)*, often sprinkled with a bit of red ochre, which is pleasing to the deities and spirits.[7] Flowers (frequently rhododendrons, the national flower of Nepal), burning titi paati leaves, a lit candle, and a small glass of home-brewed whiskey *(rakshi)* are offered to the spirits residing in the four directions, and on both sides of the right hand, symbolic of the manner in which the good and bad spirits take their offerings—palm up for those kindly disposed and palms down for the opposite. Such is the way of calling every type of spirit from every possible direction, in order to remove any hindrances to a successful pilgrimage.

There is also a sacred water vessel (Ta: bumba or *kalash*) placed on the small ritual table. The water pot is a receptacle for deity and healing power, and is sacred to the Mother Goddess ("Shakti" or wives of Shiva). We will carry a bumba with us on pilgrimage, fill it with holy water from the pond at the Shiva shrine, and return home with it. The bumba must be carried by someone who is pure, as opposed to someone ritually impure or polluted. In the Tamang belief system, the purest person is a premenstrual virgin.

There can be slight variations in the style of bumba; they come in different sizes and are made of various metals. Aama considers only bumba made of copper and fashioned by a blacksmith *(kami)* to be suitable for ritual use. The blacksmith caste is generally believed to have magical powers, alchemical abilities to transmute one substance into another, entrusted to them by the deities. They are sometimes healers or even shamans, and are thought to possess powerful mantra.

The she-rab of the bumba, as sung by shamans when they empower it on the evening before departure for the shrine, is translated as follows:

> Bishwa Karma, the son of Ghesar Gyalpo, is a blacksmith by trade … (In order to make a copper bumba), Bishwa Karma built a fire… and (in the process of crafting the bumba) burned his hand. His father in Heaven, Ghesar Gyalpo, helped him complete the work and, when done, saw that the bumba was good for healing wounds, offering water (to stave the thirst of the rising sun as it begins its daily journey across the sky) and for drinking water when having a meal…. So the bumba was thus created and given (by the God of Heaven and his son) to Ghang Selmo Lhamo, who then gave it to Selhi Häzer Bombo. Selhi Häzer Bombo said he didn't know what to do with the bumba at first, but then he knew (from revelation) the sacred nature of the bumba and he said, "I make a sacred vow, a promise to the spirit of the Earth, with the planets as my witness, to use the bumba to bring back souls of those who suffer from attacks by the evil spirits."[8]

We play our drums as we leave Aama's home and sing jubilantly and repetitively in Tamang, "Saio saio bombo bombo saio saio" (dance dance shaman shaman dance dance). On all the pilgrimages in which I have participated, we walk the half mile or so from the guru's house to the giant Tibetan Buddhist reliquary mound (stupa) at Boudhanath, entering by dancing at its dragon-gated entrance, and then around the stupa (about one-eighth of a mile in circumference), stopping midway around to again dance the shaman's dance, this time at the shrine of the grandmother goddess Ajima. We honor this dangerous Hindu and Buddhist Mother Goddess, patron of Boudha, and bow to her. Aama makes an offering of rice, flowers, and red ochre to the bronze gilded image of Ajima. She washes her hands with a little water from the bumba, then takes some of the red ochre from the offering she just made and puts it on her forehead between the eyes *(tika)* with the third finger of her right hand, as a way of sharing the offering to the goddess *(prasad)*. After completing our clockwise circumambulation of the stupa, we board our bus still singing the sacred songs and playing our drums on the way to one of the Shiva shrines and ponds.

When leaving Aama's puja room, the Tamang shamans leave their shoes behind at the door, where they had been placed the night before when the rites preceding the pilgrimage began. They will not put them on again until the pilgrimage is complete. Shoes are considered to be ritually impure or polluted in the culture, and are left outside of all homes and shrines before entering so as not to carry pollution inside. Such a firm practice is further supported by an assumption that many shoes are made from the hide of the sacred cow. Removing one's shoes honors the sanctity and ritual purity of a house or shrine.

A lay person will remove shoes before approaching Shiva's bathing pond, but the shamans with whom I journeyed walked and danced barefoot the entire way, over dirty streets littered with sharp objects, through monsoon-soaked muddy fields, leech infested forests, and dangerous mountain paths. The lay folk, like the shamans, recognize going barefoot as indicative of a protective power given by Shiva, as he knows we are on a sacred journey to see him and need to be pure. Still, going barefoot is not a demonstration of power. It is an honoring to the earth and the purity of our mission. The path to the shrine is sacred ground. It is now different from an ordinary path. It is now sacred nonordinary territory, and customary behavior for touching the earth with shoes is inappropriate. Gajendra said that, during ritual worship, anything blocking direct contact with the ground weakened his power. Pilgrimage is shamanic ritual. The path, the bus, the puja room at Aama's house, everywhere we tread on pilgrimage is sacred ground.[9]

During the pilgrimage journey, shamans sing to the earth:

Listen to me ancestors
Listen to me, Earth Mother
Sky Father and Spirits of the four directions
I am just a bombo who knows nothing and is blind.

I am just a simple person living on the Earth
following the guidance of the guru and deities.
Mother Earth
Father Sky
I am a bombo of the Earth
and I am going to dance.
Earth Mother
I will touch you with my bare feet
Know I honor you
Do not be displeased
And grant me your shakti.

I have worn shoes on almost every pilgrimage. When alone with Tamang fellow initiates, I was the only initiate wearing shoes. I never received any specific instructions to the contrary, but I did not follow their or my gurus' model either, although I was aware of the significance in the Tamang belief system. But on the Janai Purnima of 1997, events conspired against my usual behavior. We left Aama's house so quickly I was unable to put on my shoes nor carry them with drum and drumstick in hand, so I reluctantly left without them. As I left the courtyard of Aama's home after the dance, I became afraid I'd injure myself. The bottoms of my feet have always been sensitive—my "Achilles' heels" so to speak—and I feared I was about to have a miserable time. At the same time, my spirit was into the dance and song. I wanted to tell someone to go back and retrieve the shoes, yet I didn't want to break the spell and aura cast about me, to break the reality of the experience with such a mundane request.

Since Janai Purnima occurs during the monsoon period, it was raining. The path was flooded; dirt, mud, and water obscured the ground. But I remembered the sharp bricks, stones, holes, piles of filth, waste, debris, and glass that cover the ground every other day. However, it was too late and I'd made my decision. I followed Aama and my brother and sister Tamang initiates. At first I was anxious and fearful, but each passing step gave me confidence that I was protected. By the time I'd walked, danced, drummed, and sung myself down main street to the Boudhanath stupa, I had hit a stride. Normally too self-conscious to be a good dancer, I was in perfect sync, and I knew it as I watched myself drumming, spinning, with my long red and white rainbow scarves carried in the wind. And I knew the hundreds of Boudhanath residents who had come to see us shamans leave for pilgrimage noticed that I too was barefooted and empowered with spirit to complete the sacred journey upon which we were all embarking. At the end, Aama and the others told me I'd done well—that I had embodied the shakti of Shiva.

The Pilgrimage as Initiation: Transition

The "transition" part of the pilgrimage initiation is the time of learning and transformation when the old is given up and new ways of being and doing are initiated. During this transition phase, transformational contact with the divine is made. Pilgrims come for a healing and the shamans come to acquire power to impart healings to their community for the ensuing year.

As we proceed along the road by bus, divinatory signs are noted. The flight of an eagle above the bus is said to be a good sign. But if a cat crosses our path, or a dead animal is on the road, it would be a bad sign. Aama says such an omen could cause us to take another road or even abort the pilgrimage. On the bus journey to the shrine, Aama spends most of the time discussing our intention. That is, why are we going to Shiva's pond? Aama teaches that the deities grant power to achieve one's desire if one's "heart is pure," that is, if all enmity and anger is cleansed from the heart when approaching the shrine. One must pray to the deity for wisdom and love, which is the proper attitude for entering Shiva's presence. Then he will grant what our hearts desire, as long as we are not greedy and thereby do not ask for more than one thing.

When we approach the pilgrimage site and nearby rock shrine, we dance and play our drums in honor of Shiva. Typically Aama is first to approach the shrine, a stone near the pond often said to conceal its underground source. There she will light a candle and burn incense. She bathes the rock shrine with holy water and honors the presence of deity with red ochre and a rice offering. Frequently she touches her forehead to the shrine and then sometimes, if the crowd is small, will fall backward and lie below the shrine, shaking and moaning, embodying Shiva's power (shakti). Arising, still, she gives tika to her disciples, taking the red ochre from offerings made on the holy rock that embodies the gods' invisible presence and putting it between our eyes. It is a shared offering and transference of power from deity to guru to student.

On Janai Purnima in 1994, we journeyed to the Shiva shrine at Richeswar, a sacred power place where water "miraculously" oozes from a large stone that is believed to be sourced by Gosainkunda. Richeswar is not typically visited at this time of year, and, therefore, is not the site of a crowded festival. Here Aama gave my fellow initiates and me an initiation known as "lamp light" *(diyo batti)*. Approaching me, Aama said, "Open your mouth. If you are pure of heart you will not die. Om Shiva." Without a thought, I did as she had instructed and Aama poured a burning wick and oil from a small earthen lamp into my mouth. I could hear it sizzling as I felt it on my tongue. After a few seconds I inadvertently swallowed some oil, gagged, and then spit out the wick. I was baffled for what had occurred and furthermore didn't understand why I was not burned.

Later, Aama explained Shiva had given me his shakti to withstand the heat, as well as his blessing. This had been a test to divine if I could receive more teachings. A few days later, Aama added that the rite was given as a surprise as it avoided producing fear and an unwillingness to participate. Previously, I had seen Aama demonstrate a similar mastery of fire when she would threaten sorcerers and bad spirits possessing a patient with wick and fire. By first eating the flame and then threatening to force the wicked agents attacking the patient to do the same if they didn't immediately comply with her demands, she chased them away.[10] Gajendra used to put live coals into his disciples' mouths in order to drive away the bad spirits they exorcised from patients and transferred into their own bodies as part of the healing ceremony.

At this and other full moon pilgrimages, Aama gives her initiates Raksha Bandhan, as mentioned earlier, for spiritual protection. While tying the strings around the wrist seven times, Aama prayed to Shiva for his kindness to us initiates, that he fill our lives with wisdom and love, and show us the path beyond anger and greed. When she said this, I remembered her teaching that such feelings hinder the practice of shamanism as they cloud the mind so that it isn't receptive to the clear message of the spirits and deities.

Before leaving the pilgrimage power place, we dance in a line before the shrine, bringing Shiva's power into our bodies. Some of us shake. Then we do a soul-calling for ourselves, for others in the crowd, and sometimes for a particular person who has journeyed with us for the purpose of being healed. When shaking, many of us bend down and dip our drum handles into the sacred water and then sprinkle it on ourselves to purify the drum and shaman and to overcome our poisons as Shiva did in the legend. Then the drum is held out flat, one side facing up, while playing on the underside with the curved wooden stick. The guru places a small amount of white husked rice on the top side of the drum. As the drum is being beaten, the rice bounces and some of whatever chaff remains separates from the rice. If the separated part is dark, it indicates bad planets or bad days; it is a sign of misfortune. If white, all is well. If whitish yellow, it is from the sun, and is the most auspicious sign for the prosperity of the person. It is a bad sign if the rice congregates on the south side of the drum, the direction of death, or if slight beating of the underside of the drum causes the rice to bounce unexpectedly high, indicating the desire to leave the earth.

At the pilgrimage site, the rice is discarded if there are dark parts of separated husk, or if other bad signs appear. No attempt at communicating the divination is made during the pilgrimage. More rice is then placed on the drum by the guru and, when the result is good, the light separated parts and the rice are poured by the shaman over his/her own head. The process is then repeated and the white separated parts and rice poured over members of the nearby crowd or the person/patient brought for that purpose.

At one pilgrimage, a woman who was inexplicably finding it difficult to become pregnant accompanied us. Among the shamans on the pilgrimage were her father and brother. Her husband and many other family members came to show their support. When we saw the white/yellow rice, we were happy and poured it over the woman's head and danced and drummed around her.

Soul Retrieval: The Healing Work of Pilgrimage

Shamans speak of white rice as one type of soul—the chi (Ta.) or *saato*. Chi is also the ritual process of soul-calling, and the method of returning a lost soul by pouring the rice.

An individual is thought to have three souls (Peters 1995, 1998). Gajendra spoke of the chi as a soul of wisdom and as a microcosm of the High Heavenly God Ghesar Gyalpo, the source of life and creator of the universe. The chi is a whitish golden light, like the sun. It is responsible for our conscious self-awareness or mindfulness; without it a person becomes foolish with erratic behavior. There is a loss of ability to work and maintain good social relations (cf. Desjarlais 1992; Maskarinec 1995; Peters 1998). It can get lost and/or be captured by sorcerers and bad spirits when it departs the body in fear states, as well as in dreams. It is located in the middle of the forehead in the place of the third eye at times of conscious ordinary reality awareness.

Aama distinguishes chi or saato from the *atma* soul, which is immortal and, unlike saato, produces physical death when it leaves the body. Saato is also different from *hungsa*, a term used for the death-state soul. *Saato* means "presence of mind."

Saato is given to the fetus by divinity at the inception of life. It is the womb soul and human life soul. It is the dream soul and the soul the shaman sends on soul journeys. According to Aama, under normal conditions, it ceases to exist at the time of a person's physical death.[11]

When this soul has left the body and is lost, there is a consequent failure to focus and think clearly about things. My field assistant told me that saato soul loss can cause a sort of obsession, as when a person leaves a comfortable place or a loved one for a journey, a part of that person (the saato) can remain behind. When leaving home, for example, a person might do a short soul-calling ritual and then cut its path of return, that is, the connection that would obstruct presence of mind and clear thinking for the task at hand, and then does not look back in that direction until home is out of view.

Saato is described as being a sort of "breath soul" (Sanskrit: *prana*), a life energy that pervades the universe. Thus, when saato is lost, there is a lack of energy, vitality, and interest in life. The saato returning done at the Shiva shrine for the childless woman was to restore her vital reproductive saato. The life energy of reproduction was called and returned through the chi ritual.

In discussions of sorcery, the term *saato putla* is used. A *putla* can be an amulet containing a part of a person (hair, nails) or an image in the victim's likeness that is used to call the saato, fooling it into coming to the amulet or image in the belief it is "body," so that a sorcerer can capture it and use it to control and make a person ill. For example, burning the putla burns the victim. Putla also has the meaning of being the puppet of another person, as when one person is acting the agenda of another, sometimes unaware and due to saato theft by nefarious sorcerers.

In my opinion, the principle shamanic work of pilgrimage is the healing work of chi or saato retrieval. It is the ritual event that distinguishes the shamans' activities from the others who participate in the full moon festivals. Everyone approaches the sacred pond at the shrine and douses themselves with the healing waters. Many receive the threads and red tika at the shrine. Pilgrims dance and sing, but no one else does soul retrievals but the shamans.[12]

Pilgrimage No Guarantee of Shamanic Initiation

Not every pilgrimage is a successful initiation, and just going on pilgrimage with Aama is no guarantee of an initiation for the candidate shaman. Aama is a direct, spontaneous person of firm character with absolute trust in the power of her relationship to spirit. She says she looks into a person's heart and knows if it is pure or impure and dark. If the person is involved in sorcery of any kind, she has very little patience with that person.

Such is the case of Sita, a patient and potential candidate shaman. Sita claimed to be have been taken as a child as an initiate of the forest shaman *(ban jhankri)*, a half-human, small yeti-type character (see Peters 1997d). Later she had a shaman teacher who died before giving her the necessary mantra to control bad spirits. Aama's spirit divined that Sita should accompany us three months later to Nagarkot, on Janai Purnima 1997, to "become perfect." Aama seemed to like Sita.

During the ensuing three months, Aama learned that Sita and her deceased guru were involved in sorcery and were "playing" with evil cremation ground ghosts. In one divination, Aama's chief tutelary spirit diagnosed that Sita's problem was that, while she had awakened evil spirits and was attempting to use them to get revenge on her divorced husband, she had no control of them and, consequently, they were causing her physical and mental problems. In other words, Aama came to see Sita as a person capable of sorcery. This was confirmed to her on the evening before departing for the Janai Purnima initiation when Sita became possessed by a spirit who claimed to be the fearsome goddess Kali's younger sister, and a great mountain divinity. Aama and the other shamans present recognized this as a lie told by the wicked spirit causing Sita's illness and possessing her. Sita is not a shaman nor healer, and whatever relationship she has with spirit, it is not good in the shaman's view. Her behavior is motivated by anger and a desire to cause harm, which is not the behavior associated with the presence of a prestigious goddess.

Thus, when we arrived at the Shiva shrine on our pilgrimage, Aama did not give Sita the blessing, initiation, and mantra she wanted. Unlike the other initiates, Sita was not in costume and thus not giving the proper honor. So, as she stood at the pond with us white-clad and feathered candidates, Aama pushed her into the water. When Sita was soaked with mud up to her waist and began to climb out, Aama pushed her on the forehead with her bare foot, propelling her back into water over her head. I assume this was degrading and humiliating to Sita, even more than one would experience in the West, given the Nepalese cultural belief regarding the spiritually polluting effects of contact with the feet. But, in Aama's view, she was not being disrespectful to Sita nor attempting to injure her. She was "driving away" the possessing and controlling evil spirit from Sita's body. She had not kicked Sita but rather the spirit possessing her. If anyone was embarrassed or injured, it was the spirit.

The Pilgrimage as Initiation: Worldly Return

The "dangerous passage" that is initiation is not complete until a return to the world with something new, a transformed condition that benefits the initiate and the community. Turner (1967) argues that this return phase of the rite of passage enhances a feeling of oneness and solidarity with the community.

When we return to Boudhanath, we are empowered with healing power from Shiva, which we use to heal members of the community. We return with the sacred water vessel, which now contains the holy water from Shiva's pond. As mentioned before, the person who carries it should be as pure as possible in order to maintain ritual purity. The water vessel and its contents are a remedy for the ills of those who need treatment, those who leave an offering for us on the streets of Boudhanath.

Dueling Shamans

Shaman groups pass one another on the roads leading to and from the shrines. Generally, such encounters cause the groups to stop and bow to one another, as a form of honoring. Sometimes one group will challenge another group to a song "duel" in which each shaman group competes, demonstrating their knowledge of the stories and legends. A loss requires a bow and acknowledgment of the other group's proficiency. Even between competing groups, there seems to be a feeling of camaraderie. After a duel, the shamans are likely to embrace and share a laugh and a cigarette or drink together.

But problems may develop. Stories are legion. One group may desire to hinder the progress of the other through magic or *mantra-tantra*. In fact, there always seems to be a suspicion that something negative and potentially violent can occur. I've seen these initial fears compounded with shaman groups flaunting arrogance and the ready availability of strong alcohol. For two consecutive years, Aama became involved in pushing matches with groups of male shamans who unsuccessfully attempted to push her away from the Shiva shrine at Nagarkot as they advanced swiftly, dancing, drumming, pushing, and flaunting their prowess, unconcerned that Aama and a host of other supplicants were already there in line.

As one can imagine, a tall white shaman in a crowd of small dark Nepali shamans attracts a lot of attention. Quite often, the natives' cameras have turned on me, even though I try to ignore their stares and to blend in as much as possible. However, one year a drunk became angry, and accused me of sacrilege because I am not Nepali. Aama stepped in to defend me and said I was on pilgrimage as her student. When the man pushed me, Aama drew her wooden dagger from her skirt and chased him away at the same time that Maya, one of her colleagues, whisked me away from the crowd that had gathered to watch the fracas.

Other anthropologists who have participated in shaman pilgrimages also tell of potential consequences of "magical battles." Miller (1997) mentions an encounter between shaman groups that led to one group seizing the water vessel of the other. Generally, such occurrences are followed by solemn discussion and a shaking of heads. On the bus back to Boudhanath after our brief encounters, Aama said, "Why should we fight each other? When we go to the shrines, our hearts are pure and we have no evil in mind. Why should anyone attempt to stop anyone?"

Returning with Power to Heal

When we arrive in Boudhanath to complete the pilgrimage, and alight from the bus, we begin our final circle around its central shrine (the stupa) again dancing, drumming, and singing *"Saio saio bombo bombo saio saio."* Many people gather around us, and residents who want healings bring out their offering trays. We slowly dance around the stupa, stopping to perform soul-callings and returning (chi) at each person's offering, and then finally go back to Aama's home and puja room.

On Janai Purnima 1998, we performed six soul retrievals in Boudhanath. These were conducted with passion and energy, although we were very tired from the long journey we had begun over twenty-four hours earlier. The soul retrievals were done in two ways. First, all the shamans and initiates in our group completed a ten- to twelve-minute vigorous pilgrimage dance to call the soul of the patient into the water vessel. As told in the she-rab legend, the water vessel is used to retrieve souls. In some healing rituals, strings are tied to the vessel and food perched on its lips, then the shaman drums along the strings enticing the soul to enter into the vessel. During the pilgrimage soul retrievals, the shamans likewise drum the soul into the vessel but without the strings. A shaman puts the point of his/her daggers or drum handle into the water vessel, wetting it with holy water, which is then placed upon the crown of the patient's head while the shaman continues to drum and dance. These ritual gestures symbolize the return of saato soul parts.

For the second form of soul retrieval, some of us took rice from Aama, who first had the patient hold it before placing it upon the surface of our drums. Then we called the lost soul into our drums, as before, after which we discarded anything unfavorable, finally pouring the remaining white rice and flakes on the patient's head.

With the completion of the healings, the purpose of the shaman's pilgrimage has been accomplished. He/she went to the pilgrimage shrines "to beg for power" and has returned with the shakti of healing.

Initiation Concludes but the Work Goes On

After completing the healings, we return to Aama's house and puja room. Aama faces her altar, sits down, drums, and begins to shake. Then, with hand gestures, she releases the spirits that she carried (or carried her) and guided her and us disciples to the Shiva ponds. After twenty minutes or so, we help one another take off our shaman's costumes. Some of the shamans, and most of the lay folk, now leave us. The pilgrimage is complete. A few remain behind to have dinner with Aama and discuss the events of these twenty-four hours—the empowering of the costumes, the singing of the she-rab, and the resumption of playing the drum, the rejected initiate, the pilgrimage dance and songs, the soul retrievals, and the return home with power to continue the shaman's work for the next year.

Soon patients begin to arrive, having heard that the empowered shamans have returned. Some of the patients are old and ill. Another who had recently lost her father, needs her saato returned and the cords of attachment to the deceased cut. The initiation is over but the power given by Shiva to the shaman has been replenished and the work of healing goes on.

Notes

Introduction

1. On the sensory dimensions of culture and experience, see Classen 1993; Classen, Howes, and Synnott 1994; Seremetakis 1994; Stoller 1989, 1997; Taussig 1993.

2. In Turner's work on pilgrimage, he used the term *liminoid* ("liminal-like") to characterize the transition stage. Many writers who draw on Turner seem to have found this term awkward and have used *liminal* instead, a practice we will follow here.

3. Such is the case of Medjugorje in former Yugoslavia, where an apparition of the Virgin Mary led to the establishment of an internationally renowned pilgrimage site (see Bax 1992).

4. At the same time, as Greenfield and Cavalcante (this volume) rightly note, "anti-structure" is not necessarily a feature of all pilgrimage.

5. However, this does not mean that individuals who do avail themselves of the biomedical system do not also make vows and pilgrimage part of their search for healing.

6. In recent literature on pilgrimage and tourism, a number of authors have suggested that the boundaries between the two are often blurred.

7. However, we do not want to over-emphasize this dimension of pilgrimage. While we believe the fact that pilgrimage is a collective activity is an important part of its healing power, we also want to acknowledge the many critiques of Turner that emphasize the limits to communitas on many pilgrimages. Moreover, the sense of felt communitas may be variable both among individuals and groups, and over time, in the course of any particular pilgrimage.

Chapter 1

1. Maria da Fatima Batista and her cousin Laura are composites of individuals used to facilitate telling the story. Other characters represent real people whom we met and interviewed, although we have changed their names and identities.

2. The wages that are lost and the physical demands of the journey also must be considered when calculating the cost of a pilgrimage.

3. Her data, collected on the same population, although at different times, seems to lead to conclusions that differ from ours.

4. We use the masculine form for saints since our primary reference is to St. Francis.

5. See references on this point provided by King (this volume).

6. In the more than three-fourths of a millennium since, fewer than three hundred saints have been designated authentic. In contrast, *Butler's Lives of the Saints*, a standard reference, "lists over three thousand saints and beati without pretending to be exhaustive" (Kieckhafer 1988: 2), and *The Biblioteca Sanctorum*, the most comprehensive work on saints as of 1980, listed more than ten thousand saints, and many more are not included (see Kieckhafer for citations).

7. It is unfortunate that in what is perhaps the most influential anthropological book on pilgrimage, *Image and Pilgrimage in Christian Culture* (Turner and Turner 1978), the authors allowed this misconception when they applied van Gennep's model of transition to focus on the implications of the liminal experience of visitors to some of the major shrines of Christendom. Although this enabled them to make a major contribution to anthropological thinking, it decontextualized pilgrimage as an aspect of the cult of the saints to the reader unfamiliar with medieval and Latin American pilgrimage.

8. Transduction is the conversion of matter, energy, and information from one form to another.

9. For independent confirmation with children suffering from asthma, see Castes, et al. 1999. Research conducted on laboratory animals, however, has resulted in the questioning of a simple relationship between stress and depressed immune function (Dantzer 1997; Dhabhar, Miller et al. 1995; Dhabhar and McEwen 1996). Acute stress, it appears, redistributes peripheral blood leukocytes (in the rat) to other bodily compartments serving to enhance immune surveillance and ultimately immune function (Dhabhar and McEwen 1996: 2608). Only chronic stress, the kind with which we are concerned, depresses immune function.

10. Declarative learning and memory are conscious and usually easy to present verbally since they refer mostly to people, objects, and places. (Procedural memory, in contrast, is associated with perceptual and motor skills.) They are not conscious, often difficult if not impossible to express verbally, and evident only in performance rather than in conscious recall (Kandel 1999: 508). Both usually work together. Through repetition, declarative memory can be transformed into the procedural type.

11. Conceptualized as part of a schema, defined as "the organization of cognitive elements into an abstract mental object capable of being held in working memory with default values or open slots which can be variously filled with appropriate specifics" (D'Andrade 1995: 179), serial or sentential logic recodes experience into

symbols, while parallel connectionist logic transforms it into connections between neuron-like units (140). The two forms of logic lead to two ways of learning with the serial one being more explicit and much quicker since it can be verbalized in terms of rules. The connectionist one, that most likely is employed by pilgrims who have made their vows while in a religiously (self) induced ASC, leads to a result that is more permanent with more rapid and automatic execution (144).

12. Work by Stoller (1996) on the role of music and dance in conveying information and its meaning in healing rituals among the Songhay adds further support to this argument.

13. At present there are no unobtrusive ways to tell whether an individual being observed or interviewed is in trance, especially in a field situation. DNA microarrays may make this possible in the future (see T. Brown 1999; Rossi 2000a, 2000b).

Chapter 2

1. See Vieira 1991; Galán 2000; Garcia 2000.

2. For the prominence of women pilgrims at Marian shrines see, for example, Christian 1989; Taylor 1995; Warner 1990.

3. Fieldwork was carried out in 1991–1992, and during a shorter period in 1997. The dissertation based on this fieldwork is published in Gemzöe 2000. During my periods of study and fieldwork in Portugal, I have been affiliated with the Instituto de Ciências Sociais in Lisbon under the supervision of Professor João de Pina-Cabral. Fieldwork in Portugal, as well as periods of writing, were made possible by grants from the Swedish Institute; Helge Ax:son Johnsons stiftelse; Stiftelsen Lars Hiertas minne; Svenska Sällskapet för Geografi och Antropologi; Wallenbergsstiftelsens jubileumsfond; and Crafoordska Stiftelsen.

4. I use the term *popular religion* in this chapter in line with Badone's definition. According to Badone, "popular religion" refers to "those informal, unofficial practices, beliefs, and styles of religious expression that lack the formal sanction of established church structure" (1990: 5–6).

5. In Sanchis's words, "Quando está em perigo a seguranca essencial da existência, individual, familiar ou social."

Chapter 3

1. For more information about the spread of this tradition, see also Dubisch 1995; Finucane 1977; Garbini 1966; Hansen 1968; Marinatos and Hirmer 1960; Merrifield 1987; Nolan 1991; Oettinger 1997; Pina-Cabral 1986; Radford 1949; Wilson 1983.

2. See Barreto n.d.; Bercht 1989; Cardoso 1983; Della Cava 1970; Dörner 1962; Egan 1991; Forman 1975; Frota 1989; Gross 1971; Meirelles 1968; Mota 1968; Oettinger 1990, 1992; Oktavec 1995; Romano 1965; Saia 1944; Sanchis 1983; Slater 1986, 1990; Toor 1947; Turner and Turner 1978.

Chapter 4

1. Hebrew grammar marks masculine and feminine forms of both words.

2. This poem can be found in a collection of Rachel Blubstein's poems entitled *Shirat Rachel* (1950).

3. Men also come to these tombs, but they rarely come to "pour their hearts out" or to seek "understanding." At the tombs of Our Mother Rachel and Rachel the Wife of Rabbi Akiva, men typically recite prayers from the formal Jewish liturgy or they accompany women kin who have come for personal reasons. Especially at the Tomb of Rachel the Wife of Rabbi Akiva, the men who do come to make personal petitions tend to belong to subordinate ethnic or socioeconomic groups. At the tomb of Rachel the Poetess men generally come as part of tour groups, or to accompany women kin. The fact that the saint "understands" is far more dominant in the discourse of women pilgrims than in the discourse of men pilgrims.

4. I am not referring here solely to women in patriarchal societies, but also to men who are not part of the dominant group, for any reason (race, class, sexual identity, physical disabilities, etc.).

Chapter 5

1. Names of all pilgrims have been changed.

2. Walsingham lies just to the south of a number of coastal resorts, and with its medieval buildings and ruins it is a common place of resort for those seeking some "culture" to go with the sun and sand of a beach holiday.

3. Much of the debate over the ordination of women centered around the question of whether creating women ministers (and ultimately creating women bishops) would break the chain of authority established by the church over the centuries. The Anglican shrine at Walsingham, along with other pockets of conservatism in the Church of England, held out against such ordination. I do not explore in detail here the fascinating and important issue of gender symbolism (and conflict) in conceptualizations of Mary and Christ.

4. Indeed, a relic taken from the body of a holy figure mediates between personhood and materiality, especially when it is physically incorporated into the structure of a building.

5. The parallel here is with Turner's (1967: 28–30) notion of condensation in symbolism, combining ideological, emotional, and physical poles of association.

6. Of course the Walsingham story displays parallels with certain other "origin myths" of Christian pilgrimage sites. Dubisch (1995) discusses a Greek Orthodox shrine celebrating the Annunciation that also features a well discovered by builders of a church, the healing of royalty, and the rebirth of nationhood.

7. The sermon was given by Ernest Underhill, a well-known supporter of Catholic Revival.

8. So far, approximately forty interviews have been completed with pilgrims from various parts of England.

9. As one Roman Catholic woman, a middle-aged resident of Walsingham, put it: "The pilgrims coming really do get a sense of peace and…they get an answer but what I feel is that they come and they pray and they are able to face whatever it is they have got to face when they go back. I mean people know, they have told me they have been told they are terminally ill, they know they are going to face death. I have also been told that they have gone in the Slipper Chapel knowing this, knowing that there is no hope and they don't come back but they are able to go away and face it with courage and that takes a lot."

10. Compare with Preston (1992: 33) who briefly notes that cures associated with pilgrimage may be physical but also "social," such as the healing of family solidarity or the attainment of jobs.

Chapter 6

1. This is not to imply that the pilgrimages taken by members of more traditional groups are *not* flexible or idiosyncratic. Typically however, such pilgrimages are perceived by creatives as being more tightly structured and organized than creativist pilgrimages.

2. While attending a large evangelical religious meeting in San Diego, I was surprised to hear the minister in attendance claim that anyone not cured during the meeting had not had sufficient faith. In my experiences visiting Roman Catholic shrines and interviewing practicing Roman Catholics, this causal link between insufficient faith and continued illness did not seem to be made.

3. In all fairness, I should point out that I came across many American Catholics and many French creatives, although the French do tend to think of Americans as being more "New Age" than themselves.

Chapter 7

1. For a comprehensive account of the Run for the Wall, see Michalowski and Dubisch 2001.

2. The literature on PTSD is vast and more than can be covered here. For a discussion see Young 1982; also Piquet and Best 1986 for a bibliography of PTSD literature to that date.

3. Rolling Thunder is an enormous yearly event with its own organization. Ostensibly dedicated to the POW/MIA issue, it has become a yearly biker phenomenon. See Michalowski and Dubisch 2001 for a more extended discussion.

4. For a discussion of the POW/MIA issue, see Franklin 1993. However, R. Michalowski and I have a different take on this issue in our book (2001).

5. While both of these are now officially recognized consequences of the war, it was some time after the war's end that such recognition occurred; on PTSD, see Young 1995.

6. Many Vietnam veterans we know have trouble sleeping, a common symptom of PTSD.

7. For a discussion of such forms of secular, popular pilgrimage, see Reader and Walter 1993.

8. On the attraction of motorcycle riding and outlaw biker gangs for veterans, see Pierson 1997; Wolf 1991.

9. On the concept of brotherhood among outlaw bikers, see Wolf 1991. On the formation of the Hell's Angels among World War II veterans, and the later attraction of the biker gangs for returning Vietnam veterans, see Livigne 1987.

10. For an overview of anthropological work on the subject, see Young 1982.

11. For discussions of the "self-traumatized" vet—that is, the veteran whose traumas resulted from acts he himself committed during war—see Laufer et al. 1985; Haley 1974; Fontana et al. 1992; also Lifton 1992.

12. This is not to suggest, however, that the Vietnam Veterans Memorial has necessarily brought about reconciliation over the conflicts that Vietnam represented—and continues to represent—in American culture. For a discussion of some of these issues, and the conflict between the "romantic" and the "heroic" traditions of memorialization in American culture, see Morris 1990.

Chapter 8

Author's Note: Another version of this material appears in Gilmore and Van Proyen 2005.

1. Theme camps are groups that attach a particular "theme" to their campsite and that invite other festival attendees to participate in some way in their theme or installation. These camps typically have names like the Irrational Geographic Society, the Liminal Lounge, and the Cat Herders Union, Local 451. Villages are larger groupings and are typically collections of many different theme camps.

2. The other original cofounder, Jerry James, is no longer involved with Burning Man.

3. For example, one incorrect but popular legend is that Harvey initiated Burning Man because he wanted to commemorate a lost love. The popularity of this myth has necessitated a statement on Burning Man's official Web site (see Harvey 2000).

4. By their own definition, the San Francisco Cacophony Society is "a randomly gathered network of free spirits united in the pursuit of experiences beyond the pale of mainstream society. We are that fringe element which is always near the edge of reason.... We are the merry pranksters of a new decade. Our ranks include starving artists living on a diet of sacred cows, under-employed musicians listening to their own subliminal messages, post-modern explorers surveying urban environments, dada clowns working in the neural circuits, and live actors playing the theater of the street. We are nonpolitical, nonprophet and often nonsensical.... You may already be a member" (see http://www.cacophony.org; accessed August 20, 2004).

5. Bohlender returned to Burning Man in 2002 and 2004 and now lives in Kansas City where he is a minister for the Friends of the Bridegroom International House of Prayer (he was previously with the Vineyard Church in Cincinnati, Ohio).

6. Eliade was, of course, not without his own critics (see Smith 1982; Grimes 1990).

Chapter 9

Author's Note: I would like to thank James Bauml for his partnership on our field-trip pilgrimages and for his editorial comments. Susana Eger Valadez, John and Collette Lilly, Húmberto Fernandez, Patricia Díaz Romo, and Jerry and Linda Patchen have all helped make this research fruitful. The study would not have been possible without the generous assistance, guidance, and expertise of the Wixárika families mentioned. Support for this research was funded in part by a Fulbright–García Robles Fellowship; a University of Texas–Pan American Faculty Research Grant; and California State University, Chico New Faculty Research Development Funds.

1. I use the term *Wixárika*, instead of *Huichol*, because it is the term they prefer to call themselves. *Wixáritari* is the plural form. Huichol is the name Spanish explorers, conquerors, administrators, and clergy gave them; it was later adopted by the Mexican government.

2. In an e-mail message dated April 24, 1999, anthropologist Bret Blosser writes that in his archival research in Mexico City and Guadalajara he found what may be the earliest reference to the Wixárika peyote pilgrimage, written in 1869. Blosser writes "A missionary proposed that the regional political authorities use their good connections with political authorities in the peyote desert, and along the peyote route to arrest peyote pilgrims in order to give them a *"susto"* (big scare) that would stop them from bringing peyote to the Sierra. In later letters, it became clear that the political authorities contacted their superiors in Guadalajara, who responded that they should stay out of religious affairs."

3. Much of the information on peyote and tobacco and descriptions of healing activities occurring on the pilgrimage presented here comes from long-term field-work that Jim Bauml, botanist at the Arboretum of Los Angeles County, and I, have been carrying out among the Wixárika for close to two decades. In 1987 I joined a temple group of Wixáritari on this pilgrimage, and since 1998 Bauml and I have accompanied several Wixárika shamans and their families on three pilgrimages to Wirikuta. During three trips Bauml and I took with the Wixárika families, we recorded myths and locations of sacred places visited on the pilgrimage, rituals that took place, and ethnobotanical information of plant knowledge and use by our companion consultants. The actual names of these individuals have been changed for reasons of privacy.

4. Temple members holding major roles, such as the singing shaman, the keepers of the corn goddess, the fire god, the goddess of growth and vegetation, the rain gods, the god of the hunt, and the earth goddesses are required to make three pilgrimages to Wirikuta during the five years that these individuals and their families are fulfilling their ritual responsibilities in the temple. All other temple members are encouraged to participate in the pilgrimage; however, not all do. Ranch groups

usually attempt to complete five pilgrimages to Wirikuta in five years; however, this, too, can vary and families may take longer to accomplish the journeys.

5. See De Mille (1976, 1980) for his critique on the factuality of Carlos Castañeda's work as social science literature. In my own fieldwork, I have met numerous Americans, Mexicans, and Europeans who were avid readers of Castañeda's books and who had come to the Wixárika area in search of their own Don Juan. Several westerners promote themselves as Wixárika-trained shamans and capitalize on this by offering journeys to the Wixaritari, or to the San Luis Potosí desert and the lure of consuming peyote. This kind of "drug tourism" has taken its toll on Wirikuta and the surrounding environment with over harvesting in the native peyote habitat and desecration of sacred places revered by the Wixárika (see Furst and Schaefer 1996).

6. I wish to thank Drs. Johannes Wilbert (e-mail March 27, 2001) and Lisa Feintech (e-mail April, 2001) for their instructive comments on the pharmacology of peyote and nicotine and potential neurochemical actions that may arise from combining these two psychoactive plants.

7. Wixáritari go on the pilgrimage for various reasons. Some pilgrims may be fulfilling their specialist training in becoming a master musician, as was the case for Rafael, or attaining the level of master artist (see Eger 1978; Valadez 1986a, 1986b; Schaefer 1993, 2002).

Chapter 10

1. All foreign words are Nepali unless otherwise indicated. The vocational vocabulary of the Tamang shamans is a mixture of Nepali and Tamang (a Tibetan dialect). The latter will be signified as Ta. The Tamang term *bombo* is philologically related to the Tibetan term *bonpo*.

2. Shiva, whose name means "Peaceful One" or "Auspicious One," (Dowman and Bubriski 1995, Pattanaik 1997) is probably the most popular divinity in Nepal and considered by many Tamang shamans to be "god of the shamans." He is called "Mahadev" or "Great God." For most Nepalese, Hindu and Buddhist alike, he is creator and destroyer.

3. There are various styles and types of drums used by shamans in Nepal. All Tamang shamans I've met use the dhyangro, as do the shamans of quite a few other ethnic groups (see Miller 1997) although its use is certainly not universal among Nepalese shamans (see Maskarinec 1995).

4. See Zimmer (1972) for detailed discussion of the significance of the number 108 in Indian cosmology.

5. The most powerful and prototypical coin for the drum is a blacksmith-produced copper coin called a "Pasupati," another of Shiva's names, forged as long ago as the Licchavi period, which began about 300 CE, as a way of honoring the god and his principle place of worship in Nepal, also called Pasupati. Pasupati means "Lord of Beasts, Animals, and Living Beings" as well as "Remover of Fetters" and "Savior" (Dowman and Bubriski 1995).

6. *Kamnu* (to shake) is a universally recognized sign in Nepal that the spirits and/or their *shakti* (power) have entered the body ("embodying" the shaman). Kamnu is also used to describe the shaking of "possessed" patients, the victims of spirits. The shaman's controlled embodiment is ceremonial, while the victim's are spontaneous and involuntary trance states (see Bourguignon 1976: Lewis 1971). Thus, shaking is the principle feature of merging with divinity or spirit, be it good or evil, voluntary or involuntary, by shaman or patient (see Hitchcock and Jones 1976).

7. The rice used in shamanic ceremonies that I've observed is always husked (i.e., more or less removed of its husk). There are differences among various groups, and even within the same group, as to which stage of rice, husked or not, is most holy and therefore to be utilized in puja. Generally speaking, based on my experiences, husked chamal, is purest because it is white, and uncooked is purer than cooked (see Geller 1992, Miller 1997).

8. Ghesar Gyalpo is the ruler of the Universe who Gajendra said resides on a level above the ninth level of the Upper World. He sits on a throne of soul (Ta: *chi*, Nepali: *saato*) that he brings to earth to bestow life. His origins are Tibetan and pre-Buddhist, yet the name of his son is Hindu. Thus this she-rab, like so many other aspects of Tamang shamanic culture in the Kathmandu Valley represents a unique blending of ancient Tibetan and Indian spiritual sources (Peters 1998; cf. Holmberg 1989 for a description of a very different Tamang shamanic system from another area of Nepal).

Parenthetical phrases were given as commentary and explanation by my Tamang shaman teachers.

9. Not everyone barefoot is motivated by religious observance. There are always some mountain folk going to the shrines who do not wear shoes because they are too poor to buy them.

10. *Batti* or putting a flame into a deceased person's mouth is the first act of setting the body on fire during the Hindu funeral ceremony. Thus the shaman's *diyo batti* symbolizes the conquest of death. The sorcerers' fear of the fire and wick is a fear of death and immolation, as they do not have Shiva's protection.

11. To the contrary, Gajendra maintained the chi was immortal (see Peters 1998).

12. These soul retrievals do not involve a shamanic journey but a calling of the lost soul to come to the drum so it can be returned. It is completely different from the methods taught by Sandra Ingerman (1991).

References Cited

Aijmer, G., ed. 1995. Introduction to *Syncretism and the Commerce of Symbols*, 4–5. Göteborg, Sweden: The Institute for Advanced Studies in Social Anthropology.

Akstein, D. 1977. Socio-Cultural Basis of Terpsichoretrancetherapy. *American Journal of Clinical Hypnosis* 19 (4): 221–25.

Albe, E., and J. Rocacher, eds. 1996. *Les Miracles de Notre-Dame de Rocamadour au XIIe Siècle*. Toulouse, France: Le Pérégrinateur.

Allen, L. 1995. Offerings at the Wall. *American Heritage*, February/March, 94.

Avgar, A., and C. Gordon. 1997. Your Health: Results and Conclusions. *At*: 62.

Avorva, M., Z. Haklai, H. Klein, and M. Handelsman. 1996. *Health in Israel: Selected Statistics*. Israel Ministry of Health.

Azzi, R. 1978. *O Catolicismo Popular No Brasil*. Petrópolis, RJ: Editora Vozes.

Badone, E., ed. 1990. Introduction. In *Religious Orthodoxy and Popular Faith in European Society*, 3–23. Princeton: Princeton University Press.

Barber, T. X. 1984. Changing "Unchangeable Bodily" Processes by (Hypnotic) Suggestions: A New Look at Hypnosis, Cognitions, Imaging, and the Mind-Body Problem. In *Imagination and Healing*, ed. A. A. Sheikh, 69–128. Farmingdale, New York: Baywood.

Barnai, Y. 1980. *Igrot Hasidim M'Eretz Yisrael*. Jerusalem: Yad Yitzhak Ben-Zvi.

Barreto, A. de P. 1986. A Romaria e a Doença. Paper presented at the Meetings of the Latin American Studies Association, Boston, MA.

———. n.d. Ex:Votos: Os Milagres dos Santos. Unpublished manuscript.

Bastide, R. 1951. Religion and the Church in Brazil. In *Brazil: Portrait of Half a Continent*, ed. T. L. Smith and A. Marchant, 334–55. New York: Dryden.

Battiata, M. 1984. Remembrance on a Train: From Seattle and the Plains, Vietnam Veterans Make Pilgrimage to Reunion at "The Wall." *Washington Post*, November 10, 1984.

Bax, M. 1992. Female Suffering, Local Power Relations, and Religious Tourism: A Case Study From Yugoslavia. *Medical Anthropology Quarterly* 6 (2): 114–27.

Begg, E. 1996. *The Cult of the Black Virgin*. London: Penguin Books Arkana.

Ben-Ari, E., and Y. Bilu. 1987. Saints' Sanctuaries in Israeli Development Towns. *Urban Anthropology* 16:243–72.

Benítez, F. 1968. *En la Tierra Magica del Peyote.* México: D.F.

Benowitz, N. L. 1988. Pharmacological Aspects of Cigarette Smoking and Nicotine Addiction. *New England Journal of Medicine* 319:1318–1330.

Ben-Zvi, Y. 1960. *Journeys on the Paths of the Land and its Neighborhoods, Taken from Travel Notes and Diaries.* Jerusalem: Jerusalem Printing and Publishing.

Bercht, F. 1989. Miracles: Votive Offerings in Northeastern Brazil. In *House of Miracles,* 11–17. New York: Americas Society.

Berdahl, D. 1994. Voices at the Wall: Discourses of Self, History, and National Identity at the Vietnam Veterans' Memorial. *History and Memory* 6,2 (Fall, Winter): 88–124.

Best, D., and J. Haye. 2001. The Mausoleum: Temple of Memory. http://www.burningman.com/whatisburningman/2001/01_art_theme.html (accessed December 23, 2004).

Betteridge, A. H. 1992. Specialists in Miraculous Action: Some Shrines in Shiraz. In *Sacred Journeys: The Anthropology of Pilgrimage,* ed. A. Morinis, 189–210. Westport, CT: Greenwood.

Black, S. 1969. *Mind and Body.* London: William Kimber.

Blanco, V. 1991. *El Venado Azul.* Mex.: Editorial Diana. Video.

Bloch, M. 1991. Language, Anthropology and Cognitive Science. *Man* 26 (2): 183–98.

Blubstein, R. 1950. *Shirat Rachel.* Tel Aviv: Davar Publisher.

Bohlender, R. 2000. The Redefinition of My Personal Concept of Weird. http://www.next-wave.org/oct00/burningman.htm (accessed August 20, 2004).

Bourguignon, E. 1976. *Possession.* San Francisco: Chandler and Sharp.

Bowers, K. 1977. Hypnosis: An Informational Approach. *Annals of the New York Academy of Sciences* 296:222–37.

Bowman, G. 1991. Christian Ideology and the Image of a Holy Land: The Place of Jerusalem Pilgrimage in Various Christianities. In *Contesting the Sacred: The Anthropology of Christian Pilgrimage,* ed. J. Eade and M. J. Sallnow, 98–112. New York: Routledge.

Boyd, C. E., and J. P. Dering. 1996. Medicinal and Hallucinogenic Plants Identified in the Sediments and Pictographs of the Lower Pecos, Texas Archaic. *Antiquity* 7 (268): 256–75.

Boyll, L. 1991. *Huichol Sacred Pilgrimage to Wirikuta.* University of California Extension Center for Media and Independent Learning. Video.

Braithwaite, J. 1990. Cultural Communications Among Vietnam Veterans. In *Cultural Legacies of Vietnam,* ed. P. Ehrenhaus and R. Morris, 145–70. Norwood, NJ: Ablex.

Brettell, C. 1990. The Priest and His People. The Contractual Basis for Religious Practice in Rural Portugal. In *Religious Orthodoxy and Popular Faith in European Society*, ed. Badone, 55–75. Princeton: Princeton University Press.

Brill, L. 1998. The First Year in the Desert. http://www.burningman.com/whatis-burningman/1986_1996/firstyears.html (accessed December 23, 2004).

Brown, D. DeG., and M. Bick. 1987. Religion, Class, and Context: Continuities and Discontinuities in Brazilian Umbanda. *American Ethnologist* 14 (1): 73–93.

Brown, D. P. 1992. Clinical Hypnosis Research Since 1986. In *Contemporary Hypnosis Research*, ed. E. Fromm and M. R. Nash, 427–58. New York: Guilford.

Brown, D. P., and E. Fromm. 1987. *Hypnosis and Behavioral Medicine*. Hillsdale, NJ: Erlbaum.

Brown, P. 1981. *The Cult of the Saints*. Chicago: University of Chicago Press.

Brown, T. 1999. *Genomes*. NY: Wiley-Liss.

Cacophony Society. 1990. Rough Draft: The "Official" Monthly Newsletter and Calendar of Events for the San Francisco Cacophony Society.

Campbell, J. 1968. *The Hero with a Thousand Faces*. 2nd ed. Princeton: Bollingen Series/Princeton University Press.

Cardoso, C. L. 1983. Ex-voto, uma Expressao Ambigua. In *Primeira Exposicao Nacional de Paineis Votivo do Rio, do Mare do Alem-Mar*. Lisbon: Museu de Marinha.

Carroll, J. 2001. *Constantine's Sword: The Church and the Jews: A History*. Boston: Houghton Mifflin.

Cassar, P. 1964. Medical Votive Offerings in the Maltese Islands. *The Journal of the Royal Anthropological Institute of Great Britain and Ireland* 94 (I,II): 23–29.

Castés, M., I. Hagel, M. Patenque, P. Canelones, A. Corao, and N. R. Lynch. 1999. Immunological Changes Associated with Clinical Improvement of Asthmatic Children Subjected to Psychosocial Intervention. *Brain, Behavior, and Immunity* 13:1–13.

Cavalcante, A. M. 1987. As Festas da Festa. In *Diario de Noticias*, October 11.

Cavalcante, A. M., and S. M. Greenfield. 2003. *Dr Argeu: A Construção de um Santo Popular*. Fortaleza, Br.: Editora UFC.

Christian, W. 1984. Religious Apparitions and the Cold War in Southern Europe. In *Religion, Power and Protest in Local Communities: The Northern Shore of the Mediterranean*, ed. E. R Wolf, 239–66. Berlin: Mouton.

———. 1989. *Person and God in a Spanish Valley*. Rev. ed. New York: Seminar Press.

Classen, C. 1993. *Worlds of Sense: Exploring the Senses in History and Across Cultures*. New York: Routledge.

Classen, C., D. Howes, and A. Synnott. 1994. *Aroma: the Cultural History of Smell*. New York: Routledge.

Cocksworth, C. 1991. Eucharistic Theology. In *The Identity of Anglican Worship*, ed. K. Stevenson and B. Spinks, 49–68. Harrisburg, PA: Morehouse Publishing.

Coleman, S. 2000. Meanings of Movement, Place and Home at Walsingham. *Culture and Religion* 1 (2): 153–70.

Coleman, S., and J. Eade, eds. 2004. *Reframing Pilgrimage: Cultures in Motion*. New York: Routledge.

Coleman, S., and J. Elsner. 1995. *Pilgrimage Past and Present in the World Religions*. Cambridge: Harvard University Press.

———. 1998. Performing Pilgrimage: Walsingham and the Ritual Construction of Irony. In *Ritual, Performance, Media*, ed. F. Hughes-Freeland, 46–65. New York: Routledge.

———. 1999. Pilgrimage to Walsingham and the Reinvention of the Middle Ages. In *Pilgrimage Explored*, ed. J. Stopford, 189–214. York: York Medieval.

Colven, C. 1990. *England's Nazareth: A History of the Holy Shrine of Our Lady of Walsingham*. Fakenham: Iceni Press.

Cowan, D., and A. Silk. 1999. *Ancient Energies of the Earth: An Extraordinary Journey into the Earth's Natural Energy System*. London: Thorsons/Harper Collins.

Crain, M. 1992. Pilgrims, "Yuppies," and Media Men: The Transformation of an Andalusian Pilgrimage. In *Revitalizing European Rituals*, ed. J. Boissevain, 95–112. New York: Routledge.

Cranston, R. 1988. *The Miracle of Lourdes*. New York: Image, Doubleday.

Crosby, D. and J. McLaughlin. 1973. Cactus Alkaloids. XIX. Crystallization of Mescaline HC1 and 3-Methoxytryptamine HC1 from Trichocereus Pachanoi. *Lloydia* 36:416–18.

Csordas, T. J. 1983. The Rhetoric of Transformation in Ritual Healing. *Culture, Medicine and Psychiatry* 7 (4): 333–75.

———. 1994. *The Sacred Self: A Cultural Phenomenology of Charismatic Healing*. Berkeley: University of California Press.

———. 1995. Imaginal Performance and Memory in Ritual Healing. In *The Performance of Healing*, ed. C. Laderman and M. Roseman, 91–113. New York: Routledge.

D'Andrade, R. 1995. *The Development of Cognitive Anthropology*. Cambridge: Cambridge University Press.

Dahlberg, A. 1991. The Body as Principle of Holism: Three Pilgrimages to Lourdes. In *Contesting the Sacred: The Anthropology of Christian Pilgrimage*, ed. J. Eade and M. Sallnow, 30–50. New York: Routledge.

Danforth, L. 1989. *Firewalking and Religious Healing: The Anastenaria of Greece and the American Firewalking Movement*. Princeton: Princeton University Press.

Dantzer, R. 1997. Stress and Immunity: What Have we Learned from Psychoneuro-immunology. *Acta Physiol Scand Suppl* 640:43–46.

Davidson, H. 1998. *Roles of the Northern Goddess*. London: Routledge.

Davie, G. 1993. "You'll Never Walk Alone": The Anfield Pilgrimage. In *Pilgrimage in Popular Culture*, ed. I. Reader and T. Walter, 201–19. Basingstoke, UK: MacMillan.

Davis, J. 1984. The Sexual Division of Religious Labor in the Mediterranean. In *Religion, Power and Protest in Local Communities*, ed. E. Wolf, 17–50. New York: Mouton.

Dearing, T. 1966. *Wesleyan and Tractarian Worship: An Ecumenical Study*. London: Epworth.

Deep, D. K. 1993. *Popular Deities, Emblems and Images of Nepal*. Delhi: Nirala.

Della Cava, R. 1970. *Miracle at Joaseiro*. New York: Columbia University Press.

De Mille, R. 1976. *Castaneda's Journey: The Power and the Allegory*. Santa Barbara, CA: Capra.

———, ed. 1980. *Don Juan Papers: Further Castaneda Controversies*. Santa Barbara, CA: Ross-Erickson.

Desjarlais, R. R. 1992. *Body and Emotion: The Aesthetics of Illness and Healing in the Nepal Himalayas*. Philadelphia: University of Philadelphia Press.

Devereux, P. 1990. *Places of Power: Secret Energies at Ancient Sites: A Guide to Observed or Measured Phenomena*. London: Blandford/Cassell.

———. 1999. *Places of Power: Measuring the Secret Energy of Ancient Sites*. London: Blandford.

Deyts, S. 1988. Ex-voto de Guerison en Gaule. *Historie et Archologie* 23:82–87.

Dhabhar, F. S., and B. S. McEwen. 1996. Stress-induced Enhancement of Antigen-specific Cell-mediated Immunity. *Journal of Immunology* 156:2608–15.

Dhabhar, F. S., A. H. Miller, B. S. McEwen, and R. L. Spencer. 1995. Effects of Stress on Immune Cell Distribution. *Journal of Immunology* 154:5511–27.

Dias, G. M. 1978. New Patterns of Domination in Rural Brazil: A Case Study of Agriculture in the Brazilian Northeast. *Economic Development and Cultural Change* 27 (1):169–82.

Dörner, G. 1962. *Folk Art of Mexico*. New York: A. S. Barnes.

Douglas, M. 1970. *Natural Symbols: Explorations in Cosmology*. New York: Random House.

Dow, J. W. 1986. Universal Aspects of Symbolic Healing: A Theoretical Synthesis. *American Anthropologist* 88:56–69.

Dowman, K., and K. Bubriski. 1995. *Sacred Places of Kathmandu*. London: Thames and Hudson.

Dubisch, J. 1995. *In a Different Place: Pilgrimage, Gender, and Politics at a Greek Island Shrine*. Princeton: Princeton University Press.

Eade, J. 1991. Order and Power at Lourdes: Lay Helpers and the Organization of a Pilgrimage Shrine. In *Contesting the Sacred: The Anthropology of Christian Pilgrimage*, ed. J. Eade and M. Sallnow, 51–76. New York: Routledge.

Eade, J., and M. J. Sallnow, eds. 1991. *Contesting the Sacred: The Anthropology of Christian Pilgrimage*. New York: Routledge.

Egan, M. 1991. *Milagros: Votive Offerings from the Americas*. Santa Fe: Museum of New Mexico.

Eger, S. 1978. Huichol Women's Art. In *Art of the Huichol Indians*, ed. K. Berrin, 35–53. San Francisco: Fine Arts Museums of San Francisco.

Eickelman, D. 1976. *Moroccan Islam: Tradition and Society in a Pilgrimage Center*. Austin: University of Texas Press.

Eickelman, D., and J. Piscatori. 1990. *Muslim Travelers: Pilgrimage, Migration, and the Religious Imagination*. Berkeley: University of California Press.

Eisler, R. 1988. *The Chalice and the Blade: Our History, Our Future*. San Francisco: Harper.

Eliade, M. 1954. *The Myth of the Eternal Return: Or Cosmos and History*. London: Arkana.

———. 1964. *Shamanism: Archaic Techniques of Ecstasy*. Trans. W. Trask. Princeton: Bollingen Series/Princeton University Press.

———. 1976. *Myths, Dreams and Mysteries: The Encounter Between Contemporary Faiths and Archaic Reality*. London: Collins.

Eshed, H. 1991. Morbidity Factors among Women: Research Findings. In *Women's Health in Israel*, ed. A. Avgar, 35–40. Jerusalem: Israel Women's Network.

Espírito Santo, M. 1995. *Os Mouros Fatimidas e as Aparições de Fátima*. 3a Edição ed. Lisboa: Instituto de Sociologia e Etnologia das Religiões. Universidade Nova de Lisboa.

Ferguson, M. 1980. *The Aquarian Conspiracy: Personal and Social Transformation in the 1980s*. New York: St. Martin's Press.

Finucane, R. C. 1977. *Miracles and Pilgrims: Popular Beliefs in Medieval England*. Totowa, NJ: Rowman and Littlefield.

Fisher, C. 1979. *Walsingham Lives On*. London: Catholic Truth Society.

Fontana, A., R. Rosenheck, and E. Brett. 1992. War Zone Traumas and Post-Traumatic Stress Disorder Symptomatology. *Journal of Nervous and Mental Disease* 180:748–55.

Forman, S. 1975. *The Brazilian Peasantry*. New York: Columbia University Press.

Frank, G. 2000. *The Memory of the Eyes: Pilgrims to Living Saints in Christian Late Antiquity*. Berkeley: University of California Press.

Franklin, B. H. 1993. Mythmaking in America. New Brunswick, NJ: Rutgers University Press.

Frecska, E., and Z. Kulcsar. 1989. Social Bonding in the Modulation of the Physiology of Ritual Trance. *Ethos* 17 (1): 70–87.

Frey, N. 1998. *Pilgrim Stories: On and Off the Road to Santiago*. Berkeley: California University Press.

Freyre, G. 1964. *Masters and the Slaves*. Trans. S. Putnam. New York: Alfred A. Knopf.

Frota, L. C. 1989. The Ex-voto of Northeastern Brazil: Its Antecedents and Contemporary Expression. In *House of Miracles*, 25–35. New York: Americas Society.

Fulleylove, J., and J. Kilman. 1912. *The Holy Land*. London: Adam and Charles Black.

Furst, P. T. 1969a. Myth in Art: A Huichol Depicts His Reality. *The Quarterly* 7 (3): 16–26. Los Angeles: County Museum of Natural History.

———. 1969b. *To Find Our Life: The Peyote Hunt of the Huichols of Mexico*. Los Angeles: UCLA Latin American Center Media Division. Video.

———. 1972. To Find Our Life: Peyote among the Huichol Indians of Mexico. In *Flesh of the Gods: The Ritual Use of Hallucinogens*, ed. P. T. Furst, 136–84. New York: Praeger.

———. 1989. Life and Death of the Crazy Kieri: Natural and Cultural History of a Huichol Myth. *Journal of Latin American Lore* 15 (2): 155–79.

Furst, P. T., and M. Anguiano. 1976. "To Fly As Birds": Myth and Ritual as Agents of Enculturation among the Huichol Indians of Mexico. In *Enculturation in Latin America: An Anthology*, ed. Johannes Wilbert, 95–181. Los Angeles: UCLA Latin American Center Publications.

Furst, P. T., and S. B. Schaefer. 1996. Peyote Pilgrims and Don Juan Seekers: Huichol Indians in a Multicultural World. In *People of the Peyote: Huichol Indian History, Religion and Survival*, ed. S. B. Schaefer and P. T. Furst, 503–21. Albuquerque: University of New Mexico Press.

Galán, L. 2000. El Vaticano Revela el Texto Integro del Tercer Misterio de la Virgen de Fátima. *El Pais*:44.

Garbini, G. 1966. *The Ancient World*. New York: McGraw-Hill.

Garcia, J. 2000. La incógnita de las versiones cambientes. *El Pais*:44.

Geertz, C. 1973. *The Interpretation of Cultures: Selected Essays*. New York: Basic Books.

Geller, D. 1992. *Monk, Householder and Tantric Priest*. Cambridge: Cambridge University Press.

Gemzöe, L. 2000. *Feminine Matters. Women's Religious Practices in a Portuguese Town*. Stockholm: Almqvist and Wiksell.

Gillett, H. 1946. *Walsingham: The History of a Famous Shrine*. London: Burns Oates and Washbourne.

Gilmore, L. 2005. Fires of the Heart: Ritual, Pilgrimage, and Transformation at the Burning Man Festival. In *AfterBurn: Reflections on Burning Man*, ed. L. Gilmore and M. Van Proyen. Albuquerque: University of New Mexico Press (43–62).

Gilmore, L., and M. Van Proyen, eds. 2005. *AfterBurn: Reflections on the Burning Man Festival*. Albuquerque: University of New Mexico Press.

Glaser, R., S. Kennedy, W. Lafuse, R. Bonneau, C. Speicher, J. Hillhouse, and J. Kiecolt-Glaser. 1990. Psychological Stress-induced Modulation of Interleukin 2

Receptor Gene Expression and Interleukin 2 Production in Peripheral Blood Leukocytes. *Archive of General Psychiatry* 47:707–12.

Glaser, R., W. Lafuse, R. Bonneau, C. Atkinson, and J. Kiecolt-Glaser. 1993. Stress-associated Modulation of Proto-oncogene Expression in Human Peripheral Blood Leucocytes. *Behavioral Neuroscience* 107:525–29.

Gold, A. G. 1988. *Fruitful Journeys: The Ways of Rajasthani Pilgrims*. Berkeley: University of California Press.

Goodman, F. D. 1988. *Ecstasy, Ritual and Alternate Reality: Religion in a Pluralistic World*. Bloomington: Indiana University Press.

Greenfield, S. M. 1972. Charwomen, Cesspools and Road Building: An Examination of Patronage, Clientage and Political Power in Southeastern Minas. In *Structure and Process in Latin America: Patronage, Clientage and Power Systems*, ed. A. Strickon and S. M. Greenfield, 71–100. Albuquerque: University of New Mexico Press.

———. 1977. Patronage, Politics and the Articulation of Local Community and National Society in Pre-1968 Brazil. *Journal of Inter-American Studies and World Affairs* 19 (2): 139–72.

———. 1979. Domestic Crises, Schools, and Patron Clientage in Southeastern Minas Gerais. In *Brazil: Anthropological Perspectives*, ed. M. Margolis and W. Carter, 362–78. New York: Columbia University Press.

———. 1989. Pilgrimage, Therapy, and the Relationship Between Healing and the Imagination. Center for Latin America Discussion paper No. 82 Milwaukee: University of Wisconsin–Milwaukee.

———. 1990. Turner and Anti-Turner in the Image of Christian Pilgrimage in Brazil. *Anthropology of Consciousness* 1 (3–4): 1–8.

———. 1991. Hypnosis and Trance Induction in the Surgeries of Brazilian Spirit Healer-mediums. *Anthropology of Consciousness* 2 (3–4): 20–25.

Griffin, W., ed. 2000. *Daughters of the Goddess: Studies of Healing, Identity, and Empowerment*. Walnut Creek, CA: AltaMira.

Grigg, R. 1995. *When God Becomes Goddess*. New York: Continuum.

Grimes, R. L. 1990. *Ritual Criticism: Case Studies in its Practice, Essays on its Theory*. Columbia: University of South Carolina Press.

———. 2000. *Deeply Into the Bone: Re-inventing Rites of Passage*. Berkeley: University of California Press.

Gross, D. R. 1971. Ritual and Conformity: A Religious Pilgrimage to Northeastern Brazil. *Ethnology* 10 (2): 129–48.

Haley, S. 1974. When the Patient Reports Atrocities: Specific Considerations of the Vietnam Veteran. *Archives of General Psychiatry* 30:191–96.

Hansen, H. J. 1968. *European Folk Art in Europe and the Americas*. Trans. M. Whittall. London: Thames and Hudson.

Harel, Y., D. Kaneh, and G. Rahav. 1997. *Youth in Israel: Social Welfare, Health, and Risk Behavior from an International Perspective*. Jerusalem: Brookdale Institute.

Harner, M. 1990. *The Way of the Shaman*. 2nd ed. San Francisco: Harper and Row.

Harvey, L. 1998. Larry Harvey's 1998 Speech: Saturday, September 5, 1998, Center Camp Stage–Black Rock City, NV. http://www.burningman.com/whatisburningman/1998/98_speech_1.html (accessed August 20, 2004).

———. 2000. Setting the Record Straight on Burning Man Myths (and a Few New Ideas). http://www.burningman.com/press/myths.html (accessed December 23, 2004).

Hass, K. 1998. *Carried to the Wall: American Memory and the Vietnam Veterans Memorial*. Berkeley: University of California Press.

Hirschon, R. 1983. Women, the Aged, and Religious Activity: Oppositions and Complementarity in an Urban Locality. *Journal of Modern Greek Studies* 1 (1): 113–30.

Hitchcock, J., and R. Jones, eds. 1976. *Spirit Possession in the Nepal Himalayas*. New Delhi: Vikas.

Holmberg, D. 1989. *Order and Paradox*. Ithaca, NY: Cornell University Press.

Holroyd, J. 1992. Hypnosis as a Methodology in Psychological Research. In *Contemporary Hypnosis Research*, ed. E. Fromm and M. R. Nash, 201–26. New York: Guilford.

Hooneart, E. 1987. *A Teologia das Romarias*. Diário do Nordeste. October 11.

Hooper, J., and D. Teresi. 1986. *The 3-Pound Universe*. New York: G. P. Putnam's Sons.

Hutchinson, B. 1966. The Patron-dependent Relationship in Brazil: A Preliminary Examination. *Sociologia Ruralis* 6 (1): 3–29.

Hyde, L. 1979. *The Gift: Imagination and the Erotic Life of Property*. New York: Random House.

Ingerman, S. 1991. *Soul Retrieval*. San Francisco: Harper Collins.

Instituto Nacional Indigenista. 1992. *Lugares Sagrados: Relato Wirrarika*. México, D. F.: Instituto Nacional Indigenista.

Israel Center for Disease Control. 1997. *Condition of Health in Israel*. Tel HaShomer.

Jackowski, A., and V. Smith. 1992. Polish Pilgrim Tourists. *Annals of Tourism Research* 19:92–106.

Jackson, M. 1989. *Paths toward a Clearing: Radical Empiricism and Ethnographic Enquiry*. Bloomington: Indiana University Press.

Jackson, R. 1988. *Doctors and Diseases in the Roman Empire*. Norman: University of Oklahoma Press.

Janet, P. 1925. *Psychological Healing*. New York: MacMillan.

Jaschke, H. 1972. *A Tibetan-English Dictionary*. London: Routledge and Kegan Paul.

Jennings, D. 1992. Walsingham and its Contribution to English Marian Devotion

Principally From 1897 to the Present-Day. Bachelor's Thesis. Ordinary, St. John's Seminary, Wonersh.

Jilek, W. G. 1989. Religious Experiences as Self-Healing Mechanisms. In *Altered States of Consciousness and Mental Health: A Cross Cultural Perspective*, ed. C. A. Ward. Newbury Park, CA: Sage.

Justice, Christopher. 1997. *Dying the Good Death: The Pilgrimage to Die in India's Holy City*. Albany: State University of New York Press.

Kandel, E. R. 1998. A New Intellectual Framework for Psychiatry. *American Journal of Psychiatry* 155 (4): 457–69.

———. 1999. Biology and the Future of Psychoanalysis: A New Intellectual Framework for Psychiatry Revisited. *American Journal of Psychiatry* 156 (4): 505–24.

Keast, H. 1984. *Our Lady in England. A Panorama of Marian Culture and Devotion in England from Anglo-Saxon Times Down to the Present*. Helston, UK: Helston Printers.

Kemp, E. 1990. Foreword to *Nazareth: A History of the Holy Shrine of Our Lady of Walsingham*, by C. C. England, 5–6. Fakenham: Iceni.

Khalsa, P. S., ed. 1981. *A Pilgrim's Guide to Planet Earth: A Traveler's Handbook and New Age Directory*. London: Wildwood House.

Kieckhafer, R. 1988. Imitators of Christ: Sainthood in the Christian Tradition. In *Sainthood: Its Manifestations in World Religions*, ed. R. Kieckhafer and G. D. Bond, 1–42. Berkeley: University of California Press.

King, C. 1993. His Truth Goes Marching On: Elvis Presley and Pilgrimage to Graceland. In *Pilgrimage in Popular Culture*, ed. I. Reader and T. Walter, 92–114. Basingstoke, UK: MacMillan.

King, C. L. 1999. Ex-votos: Religious and Social Commentaries in Northeast Brazil. PhD diss., University of Tennessee.

King, S. K. 1992. *Earth Energies*. Wheaton, Illinois: Quest Books.

Kirmayer, L. J. 1993. Healing and the Invention of Metaphor: The Effectiveness of Symbols Revisited. *Culture, Medicine, and Psychiatry* 17:161–95.

Kleinman, A. 1988. *The Illness Narratives: Suffering, Healing and the Human Condition*. New York: Basic Books.

Kleinman, A., V. Das, and M. Lock, eds. 1997. *Social Suffering*. Berkeley: University of California Press.

Kozinets, R. V. 2002. Can Consumers Escape the Market?: Emancipatory Illuminations from Burning Man. *Journal of Consumer Research* 29:20–38.

Kritz, R. 1976. *Al Shirat Rachel*. Kiryat Motskin: Poreh.

Laderman, C., and M. Roseman, eds. 1996. Introduction. In *The Performance of Healing*, 1–16. New York: Routledge.

Lanciani, R. 1893. *Pagan and Christian Rome*. New York: Houghton Mifflin.

Larkin, M. 1995. *Religion, Politics and Preferment in France since 1890: La Belle Epoque and its Legacy*. Cambridge: Cambridge University Press.

Laufer, R. S., E. Brett, and M. S. Gallops. 1985. Symptom Patterns Associated with Post-Traumatic Stress Disorder Among Vietnam Veterans Exposed to War Trauma. *American Journal of Psychiatry* 142:1304–11.

LeDoux, J. 2002. *Synaptic Self: How Our Brains Become Who We Are*. New York: Viking.

Lévi-Strauss, C. 1963. The Effectiveness of Symbols. In *Structural Anthropology*, 186–205. Trans. C. Jacobson and B. G. Scheepf. New York: Basic Books.

———. 1979. *The Raw and the Cooked: Introduction to a Science of Mythology: I*. Trans. John and Doreen Weightman. New York: Octagon Books.

Lewis, I. M. 1971. *Ecstatic Religion*. Harmondsworth, UK: Penguin Books.

Ley, R. G., and R. G. Freeman. 1984. Imagery, Cerebral Laterality, and the Healing process. In *Imagination and Healing*, ed. A. A. Sheikh, 51–68. Farmingdale, NY: Baywood.

Lifton, R. J. 1992. *Home From the War: Learning from Vietnam Veterans*. 2nd ed. Boston: Beacon.

Livigne, Y. 1987. *Hell's Angels: Taking Care of Business*. Toronto: Ballantine.

Lock, M. 1993. Cultivating the Body: Anthropology and Epistemologies of Bodily Practice and Knowledge. *Annual Review of Anthropology* 22:133–55.

Lock, M., and N. Scheper-Hughes. 1987. The Mindful Body. *Medical Anthropology Quarterly* 1 (1): 6–41.

Low, S. M. 1988. The Medicalization of Healing Cults in Latin America. *American Ethnologist* 15 (1): 136–54.

Luhrmann, T. M. 1989. *Persuasions of the Witch's Craft: Ritual Magic in Contemporary England*. Cambridge: Harvard University Press.

Macklin, J. 1974. Folk Saints, Healers and Spiritist Cults in Northern Mexico. *Revista/Review Interamericana* 3:351–67.

Macklin, J., and R. Crumrine. 1973. Structural Development and Conservation in Three North Mexican Folk Saint Movements. *Comparative Studies in Society and History* 5:89–105.

MacLean, P. D. 1990. *The Triune Brain in Evolution: Role in Paleocerebral Functions*. New York: Plenum.

Mandell, A. 1980. Toward a Psychobiology of Transcendence: God in the Brain. In *The Psychobiology of Consciousness*, ed. D. Davidson and R. Davidson, 379–464. New York: Plenum.

Mangrum, S. 1998. What is Burning Man? http://www.burningman.com/whatis-burningman/1998/98n_letter_sum_1.html (accessed December 23, 2004).

Margolis, L. 1984. José Gregorio Hernández: The Historical Development of a Venezuelan Popular Saint. *Studies in Latin American Popular Culture* 3:28–46.

Marinatos, S., and M. Hirmer. 1960. *Crete and Mycenae*. New York: Harry N. Abrams.

Martin, E. 1987. *The Woman in the Body: A Cultural Analysis of Reproduction*. Boston: Beacon.

Maskarinec, G. 1995. *The Rulings of the Night*. Madison: University of Wisconsin Press.

Maybury-Lewis, D. 1992. *Touching the Timeless*. Millennium Series no. 6. Alexandria, VA. P.B.S. Video.

McBrien, R. P. 1995. *The Harper Collins Encyclopedia of Catholicism*. New York: Harper.

McCleary, J. A., P. S. Sypherd, and D. L. Walkington. 1960. Antibiotic Activity of an Extract of Peyote (*Lophohora williamsii* [Leamire] Coulter). *Economic Botany* 14:247–49.

McDonald, T., ed. 1997. *Walsingham: 100 Years of Pilgrimage*. Fakenham, UK: Lanceni Press.

McGuire, M. B. 1988. *Ritual Healing in Suburban America*. New Brunswick: Rutgers University Press.

McKevitt, C. 1991. San Giovanni Rotondo and the Shrine of Padre Pio. In *Contesting the Sacred: The Anthropology of Christian Pilgrimage*, ed. J. Eade and M. Sallnow, 77–97. New York: Routledge.

McKim, W. A. 1991. *Drugs and Behavior*. Upper Saddle River, NJ: Prentice Hall.

McLaughlin, E. 1974. Equality of Souls, Inequality of Sexes: Women in Medieval Theology. In *Religion and Sexism: Images of Woman in the Jewish and Christian Traditions*, ed. R. R. Ruether, 213–66. New York: Simon and Schuster.

Meirelles, C. 1968. *As Artes Plásticas no Brasil: Artes Populares*. Rio de Janeiro: Edições de Ouro.

Merchant, K. 1996. *Pharmacological Regulation of Gene Expression in the CNS*. Boca Raton: CRC.

Mernissi, F. 1977. Women, Saints, and Sanctuaries. *Signs*. 3 (2): 101–12.

Merrifield, R. 1987. *The Archaeology of Ritual and Magic*. New York: New Amsterdam Books.

Merz, B. 1985. *Points of Cosmic Energy* W. Essex, UK: Daniel.

Michalowski, R., and J. Dubisch. 2001. *Run For the Wall: Remembering Vietnam on a Motorcycle Pilgrimage*. New Brunswick: Rutgers University Press.

Miller, C. 1997. *Faith-healers in the Himalayas*. Delhi: Book Faith India.

Milner, B., L. R. Squire, and E. R. Kandel. 1998. Cognitive Neuroscience and the Study of Memory. *Neuron Review* 20:445–68.

Milstein, U. 1985. *Rachel*. Tel Aviv: Zmora, Bitan.

Miron, D. 1991. *Founding Mothers, Stepsisters: The Emergence of the First Hebrew Poetesses and Other Essays*. Tel Aviv: HaKibbutz Ha Meuchad.

Mitchell, S. 1981. Introduction to *The Logic of Poverty: The Case Study of the Brazilian Northeast*, ed. S. Mitchell, 1–9. London: Routledge and Kegan Paul.

Morinis, A. 1984. *Pilgrimage in the Hindu Tradition: A Case Study of West Bengal*. Delhi: Oxford University Press.

Morris, R. 1990. The Vietnam Veterans Memorial and the Myth of Superiority. In *Cultural Legacies of Vietnam: The Use of the Past in the Present*, ed. R. Morris and P. Ehrenhaus, 199–219. Norwood, NJ: Ablex.

Morrison, S. S. 2000. *Women Pilgrims in Late Medieval England: Private Piety as Public Performance*. London: Routledge, Taylor, and Francis Group.

Mota, M. 1968. *Votos e Ex-votos: Aspectos da Vida Social do Nordeste*. Recife: Universidade de Pernambuco.

Muller, K. 1977. *Huichols: People of the Peyote*. Tucson: Stonedge Productions, Southwest Media. Video.

Murphy, M. D. 1993. Politics of Tumult in Andalusian Ritual. *Political and Legal Anthropology Review* 16 (2): 75.

Myerhoff, B. G. 1974. *Peyote Hunt: The Sacred Journey of the Huichol Indians*. Ithaca: Cornell University Press.

———. 1975. Organization and Ecstasy: Deliberate and Accidental Communitas among Huichol Indians and American Youth. In *Symbol and Politics in Communal Ideology: Cases and Questions*, ed. S. Moore and B. Myerhoff, 33–67. Ithaca: Cornell University Press.

———. 1978a. Return to Wirikuta: Ritual Reversal and Symbolic Continuity on the Peyote Hunt of the Huichol Indians. In *The World Upside Down: Studies in Symbolic Inversion*, ed. B. Babcock, 33–67. Ithaca: Cornell University Press.

———. 1978b. Peyote and the Mystic Vision. In *Art of The Huichol Indians*, ed. Kathleen Berrin, 56–70. San Francisco: The Fine Arts Museums of San Francisco.

Naquin, S. and C-F. Yu. 1992. *Pilgrimas and Sacred Sites in China*. Berkeley: University of California Press.

Nations, M. K., and L. A. Rebhun. 1988. Angels with Wet Wings Won't Fly: Maternal Sentiment in Brazil and the Image of Neglect. *Culture, Medicine, and Psychiatry* 12:141–200.

Ngokwey, N. 1995. Naming and Grouping Illnesses in Feira (Brazil). *Culture, Medicine, and Psychiatry* 19:385–408.

Niman, M. I. 1997. *People of the Rainbow: A Nomadic Utopia*. Knoxville: University of Tennessee Press.

Nolan, M. L. 1991. The European Roots of Latin American Pilgrimage. In *Pilgrimage in Latin America*, ed. R. Crumrine and A. Morinis, 19–47. New York: Greenwood.

Oettinger, M. 1990. *Folk Treasures of Mexico: The Nelson A. Rockefeller Collection*. New York: Harry N. Abrams.

———. 1992. *The Folk Art of Latin America: Visiones Del Pueblo*. New York: Dutton Studio Books.

———, ed. 1997. *Folk Art of Spain and the Americas: El Alma del Pueblo*. New York: Abbeville.

Oktavec, E. 1995. *Answered Prayers: Miracles and Milagros along the Border*. Tucson: University of Arizona Press.

Ousterhout, R. 1990. Loca Sancta and the Architectural Response to Pilgrimage. In *The Blessings of Pilgrimage*, ed. R. Ousterhout, 108–24. Urbana: University of Illinois Press.

Pandian, J. 1991. *Culture, Religion, and the Sacred Self*. Englewood Cliffs, NJ: Prentice-Hall.

———. 1997. The Sacred Integration of the Cultural Self: An Anthropological Approach to the Study of Religion. In *The Anthropology of Religion*, ed. S. Glazier, 505–16. Westport, CT: Greenwood.

Pang, E. 1989. Agrarian Change in the Northeast. In *Modern Brazil: Elites and Masses in Historical Perspective*, ed. M. L. Conniff and F. D. McCann, 123–39. Lincoln: University of Nebraska Press.

Pattanaik, D. 1997. *Shiva: An Introduction*. Mumbai, India: Vakils, Feffer and Simons.

Pelletier. 1977. *Mind as Healer, Mind as Slayer*. New York: Dell.

Peters, L. 1989. Shamanism: Phenomenology of a Spiritual Discipline. *Journal of Transpersonal Psychology* 21 (2): 115–37.

———. 1990. Mystical Experience in Tamang Shamanism. *ReVision: The Journal of Consciousness and Change* 13 (2): 71–85.

———. 1995. Karga Puja. *Alternative Therapies* 1 (5): 53–61.

———. 1997a. A Promise to the Goddess Kali. *Shamans Drum* 44:35–41.

———. 1997b. The Healing Rituals of Dorje Yudroma. *Shamans Drum* 45:37–47.

———. 1997c. Some Elements of the Tibetan Shamanism of Pau Wanchuk. *Journal of the Foundation for Shamanic Studies*. 10 (2): 21–23.

———. 1997d. The "Calling," the Yeti, and the Ban Jhakri (Forest Shaman) in Nepalese Shamanism. *The Journal of Transpersonal Psychology* 29 (1): 47–62.

———. 1998. *Tamang Shamans*. New Delhi: Nirala.

Pettis, C. 1999. *Secrets of Sacred Space*. St. Paul, MN: Llewellyn.

Pierson, M. H. 1997. *The Perfect Vehicle: What Is It about Motorcycles*. New York: Norton.

Pike, S. M. 2001. *Earthly Bodies, Magical Selves: Contemporary Pagans and the Search for Community*. Berkeley: University of California Press.

———. 2005. No Novenas for the Dead: Ritual Action and Communal Memory at the Temple of Tears. In *AfterBurn: Reflections on Burning Man*, ed. L. Gilmore and M. Van Proyen. Albuquerque: University of New Mexico Press.

Pina-Cabral, J. 1986. *Sons of Adam, Daughters of Eve: The Peasant Worldview of the Alto Minho.* Oxford: Clarendon.

Pinkson, T. 1995. *Flowers of Wiricuta: A Gringo's Journey to Shamanic Power.* Mill Valley, CA: Wakan.

Piquet, C., and R. A. Best. 1986. *Post Traumatic Stress Disorder, Rape Trauma, Delayed Stress, and Related Conditions: A Bibliography.* Jefferson, NC: McFarland.

Post, P., J. Pieper, and M. van Uden. 1998. *The Modern Pilgrim: Multidisciplinary Explorations of Christian Pilgrimage.* Leuven, Neth.: Peeters.

Preston, J. 1992. Spiritual Magnetism: An Organizing Principle for the Study of Pilgrimages. In *Sacred Journeys: The Anthropology of Pilgrimage,* ed. A. Morinis, 31–46. Westport, CT: Greenwood.

Prince, R. 1982. Shamans and Endorphins. *Ethos* 10 (4): 409.

Queiroz, M. E. P. De. 1973. *O Campesinato Brasileiro.* Petróoplis, Brazil: Editora Vozes.

Rabinow, Paul. 1975. *Symbolic Domination: Cultural Form and Historical Change in Morocco.* Chicago: University of Chicago Press.

Radford, U. M. 1949. The Wax Images Found in Exeter Cathedral. *The Antiquaries Journal* 29:164–69.

Ravitch, N. 1990. *The Catholic Church and the French Nation 1589–1989.* New York: Routledge.

Ray, P. H. 1997. The Emerging Culture. *American Demographics* 19 (2): 28–34.

Reader, I., and T. Walter, eds. 1993. *Pilgrimage in Popular Culture.* Basingstoke, UK: MacMillan.

Rebhun, L. A. 1993. Nerves and Emotional Play in Northeast Brazil. *Medical Anthropology Quarterly* 7 (2): 131–51.

———. 1994. Swallowing Frogs: Anger and Illness in Northeast Brazil. *Medical Anthropology Quarterly* 8 (4): 360–82.

Redfield, R. 1960. The Social Organization of Tradition. In *The Little Community and Peasant Society and Culture,* 40–59. Chicago: University of Chicago Press.

Reis, J. 1981. Hunger in the Northeast: Some Historical Aspects. In *The Logic of Poverty: The Case of the Brazilian Northeast,* ed. S. Mitchell, 41–57. London: Routledge and Kegan Paul.

Robock, S. H. 1963. *Brazil's Developing Northeast: A Study of Regional Planning and Foreign Aid.* Washington, DC: Brookings Institute.

———. 1975. *Brazil: A Study in Development and Progress.* Lexington, MA: Lexington Books.

Rocacher, J. 1979. *Rocamadour et son Pèlerinage: Étude Historique et Archéologique, vol. 2.* Toulouse, Fr.: Edouard Privat.

Rodman, M. C. 1992. Empowering Place: Multilocality and Multivocality. *American Anthropologist* 94 (3): 640–56.

Romano, O. I. 1965. Charismatic Medicine, Folk-Healing, and Folk-Sainthood. *American Anthropologist* 67 (2): 1151–73.

Roniger, L. 1990. *Hierarchy and Trust in Modern Mexico and Brazil*. New York: Praeger.

Rosaldo, M. Z. 1974. Women, Culture, and Society: A Theoretical Overview. In *Women, Culture, and Society*, ed. M. Z. Rosaldo and L. Lamphere, 17–42. Stanford: Stanford University Press.

Rosaldo, R. 1989. *Culture and Truth: The Remaking of Social Analysis*. Boston: Beacon.

Rossi, E. L. 1993. *The Psychobiology of Mind-Body Healing: New Concepts of Therapeutic Hypnosis*. Rev. ed. New York: Norton.

———. 1998. Mindbody Healing in Hypnosis: Immediate-Early Genes and the Deep Psychobiology of Psychotherapy. *Japanese Journal of Hypnosis* 43 (1): 1–10.

———. 2000a. In Search of a Deep Psychobiology of Hypnosis: Visionary Hypotheses for a New Millennium. *American Journal of Hypnosis* 42 (3): 178–206.

———. 2000b. Exploring Gene Expression in Sleep, Dreams and Hypnosis with the New DNA Microarray Technology: A Call for Clinical-experimental Research. *Sleep and Hypnosis* 1:40–46.

———. 2002. *The Psychobiology of Gene Expression: Neuroscience and Neurogenesis in Hypnosis and the Healing Arts*. New York: Norton.

Rossi, E. L., and K. L. Rossi. 1996. *The Symptom Path to Enlightenment: The New Dynamics of Self-Organization in Hypnotherapy: An Advanced Manual for Beginners*. Pacific Palisades, CA: Palisades Gateway.

Rouse, W. H. D. 1902. *Greek Votive Offerings: An Essay in the History of Greek Religion*. Cambridge: Cambridge University Press.

Ruddick, S. 1980. Maternal Thinking. *Feminist Studies* 6 (2): 342–67.

Ruether, R. 1993. *Sexism and God-Talk. Toward a Feminist Theology*. Boston: Beacon.

Ruiz de Alarcón, H. 1984. *The Treatise on the Heathen Superstitions that Today Live among the Indian Natives to this New Spain, 1629*. Trans. and ed. J. R. Andrews and R. Hassig. Tulsa: University of Oklahoma Press.

Ruzalya-Smith, P., A. Barabasz, M. Barabasz, and D. Warner. 1995. Effects of Hypnosis on the Immune Response: B-cells, T-cells, Helper and Supressor Cells. *American Journal of Clinical Hypnosis* 38 (2): 71–79.

Sahagun, Fray Bernardino de. 1950–1969. *Florentine Codex: A General History of the Things of New Spain* 12 Volumes. Trans. C. E. Dibble and A. J. O. Anderson. Salt Lake City: University of Utah Press.

Saia, L. 1944. *Escultura Popular Brasileira*. São Paulo: Edicoes Graveta.

Sallnow, M. J. 1981. Communitas Reconsidered: The Sociology of Andean Pilgrimage. *Man* 16:163–82.

Sambon, L. 1895. Donaria of Medical Interest in the Oppenheimer Collection of Etruscan and Roman Antiquities. *British Medical Journal* 2:146–50, 216–19.

Sánchez, V. 1996. *Toltecs of the New Millennium.* Trans. Robert Nelson. Santa Fe: Bear.

Sanchis, P. 1983. *Arraial: Festa de um Povo. As Romarias Portuguesas. Portugal de Perto.* Lisboa: Publicacões dom Quixote.

———. 1983. The Portuguese Romarias. In *Saints and Their Cults: Studies in Religious Sociology, Folklore and History,* ed. S. Wilson, 261–90. Cambridge: Cambridge University Press.

Sasson, A. 1997. The Process of Sanctification of Tombs in the South Coastal Plain. In *New Studies on the Coastal Plain,* ed. E. Regev, 97–113. Ramat Gan: Bar Ilan University.

Schaefer, S. B. 1993. Loom as a Sacred Power Object in Huichol Culture. In *Art in Small-Scale Societies: Contemporary Readings,* ed. R. Anderson and K. L. Field, 118–30. Englewood Cliffs, NJ: Prentice Hall.

———. 1996a. The Crossing of the Souls: Peyote, Perception, and Meaning among the Huichol Indians. In *People of the Peyote: Huichol Indian History, Religion and Survival,* ed. S. B. Schaefer and P. T. Furst, 138–68. Albuquerque: University of New Mexico Press.

———. 1996b. Pregnancy and Peyote among the Huichol Indians of Mexico: A Preliminary Report. *Yearbook for Ethnomedicine and the Study of Consciousness* 5:67–78.

———. 1998. Freedom of Expression: Huichol Indians: Their Peyote-Inspired Art and Mexican Drug Laws. *Yearbook for Ethnomedicine and the Study of Consciousness* 7:205–21.

———. 2000. The Peyote Religion and Mescalero Apache: An Ethnohistorical View From West Texas. *Journal of Big Bend Studies* 12:51–70.

———. 2002. *To Think with a Good Heart: Wixárika Women, Weavers and Shamans.* Salt Lake City: University of Utah Press.

Schaefer, S. B., and P. T. Furst. 1996. Introduction. In *People of the Peyote: Huichol Indian History, Religion and Survival,* ed. S. B. Schaefer and P. T. Furst, 1–25. Albuquerque: University of New Mexico Press.

Scheper-Hughes, N. 1986. Culture, Scarcity, and Maternal Thinking: Maternal Detachment and Infant Survival in a Brazilian Shantytown. *Ethos* 13 (4): 291–317.

———. 1992. *Death Without Weeping.* Berkeley: University of California Press.

Scheper-Hughes, N., and M. Lock. 1987. The Mindful Body: A Prolegomenon to Future Work in Medical Anthropology. *Medical Anthropology Quarterly* 1:1.

Sellers, R. W., and T. Walter. 1993. From Custer to Kent State: Heroes, Martyrs, and the Evolution of Popular Shrines in the U.S.A. In *Pilgrimage in Popular Culture,* ed. I. Reader and T. Walter, 179–200. Basingstoke, UK: MacMillan.

Sered, S. S. 1992. *Women as Ritual Experts. The Religious Lives of Elderly Jewish Women in Jerusalem*. Oxford: Oxford University Press.

———. 1994. *Priestess, Mother, Sacred Sister: Religions Dominated by Women*. Oxford: Oxford University Press.

———. 1995. Rachel's Tomb: The Development of a Cult. *Jewish Studies Quarterly* 2 (2): 103–48.

———. 2000. *What Makes Women Sick?: Maternity, Modesty and Militarism in Israeli Society*. Hanover, NH: University Press of New England.

Seremetakis, C. N., ed. 1994. *The Senses Still: Perception and Memory as Material Culture in Modernity*. Boulder: Westview.

Shay, J. 1994. *Achilles in Vietnam: Combat Trauma and the Undoing of Character*. New York: Atheneum.

Siegel, R., P. Collings, and J. Diaz. 1977. On the Use of Tagetes Lucida and Nicotiana Rustica as a Huichol Smoking Mixture: The Aztec "Yahuatil" with Suggestive Hallucinogenic Effects. *Economic Botany* 31:16–23.

Slater, C. 1986. *Trail of Miracles: Stories from a Pilgrimage in Northeast Brazil*. Berkeley: University of California Press.

———. 1990. Miracle Stories and Milagres in Northeast Brazil. *Journal of Latin American Lore* 16 (1): 109–27.

Smith, J. Z. 1982. *Imagining Religion: From Babylon to Jonestown*. Chicago: University of Chicago Press.

———, ed. 1995. *The Harper Collins Dictionary of Religion*. San Francisco: Harper.

Snyder, S. 1996. *Drugs and the Brain*. New York: Scientific American Library.

Starbird, M. 1993. *The Woman with the Alabaster Jar: Mary Magdalen and the Holy Grail*. Santa Fe: Bear.

Stark, R. 1997. A Taxonomy of Religious Experience. In *The Psychology of Religion: Theoretical Approaches*, ed. B. Spilika and D. N. McIntosh, 209–21. Boulder: Westview.

Stephenson, C. 1970. *Walsingham Way*. London: Darton, Longman and Todd.

Stoller, P. 1989. *The Taste of Ethnographic Things: The Senses in Anthropology*. Philadelphia: University of Pennsylvania Press.

———. 1996. Sounds and Things: Pulsations of Power in Songhay. In *The Performance of Healing*, ed. C. Laderman and M. Rosman, 165–84. New York: Routledge.

———. 1997. *Sensuous Scholarship*. Philadelphia: University of Pennsylvania Press.

Strathern, A. J. 1996. *Body Thoughts*. Ann Arbor: University of Michigan Press.

Strauss, C., and N. Quinn. 1994. A Cognitive/Cultural Anthropology. In *Assessing Cultural Anthropology*, ed. R. Borofsky, 284–300. New York: McGraw-Hill.

Taussig, M. 1993. *Mimesis and Alterity: A Particular History of the Senses*. London: Routledge.

Taylor, L. J. 1995. *Occasions of Faith: An Anthropology of Irish Catholics*. Philadelphia: University of Pennsylvania Press.

Toor, F. 1947. *A Treasury of Mexican Folkways*. New York: Crown.

Trölle, T. R., J. Schadrack, and W. Zieglgänsberger. 1995. Preface to *Immediate-Early Genes in the Central Nervous System*, ed. T. R. Trölle, J. Schadrack and W. Zieglgänsberger. New York: Springer.

Turner, V. 1964. Betwixt and Between: The Liminal Period in Rites de Passage. In *Symposium on New Approaches to the Study of Religion: Proceedings of the 1964 Annual Spring Meeting of the American Ethnological Society*, 1994, ed. J. Helm, 2–20. New York: AMS Press.

———. 1967. *The Forest of Symbols: Aspects of Ndembu Ritual*. Ithaca: Cornell University Press.

———. 1969. *The Ritual Process: Structure and Anti-Structure*. Chicago: Aldine.

———. 1974. *Dramas, Fields, and Metaphors: Symbolic Action in Human Society*. Ithaca: Cornell University Press.

Turner, V., and E. Turner. 1978. *Image and Pilgrimage in Christian Culture: Anthropological Perspectives*. New York: Columbia University Press.

Valadez, S. 1986a. Dreams and Visions from the Gods: An Interview with Ulu Temay, Huichol Shaman. *Shaman's Drum* 6:18–23.

———. 1986b. Mirrors of the Gods: The Huichol Shaman's Path of Completion. *Shaman's Drum* 6:29–39.

van Alphen, E. 1999. Symptoms of Discursivity: Experience, Memory, and Trauma. In *Memory: Cultural Recall in the Present*, ed. J. Crew, M. Bal, and L. Spitzer, 24–38. Hanover, NH: University of New England Press.

van Gennep, A. 1960 [1908]. *The Rites of Passage*. Trans. M. B. Vizedom and G. L. Caffee. Chicago: University of Chicago Press.

Van Rhey, D. 1999. The Art of Burning Man. http://www.burningman.com/art_of_burningman/art_of_bm.html (accessed December 23, 2004).

———. 2000. The Meaning of Participation, An Interview with Larry Harvey. *Burning Man Journal*, Summer 2000 Newsletter. http://www.burningman.com/whatisburningman/2000/00n_letter_sum_1.html (accessed December 23, 2004).

Vernette, J. 1989. *Le Nouvel Age: À l'Aube de l'Ere du Verseau*. Paris: Pierre Tequi.

Vieira, M. J. 1991. O triunfo do Coração. *O Público Sábado*: 10–14.

Walker, M. U. 1998. *Moral Understandings*. New York: Routledge.

Walter, T. 1993. War Grave Pilgrimage. In *Pilgrimage in Popular Culture*. I. Reader and T. Walter, eds. Pp.63–91. Basingstoke, England: MacMillan.

Walton, K., and D. Levitsky. 1994. A Neuroendocrine Mechanism for the Reduction of Drug Use and Addictions by Transcendental Meditation. *Alcoholism Treatment Quarterly* 11 (1/2): 89–117.

Warner, M. 1976 [1990]. *Alone of All Her Sex: The Myth and the Cult of the Virgin Mary*. London: Pan Books.

———. 1996. *Walsingham: An Ever-circling Year*. Oxford: Oxford University Press.

Watson, C. G., J. Tuorila, E. Detra, L. P. Gearhart, and R. M. Wielkiewicz. 1995. Effects of a Vietnam Memorial Pilgrimage on Veterans with Post Traumatic Stress Disorder. *Journal of Nervous and Mental Disease* 183 (5): 315–19.

Weingrod, A. 1990. *The Saint of Beer Sheva*. Albany, NY: SUNY Press.

White, J. 1989. *Protestant Worship: Traditions in Transition*. Louisville: Westminster/John Knox.

Wilbert, J. 1987. *Tobacco and Shamanism in South America*. New Haven: Yale University Press.

Williams, A. 1996. Foreword to *Walsingham: An Ever-Circling Year*, by M. Warner, vii–x. Oxford: Oxford University Press.

Wilson, S., ed. 1983. *Saints and Their Cults: Studies in Religious Sociology*. Cambridge: Cambridge University Press.

Winkelman, M. 1992. *Shamans, Priests and Witches: A Cross-Cultural Study of Magico-religious Practitioners*. Tempe: Arizona State University.

———. 1996. Psychointegrator Plants: Their Roles in Human Culture and Health. *Yearbook of Cross-Cultural Medicine and Psychotherapy* 5:9–53.

———. 1997. Altered States of Consciousness and Religious Behavior. In *Anthropology of Religion: A Handbook of Method and Theory*, ed. S. Glazier, 393–428. Westport, CT: Greenwood.

———. 2000. *Shamanism: The Neural Ecology of Consciousness and Healing*. Westport, CT: Bergin and Garvey.

Winkelman, M., and C. Winkelman. 1991. Shamanistic Healers and Their Therapies. In *Yearbook of Cross-Cultural Medicine and Psychotherapy 1990*, ed. W. Andritzky, 163–82. Berlin: Verlag and Vertrieb.

Wolf, D. 1991. *The Rebels: A Brotherhood of Outlaw Bikers*. Toronto: University of Toronto Press.

Wolf, E. R. 1958. The Virgin of Guadelupe: A Mexican National Symbol. *Journal of American Folklore* 71:34–39.

Woodward, K. L. 1990. *Making Saints: How the Catholic Church Determines Who Becomes a Saint, Who Doesn't, and Why*. New York: Simon and Schuster.

Young, A. 1982. The Anthropologies of Illness and Sickness. *Annual Review of Anthropology* 11:257–85.

———. 1995. *The Harmony of Illusions: Inventing Post Traumatic Stress Disorder*. Princeton: Princeton University Press.

Zimdars-Swartz, S. L. 1991. *Encountering Mary: Visions of Mary from La Salette to Medjugorje*. New York: Avon Books.

Zimmer, H. 1972. *Myths and Symbols in Indian Art and Civilization*. Princeton: Princeton University Press.

Zimmermann, M. 1989. The Nervous System in the Context of Information Theory. In *Human Physiology*. 2nd ed., ed. R. F. Schmidt and G. Thews, 166–73. Berlin: Springer-Verlag.

About the Editors

Jill Dubisch received her Ph.D. from the University of Chicago in 1972, and is currently Regents' Professor of Anthropology at Northern Arizona University. Her research interests include Europe, with a particular focus on Greece, and the United States. Her work in Greece has resulted in a number of articles and two books, *Gender and Power in Rural Greece* (Princeton 1986) and *In a Different Place: Pilgrimage, Gender and Politics at a Greek Island Shrine* (Princeton 1995). Her more recent work on motorcycle pilgrimage is presented in *Run for the Wall: Remembering Vietnam on a Motorcycle Pilgrimage* (Rutgers 2001), jointly authored with Raymond Michalowski. She has taught at Trinity College, Hartford, the University of North Carolina at Charlotte, and Northern Arizona University, where she has served as department chair. She has also served as president for the Society for the Anthropology of Europe, on the Executive Board of the Modern Greek Studies Association, and on the board of the Society for the Anthropology of Religion. She is currently doing research on New Age and alternative healing practices, including New Age spiritual pilgrimage. Her most recent article in this area is "Body, Self and Cosmos in 'New Age' Energy Healing," in *Corporeal Inscriptions* (eds. Edyta Lorek-Jezinska and Katarzyna Wieckowska) She is also a Reiki master and a practitioner of Jin Shin Jyutsu energy healing.

Michael Winkelman received his Ph.D. from the University of California, Irvine, in 1985, and his M.P.H. in Community Health Practice from the University of Arizona in 2002. He is currently Director of the Ethnographic Field School, Department of Anthropology at Arizona State University, which is held annually in Ensenada, Baja California Mexico. He also serves as the Head of the Sociocultural Subdiscipline in the Department. His primary research and teaching areas are in medical anthropology, particularly shamanic healing, and in cross-cultural relations. He is the author of several books, including *Shamans, Priests and Witches* (1992); *Shamanism: The Neural Ecology of Consciousness and Healing* (2000); and *Ethnic Relations in the US* (1998). He has recently examined the role of shamanism in human cognitive evolution (e.g., see "Shamanism and Cognitive Evolution," *Cambridge Archaeological Journal* 12, 2002) and as a part of an evolved human psychology (e.g., see "Shamanic Universals and Evolutionary Psychology," *Journal of Ritual Studies* 16, 2002). Winkelman has also explored the applications of this biological paradigm of shamanism to development of perspectives on "neurotheology" (e.g., see "Shamanism as the Original Neurology Theology," *Zygon* 39, 2004). His Web site is at www.public.asu.edu/~atmxw.

About the Contributors

Simon Coleman gained his Ph.D. from Cambridge University in 1989, and was subsequently a Research Fellow at both St. John's and Churchill Colleges, Cambridge. Currently Professor of Anthropology at the University of Sussex, he has conducted fieldwork in Sweden, the United States, and the United Kingdom. His professional interests include pilgrimage, conservative Protestantism, biomedical models of healing, and aesthetics. His books include *Pilgrimage Past and Present in the World Religions* (Harvard 1995, with J. Elsner); *The Anthropology of Friendship* (Berg 1999, coedited with S. Bell); *The Globalisation of Charismatic Christianity* (Cambridge 2000); *Tourism: Between Place and Performance* (Berghahn 2002, coedited with M. Crang); and *Reframing Pilgrimage: Cultures in Motion* (Routledge 2004, coedited with J. Eade).

Lena Gemzöe earned her Ph.D. in social anthropology at Stockholm University in 2000 and is currently affiliated with the Centre for Gender Studies at Stockholm University. Apart from her dissertation, *Feminine Matters: Women's Religious Practices in a Portuguese Town* (Almqvist & Wiksell International), she has published two books in Swedish: an introduction to feminist thinking, *Feminism* (Bilda förlag 2002), and an edited volume, *Contemporary Ethnography: Reflections from the Field of Media Consumption* (Nya Doxa 2004). She is currently working on a project on female saints in Portugal, part of which is in *Fat: The Anthropology of an Obsession* (ed. D. Kulick and A. Meneley, Tarcher/Penguin 2005). She is also engaged in research on cultural policy and cultural politics in two Swedish towns.

Lee Gilmore completed her Ph.D. in cultural and historical studies of religion at the Graduate Theological Union in Berkeley, California, in 2005. She currently teaches at Chabot College in Hayward, California, and at Starr King School for the Ministry in Berkeley. Previously, she served as Assistant Editor for the journal *Anthropology of Consciousness*. A participant in the Burning Man Festival since 1996, she was inspired to begin formally researching the event after witnessing the powerful and far-reaching transformations the festival had on members of her community and in her own life.

Sidney M. Greenfield is Professor Emeritus at the University of Wisconsin–Milwaukee (email egreenF222@aol.com). He has conducted ethnographic research in the West Indies; New Bedford, Massachusetts; and Brazil, and ethnohistorical and historical research in Portugal and the Atlantic Islands on issues ranging from family and kinship, patronage and politics, the history of plantations and plantation slavery and entrepreneurship, to Spiritist surgery and healing and syncretized religions in Brazil. Author and/or editor of 7 books, he has published some 120 articles and reviews in books and professional journals. Among his more recent works are *Cirurgias do Além: Pesquisas Antropológicas Sobre Curas Espirituais* (Editora Vozes 1999), a book in Portuguese about his studies of Spiritist healing; *Argeu: A Construção de um Santo Popular* (2nd edition, Editora UFC 2003), about the making of a popular saint coauthored with A. M. Cavalcante; *Reinventing Religions: Syncretism in Africa and the Americas* (Rowman & Littlefield 2001), coedited with A. Droogers; "Treating the Sick with a Morality Play: The Kardecist-Spiritist Disobsession in Brazil" (*Social Analysis* 48, summer 2004); and "Trance States and Accessing Implicit Memories: A Psychosocial Genomic Approach to Reconstituting Social Memory During Religious Rituals," (*Bodily Order and Social Memory in Digital Societies*, ed. B. M. Pirani and I. Varga, 2005). He has also produced, directed, and authored five video documentaries, including most recently *Spirits, Medicine, and Charity: A Brazilian Woman's Cure for Cancer* (Media Resource Department of the University of Wisconsin–Milwaukee 1995).

C. Lindsey King received her Ph.D. in cultural anthropology from The University of Tennessee, Knoxville, in 1999. Her dissertation fieldwork documenting the ex-voto tradition in Northeast Brazil combined her interests of folk art and religious tradition. She is the author of *Evolution of a Potter: Conversations with Bill Gordy* (Bartow History Center 1992), and her recent research has included early craft traditions in the Great Smoky Mountains as well as Appalachian textiles. She is a Lecturer in the Sociology and Anthropology Department at East Tennessee State University.

Antonio Mourão Cavalcante (email a_morao@hotmail.com) is a practicing psychiatrist, Professor of Psychiatry at the Faculty of Medicine of the Federal University of Ceará and Chief of Psychiatric Services at the University's Hospital in Fortaleza, Brazil. He holds a doctorate in psychiatry from the Catholic University in Louvain, Belgium and a second doctorate in anthropology from the University of Lyon in France. His major interests are in family therapy, ethnopsychiatry, and cultural psychiatry. Among his many publications, mostly in Portuguese and French, are *Ciúme Patologico* (Editora Record 1997); *Drogas, Esse Barrato Sai Carro* (Editora Record 1997); *Argeu: A Construção de um Santo Popular* (Terceira Margem 2000), co-authored with Sidney M.

Greenfield; and *L'homme jaloux, essai sur la jalosie pathologique* (Araknow Editions 2000).

Larry G. Peters holds a Ph.D. in anthropology from UCLA, and conducted postdoctoral ethnographic research for NIMH at UCLA's Neuropsychiatric Institute. He also earned an advanced degree in psychology at the California Graduate Institute of Psychology and Psychoanalysis, and is a licensed psychotherapist in private practice. Initiated as a shaman in the Tibetan tradition, he has conducted ethnographic field research working with shamans in Nepal, China, Mongolia, Tuva, and Siberia. Numerous articles and three books document this work. He is also a former Board Member of the Society for the Anthropology of Consciousness and a Research Associate of the Foundation for Shamanic Studies. He conducts workshops in cities across the United States teaching techniques of healing used in Tibetan Shamanism, and brings several groups to Nepal each year for Initiation Pilgrimages with Aama Bombo, including Janai Purnima. For clients in his private practice, he employs shamanic counseling methods to promote psycho-spiritual integration.

Stacy B. Schaefer received her Ph.D. in anthropology from UCLA in 1990, and has been carrying out ethnographic research among the Wixárika (Huichol) Indians of Mexico since 1977. In the course of her fieldwork, she has studied the role of Wixárika women as weavers and shamans. She has also followed the path of becoming a master weaver, which closely parallels the training to become a shaman. A Fulbright García Robles Fellow in 1998, she conducted a holistic study on healing beliefs and practices related to the toxic scorpions in the Wixárika sierra. Another area of her ongoing research is the evolution of the Native American Church, the beliefs and practices associated with this religion, and the interaction between its members and federally licensed Mexican American peyote dealers. Currently, her research is on shamans, medicine men, and the religious use of peyote and peyote-inspired art among Wixáritari and members of the Native American Church. She is the author of *To Think With A Good Heart: Wixárika Women, Weavers and Shamans* (Utah 2002) and coeditor of *People of the Peyote: Huichol Indian History, Religion and Survival* (University of New Mexico Press 1996), with P. Furst. She is presently Co-Director of the Museum of Anthropology and Associate Professor at California State University, Chico.

Susan Sered received her Ph.D. from Hebrew University, Jerusalem, in 1985. Her work spans the fields of medical anthropology, religious studies, and gender studies, and has incorporated fieldwork in Israel, Okinawa (Japan), and the United States. Her publications include *Women as Ritual Experts: The Religious Lives of Elderly Jewish Women in Jerusalem* (Oxford University Press 1992); *Priestess, Mother, Sacred Sister: Religions Dominated by Women* (Oxford University Press 1994); *Women of the Sacred Groves: Divine Priestesses of Okinawa* (Oxford University Press 1999); *What Makes Women Sick?: Militarism, Maternity and Modesty in Israeli Society* (University Press of New England 2000); *Religion and Healing in America* (Oxford University Press 2004); and *Uninsured in America: Life and Death in the Land of Opportunity* (University of California Press 2005); as well as dozens of articles in religion, anthropology, and women's studies journals. She currently is Senior Researcher at Suffolk University's Center for Women's Health and Human Rights.

Deana L. Weibel received her Ph.D. in anthropology at the University of California, San Diego, in 2001. Her dissertation, entitled "Kidnapping the Virgin: The Reinterpretation of a Roman Catholic Shrine by Religious Creatives," was based primarily on fieldwork conducted in Rocamadour, France, from October 1998 through June 1999, funded by a Fulbright grant. She has also conducted research at other shrines in France, most notably Lourdes, and at the shrine of Chimayó in New Mexico. She is an assistant professor of Grand Valley State University in Allendale, Michigan. Recent publications include "The New Age and the Old World: the Interpretation and Use of European Shrines by Religious Creatives" and "The Energy We Call the Goddess: the Religious Creativist Use of a Roman Catholic Shrine" (*Maria: A Journal of Marian Studies* 2:2, 2002); "Controlling Chance, Creating Chance: Magical Thinking in Religious Pilgrimage" (*Journal for the Academic Study of Magic* 1, 2003); and "The Virgin Mary Versus the Monkeys" (*Religious Innovation in a Global Age: Essays on the Construction of Spirituality*, ed. G. N. Lundskow, McFarland, 2005). She is currently studying pilgrimage to the "Cross in the Woods" shrine in Indian River, Michigan, and is researching the place of religion in the American and Russian space programs with historian G. E. Swanson.

Index